The SECRET

TO LIFETIME

FINANCIAL SECURITY

Published by CelebrityPress®, Orlando, FL

CelebrityPress® is a registered trademark

Printed in the United States of America.

ISBN: 978-0-9895187-1-0
LCCN: 2013942085

Most CelebrityPress® titles are available at special quantity discounts for bulk purchases for sales promotions, premiums, fundraising, and educational use. Special versions or book excerpts can also be created to fit specific needs.

For more information, please write:
CelebrityPress®
520 N. Orlando Ave, #2
Winter Park, FL 32789
or call 1.877.261.4930

Visit us online at: www.CelebrityPressPublishing.com

IMPORTANT NOTICE

The SECRET TO LIFETIME FINANCIAL SECURITY

CELEBRITY PRESS
Winter Park, Florida

CONTENTS

CHAPTER 35
THE LONG ROAD TO INSURANCE BLISS

FOREWORD

I don't know at what point in time you'll be reading this book, or what the economic conditions will be. None of us knows for sure what the economy will be like one year, 10 years or 30 years from now.

And that's the problem this book addresses. You see, if we could know the future, our traditional financial and retirement planning strategies might actually have a chance of working. But without a crystal ball, those strategies can only rely on hope and guesswork.

The idea of having a comfortable, worry-free retirement has become a distant dream for many—even for those who did "all the right things" that the financial gurus told them to do. Many of us feel like we have very little control over our money and finances.

The poet Robert Frost wrote,

> *"Two roads diverged in a wood, and I,*
> *I took the one less traveled by,*
> *And that has made all the difference."*

The advisors who contributed to this book have all taken the road less traveled…and they've become heroes to their clients in the process.

They use time-tested, proven strategies that take the guesswork out of planning for your financial future.

Going against the conventional wisdom takes courage and conviction—

and when you meet these advisors, it's instantly clear they have those traits. They are determined to help their clients reach their short-term and long-term financial goals and dreams and avoid disappointment.

Each of these advisors has met the requirements and completed the rigorous training to be a Bank On Yourself Authorized Advisor. Here is a partial list of the ways they can help you:

• Grow your wealth safely and predictably every year—even when the markets tumble.

• Have a retirement income you can predict and count on.

• Become your own source of financing for your cars, vacations, home improvements and more—and get access to capital when you want, for whatever you want.

• Give you a better way to save and pay for college.

• Create an emergency fund.

• Finance business and professional expenses—even when banks aren't lending.

• Offer special programs just for seniors up to age 85.

• Create a financial legacy for your children, grandchildren and your favorite charities.

• Take the guesswork out of financial planning and free up more time to enjoy your family and do the things you love.

These advisors can also show you ways to free up capital to fund your plan by helping you restructure your finances.

And they can help you achieve the financial security and peace of mind you want and deserve.

Yours in prosperity,

Pamela Yellen, President of Bank On Yourself, and author of *The New York Times* best-seller, *Bank on Yourself: The Life-Changing Secret to Growing and Protecting Your Financial Future*

CHAPTER 1

THE SECRET TO LIFETIME FINANCIAL SECURITY

BY PAMELA YELLEN,
PRESIDENT, BANK ON YOURSELF

What does financial security mean to you?

Knowing the value of your nest egg on the day you plan to tap into it? Having the peace of mind that comes with knowing you'll be able to enjoy a comfortable lifestyle in retirement and that your money will last as long as you do?

Having a sizable "rainy day" fund that ensures you'll be able to easily cover unexpected expenses due to a medical emergency, disability, broken major appliance or leaky roof that needs to be replaced, loss of a job, a family member needing assistance…or whatever curve ball life may throw you?

Maybe financial security means being able to send your kids or grandkids to the schools of their choice without spending your life's savings. Or being able to get your hands on money to make purchases, build a business, or take advantage of an opportunity—without having to beg for it or be forced to sell assets at the wrong time.

I believe you can—and should—have the financial security you want and deserve—however you define it.

The problem with the conventional financial and retirement planning wisdom is that it is based on the "hope and pray" method. And the results have been disastrous. Most people don't have a clue what their nest egg will be worth on the day they retire. Many say they'd have trouble coming up with even $2,000 to cover an emergency expense in the next 30 days, according to a survey by the Employee Benefit Research Institute.

Following the conventional wisdom has only created massive financial *in*security.

DOING ALL THE "RIGHT THINGS" WITH LITTLE TO SHOW FOR IT

My search for alternatives to the risk and volatility of traditional investment strategies started when my husband and I finally realized that although we'd been doing everything we'd been taught to do, we weren't getting anything close to the long-term gains we were promised.

I stumbled across Bank On Yourself almost by accident. I'm not a financial advisor, but as a business-building consultant who has worked with more than 40,000 financial advisors since 1990, I've been exposed to just about every financial product, tool, concept or method for growing wealth. Frustrated by my own experience following the conventional financial wisdom, I ended up investigating over 450 financial products and strategies, only to find most weren't even worth the paper they were printed on.

Finally, one of my financial advisor clients told me about a concept. I was intrigued. It almost sounded too good to be true, but luckily I decided to keep an open mind. Since then, the Bank On Yourself method has enabled my family, and hundreds of thousands of others, to:

- **Never miss a single beat while growing your retirement fund**

- **Become your *own* source of financing and recapture interest you pay to banks and finance companies** (this method of paying for major purchases is actually better than directly paying cash for things)

- **Have a financial safety net to see you through challenging times**

- **Ensure your kids and grandkids will be able to go to colleges of their choice**—using the Bank On Yourself method beats 529 Savings Plans, UGMAs, UTMAs, investment accounts and student loans by a country mile

BEST OF ALL, BANK ON YOURSELF LETS YOU STOP *HOPING* YOU'LL REACH YOUR FINANCIAL GOALS AND DREAMS AND START *KNOWING* YOU WILL!

Once I knew from personal experience the extraordinary power of Bank On Yourself, I felt it would be unfair to keep it to myself. And that's why it became my mission to educate people about this and do my best to ensure no one ever again needlessly suffers another lost decade in their financial plan…or even a single lost day.

However, I must warn you that Bank On Yourself is not a magic pill. There is nothing you can put under your pillow at night and wake up rich the next morning (other than a winning lottery ticket). Anyone who claims such a thing exists is a shameless huckster. The Bank On Yourself method takes a little patience and discipline. But for those who have those traits, it pays a lifetime of benefits.

It can help almost anyone—regardless of age, income or financial sophistication—reach their financial goals and dreams without losing sleep. *However, if you spend more than you make, this is not for you. And if you're looking for a get-rich-quick scheme, you will surely be disappointed.*

SO WHAT IS THE BANK ON YOURSELF METHOD?

Bank On Yourself uses a supercharged variation of a financial asset that has increased in value during EVERY single market crash and in EVERY period of economic boom and bust for more than 160 years—dividend-paying whole-life insurance.

But this is NOT the kind of whole-life policy most advisors and experts talk about! With this little-known variation, you don't have to die to "win."

Policies structured properly to maximize the power of the Bank On Yourself concept squash the arguments you may have heard that your money in a whole-life policy grows too slowly or that the agents' commissions are too high.

That's because Bank On Yourself requires a dividend-paying whole-life policy with some features added on to it that, in my experience, maybe 1 in 1,000 financial advisors or experts knows about or fully understands. A large portion of your premium goes into riders that significantly supercharge the growth of your money in the policy AND reduce the commission the agent receives by 50 to 70 percent.

Are you still skeptical? That's not really surprising, since you've probably heard people like Dave Ramsey, Suze Orman and other financial experts say that whole-life insurance is a lousy place to put your money. However, a Bank On Yourself-type policy is a totally different "animal" that most financial advisors and experts don't even know about.

Here's a quick summary of the three key differences between a Bank On Yourself-type policy and the ones Suze, Dave and others talk about:

Key Difference #1: The policies they describe usually have no "cash value" (equity you have access to) for the first several years of the policy. However, as I just noted, a Bank On Yourself-type policy incorporates riders or options that supercharge the growth of your money in the policy, **especially** in the early years of the policy. As a result, **you could have significantly more cash value** than the whole-life policies Suze and Dave describe. This allows you to use the policy as a powerful financial management tool right from Day One.

Key Difference #2: Unlike the policies most experts describe, where your death benefit stays level for the life of the policy, **both your death benefit and your cash value in a Bank On Yourself-type policy grow at a steeper pace every year**. Which means the growth is at its peak at the time you need it most—during your retirement years. (I'll show you what that growth curve looks like in a bit.)

This gives you some built-in protection against inflation, *unlike* a term insurance policy, *which loses real value every year*, due to inflation. And since your premium stays level in a whole-life policy, you're paying those premiums with ever-cheaper dollars.

Key Difference #3: Those who complain that, when you die, the company "only" pays you the death benefit and "keeps" your cash value have apparently never seen a dividend-paying whole-life policy!

On BankOnYourself.com, I have a copy of one of my policy statements that clearly shows that if I died on the date of that policy statement, my family would have gotten a check for an amount equal to the original death benefit of the policy, PLUS the current cash value of the polic... and then some! In fact, they'd get a total of over $130,000 more than the original death benefit!

Here's what many experts don't realize about dividend-paying whole-life insurance:

1.. You build up equity in the policy at a guaranteed and predictable rate. [1]

2. You can use your equity in the plan *however* and *whenever* you wish and for whatever you want. [2]

3. You don't have to apply for or beg to use your money in the policy, or fill out any nosy credit applications, and you can't be turned down for a loan.

4. You can pay your loans back on your *own* schedule, *not* someone else's.

5. If an emergency arises or you get sick or lose your job, you can reduce or skip some loan payments until you get back on your feet.[3]

Bank On Yourself-type policy owners have never had a losing year. Both your principal *and gains* are locked in—they don't vanish when stocks, real estate and other investments crash.

---

1. Guarantees are based on the claims-paying ability of the insurer.
2. Policy loans accrue interest, and if not repaid, will lower policy values. If your loan balance exceeds the cash value, outside funds may be needed to keep the policy from lapsing.
3. Excess loans can terminate a policy. A policy that lapses or is surrendered can potentially result in tax consequences.

The chart below shows you the growth curve in a properly designed Bank On Yourself policy. *It gets better every single year simply because you stick with it*—no luck, skill or guesswork required:

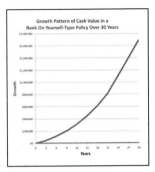

This chart is based on one of my *own* Bank On Yourself policies, showing the *actual growth* I've already received in the policy, and the projected future growth, based on the current dividend scale (dividends are not guaranteed and are subject to change).

While your plan won't look exactly like mine, what would look similar is the growth curve. If you take another look at the chart, you can see how it grows more slowly in the early years, and then the growth begins to steepen at an ever accelerating pace.

Compare that with a graph of the whip-sawing growth of the stock market, real estate or any other traditional investment—which make a day on the roller coasters at Great Adventure look tame. Those investments can (and do) plunge just when you planned to tap into them, dashing your dreams of a comfortable retirement along with them.

WHERE DO YOU FIND THE MONEY TO FUND A BANK ON YOURSELF POLICY?

If you're like many people, you may not have much money left at the end of the month and may be wondering where on earth you'll find the seed money to fund a Bank On Yourself plan. There are at least eight common places to free up money to fund a plan, and your Bank On Yourself Authorized Advisor is very skilled at helping you restructure your finances, *sometimes freeing up dollars without impacting your lifestyle.*

DOES YOUR AGE OR HEALTH MATTER?

Folks of all ages use Bank On Yourself. Many people in their 60s start Bank On Yourself policies, and special programs exist for people up to age 85. After all, with people living longer, wouldn't you rather plan on having your money last until you're 90 or 100 years young, rather than risk having your money run out before you do?

And don't rule yourself out because of your age or health problems, because you don't have to be the insured on the policy. What's important is that you own and control the policy—someone else can be the insured, typically a spouse, child, grandchild, parent or business partner. Your Authorized Advisor can discuss your options with you.

HOW MUCH DOES IT COST TO START A BANK ON YOURSELF POLICY?

There's *no set amount* you need to put into the plan—each plan is custom-tailored and you can begin at whatever level is comfortable for you.

Bank On Yourself Advisors don't charge a fee to review your situation and design your policy. If you decide to implement the policy they design for you, they receive a commission from the insurance company, which has already been taken into account in the bottom-line numbers and results you will see when you receive your Bank On Yourself Analysis. And remember—when your Bank On Yourself Authorized Advisor structures your policy this way, *their commission is reduced by 50 to 70 percent.*

Why would these advisors deliver more and get paid way less? Because by providing such a high level of advice, well-structured personalized plans and unique services, their clients do more business with them, as well as happily and voluntarily refer family, friends, neighbors and colleagues.

WHY USE A BANK ON YOURSELF AUTHORIZED ADVISOR?

If your policy isn't structured correctly, or the wrong product is used, your policy could grow *much* more slowly, or it could *lose* the tax advantages, or *both*. Out of more than 1,500 major life insurance companies, there are only a handful offer policies that have **all** the features required to maximize the power of the Bank On Yourself method.[4]

Unfortunately, most advisors "don't know what they don't know" and, in my experience, a little knowledge can be a dangerous thing. I found this out the hard way when an advisor structured my first policy incorrectly, causing it to lose its tax advantages.

The unfortunate and costly experiences I had, along with requests from folks all over the country for a referral to an Advisor who truly understands all the ins and outs of the Bank On Yourself method and could act as their professional guide, led to the creation of the Bank On Yourself Authorized Advisor Training Program. Today, there are about 200 advisors in the United States and Canada that form the core of Bank On Yourself Authorized Advisors.

THE BANK ON YOURSELF ADVISOR TRAINING PROGRAM INCLUDES...

- Rigorous, advanced training on policy design and the technical aspects make these policies a powerful financial tool.

- Advisors must pass a test and take continuing education classes.

- The advisors work under the guidance of technical and policy-design experts who have designed thousands of Bank On Yourself-type policies.

- Extensive training is focused on how to coach clients through the years to become their own source of financing—ultimately, for much of their lifestyle.

So you can rest assured that you are in excellent hands with your Bank On Yourself Authorized Advisor. They can design a custom-tailored plan to help you reach as many of your short-term and long-term financial goals and dreams as possible, in the shortest time possible.

Bank On Yourself is about building a solid foundation and taking back control of your financial future so you can enjoy real wealth and financial security for long as you live.

---

4. The Bank On Yourself system uses generally available whole-life policies and riders.

About Pamela

Pamela Yellen is president and founder of Bank On Yourself. She's a best-selling author and financial security expert who investigated more than 450 savings and retirement planning products, strategies and vehicles seeking an alternative to the risk and volatility of stocks and other investments. Her research led her to a time-tested, predictable method of growing and protecting wealth now used by more than half a million families, professionals and business owners.

Pamela also helps people fire their banker and become their own source of financing so they can get access to capital for whatever they want by answering just one question: "How much do you want?"

Pamela is the author of *The New York Times* best-seller, *Bank On Yourself: The Life-Changing Secret to Growing and Protecting Your Financial Future*, and *The Bank On Yourself Revolution* (February 2014). She has appeared on every major TV and radio network and served as a source for organizations from the Associated Press and FoxNews to Bloomberg Businessweek and AARP. Her articles have been featured in thousands of major publications and websites.

CHAPTER 2

CHANGING LIVES ONE CLIENT AT A TIME

BY W. BRUCE SPENCER

I have been involved in the financial arena for more years than I would like to admit. In fact, I just started my seventh decade of life with all its rich experiences and lessons. One of the financial "truths" I have learned along the way is that the "return of your money" is more important than the "return on your money." Another truth came from a wise Chinese man who said, "The best time to plant a tree was 20 years ago; the second best time is now." Another wise man said, "To thine ownself be true," and an even wiser one said, "Do unto others as you would want them do unto you." These "truths" have had a great influence on my life and my financial planning for others.

Another life-changing event that has influenced what and how I practice my profession happened on April 7, 1997. That day, at the age of 55, my beautiful wife, Bonnie, suffered a catastrophic brainstem stroke, which left her with quadriplegia. It was so devastating that she was initially in a "trapped brain syndrome" for several months. During that time the only thing she could do was blink her eyes. So, to communicate, we learned how to use an alphabet board. I would point at a letter and she would blink once for "yes" and twice for "no," and I would painstakingly write down each letter, eventually forming words, sentences, thoughts and ideas. As you can imagine, Bonnie became very frustrated trying to communicate with me this way.

After about 45 days of visiting her every day in the skilled nursing facility, meeting with the staff and realizing she was not going to improve in that environment, I made the decision to bring Bonnie home and to become her constant caregiver. I was absolutely terrified at the beginning because I had no experience or training in caregiving. She came home with a stomach tube surgically inserted. I had to learn how to feed her through this tube, which included grinding up all her medications so they could be administered through the tube. I had to learn how to attend to all of her physical needs around the clock.

After extensive physical and occupational therapy, my wife eventually learned how to swallow and speak again. She also recovered the ability to move her right hand and forearm, allowing her to bring her hand towards her face, provided her elbow is propped up. The significance of this is that today, she is able to operate her bed control to raise and lower her head and feet as long as I position the control within her reach. It allows her to operate the remote control for her TV. It allows her to reach a plastic glass of iced water on the hospital tray by her bed so she can sip water from a straw. It allows her to call me from her lifeline phone by touching a touch pad, and, more importantly, to call QVC. The lifeline phone has a microphone with an amplifier that allows the QVC operator to understand her and empowers her to be able to shop independently of me. It also allows her to operate her electric wheelchair independently.

So, today, despite her limitations and because of her amazing attitude, Bonnie and I go out often, facilitated by her electric wheelchair and a van conversion. We enjoy eating out, going to movies and live jazz events, and going on cruises. She inspires others and me. She has made me a better person, which benefits my prospects and clients.

Our situation required me to find a way to continue to utilize my skills, experience, schooling and training to make a living while still making myself available to tend to her needs 24/7. That meant I needed to be able to work from a home office, and I needed to find a financial concept that would guarantee my clients a return of their money (remember that life lesson?).

As luck would have it (when preparation and opportunity meet), I received an email inviting me to listen to a gentleman named R. Nelson Nash, who wrote a book called *Becoming Your own Banker: The*

Infinite Banking Concept. It was my next major life-changing event. The concept resonated so true that I signed up to take a webinar class over the following 10 weeks to learn how to teach people how to create their own "financing system." Imagine what a difference I could make in people's lives if I could show them how to create their own financing system with dividend paying whole life insurance (an asset class that would insure a return of their money), enable them to recapture interest charges they had been paying to someone else, and eliminate banks, credit card companies and financing companies from their lives.

I also had to find a way to do this from my home office so I could be available to my wife whenever she needed me. Initially I had prospective clients come to my home and I would meet with them at our dining room table. This was okay, but was intrusive for my wife. Fortunately, as technology has advanced, virtual meetings became possible and I have evolved my practice to be exclusively virtual. It has allowed me to work successfully with clients all around the country.

One of the unique services I provide my clients is a "personalized financial statement" that I prepare based on the information I gather from them during a comprehensive telephone interview about their current financial condition. This statement gives me and the client a snapshot of where they really are financially. This information, together with their goals and aspirations, helps me to formulate a Bank On Yourself personalized solution that is unique to them and their circumstances.

I would like to share some of my clients' goals and objectives so that you can see how this wonderful concept might work for you. Here are some of their stories:

Client #1: One of my early challenges for using Bank On Yourself came from a couple in their middle 40s who had several daughters who needed financial assistance with college and weddings. After conducting a comprehensive interview about their financial condition and preparing a personal financial statement for them, it was apparent that their only major financial asset was the equity in their home. Fortunately, this was before the real estate market correction. We devised a plan that allowed them to "harvest" the equity in their home and move it into a dividend-paying whole-life policy designed to be cash-rich, which allowed them to self-finance those upcoming events. They have successfully employed those transferred equity dollars to accomplish all those goals for their daughters, and had we not harvested the equity when we did, it would not have been available to pay for these goals because it all disappeared in the real estate market correction. And, in the true "Bank On Yourself" sense, they are sending loan payments back to their policy with interest that they will recapture and from which they will profit. When the daughters are all successfully employed and self-sufficient, they will also help repay the family self-financing system.

Client #2: Another interesting case involves one of my clients who is a very successful commercial real estate investor. Because of his successes, he had major resources available for capitalizing a family self-financing system. He took his time evaluating the concept. If my memory serves me correctly, it took more than a year from when I first talked to him about the concept before he moved forward.

My client's long-term goal is to be able to capitalize his self-financing system sufficiently to permit him to refinance his commercial projects and let the cash flow from those projects make the loan payments back to his financing system. After a comprehensive interview regarding his personal financial situation, I prepared a personal financial statement for him that we could use as the foundation for determining the major policies that we started on him and his wife to accomplish his goals. We have since added policies on all of his adult children. My client is the owner of all the policies so he controls the cash in all the policies. Imagine what it is going to be like for him when he no longer has to go to outside financial institutions for his financing needs. He no longer has to jump through hoops to get money to fund his projects. He is well on his way.

Client #3: My next client story is about a successful executive at a major company who researched the Bank On Yourself system enough to convince him that this concept might be a better way to pay for his sons college educations than his current method, and over time provide him and his wife with a substantial six-figure, passive tax-free income when he was ready to retire. After a comprehensive analysis of his current assets, liabilities and cash flow, we came to a mutual decision on what would be the ideal amount to fund his Bank On Yourself policy. I was then able to show him exactly how it would work and project the dollars he would have available for all of his banking and retirement goals. He likes how this anchors his overall financial plan and provides a stable foundation for everything else he is doing. He knows this portion of his financial plan is predictable and not subject to the ups and downs of the stock and real estate markets. He likes this so much that he is considering another substantial policy on his wife in the not-too-distant future.

Client #4: This case didn't involve big premiums, just a big heart. A young man came to me after hearing about Bank On Yourself, wanting to know if it could help him achieve his goal. He shared with me that he didn't make very much money, but rented an inexpensive apartment and slept on the floor so that he could save $200 each month. It turns out that he is a gifted mechanic and could find old cars in need of repair, buy them at a fair price, fix them up and then sell them for a profit. His problem was that he could not do this in enough volume to make a living, so he worked another minimum wage job and did the fixer-uppers in his spare time. He estimated that if he could afford to buy a bigger truck, which could pull a big enough trailer to haul several vehicles at once, he could go to car auctions and purchase several fixer-uppers at once. He could fix all of them in a reasonably short time and sell them. You get the idea. Soon he would be able to do this full time, make a better living and capitalize a significant Bank On Yourself financing program.

I'm proud to say he stuck with the program and today, due to his persistence and his Bank On Yourself policy, he has a thriving business. And he always pays his policy loans back from his profits. He truly gets the Bank On Yourself concept.

Client #5: Though still a prospect, not a client, this husband and wife have several existing policies and annuities they asked me to analyze. One of the policies is a whole-life policy that has been in force for 10 years and the company is a very well-known insurance company. Because the policy was not designed to make it grow cash-rich initially through the use of paid up additions riders, they thought I might be able to replace it with a better designed policy.

I told them the only way I could give them an accurate answer was for them to request an "in-force" illustration for the existing policy. The in-force illustration uses the current policy values and projects how the policy should perform in the future, given different dividend assumptions.

Once I know that, I can illustrate a policy using our assumptions and kick start it with the existing net cash surrender value transferring into the policy as a 1035 exchange, a method used to move cash values from like policies to another policy without tax consequences, and then compare my projected future values to their existing policy projections. In this case, because their policy was in force for so many years, my policy design could not outperform their existing policy (numbers do not lie). Consequently, I explained why I could not provide a better design and told them it was in their best interest to stick with their existing policy. I bring this up because you should never allow someone to approach you with the idea of replacing an existing policy without doing this analysis. Remember this is your money, not theirs.

They also had a variable universal life policy for which I also insisted they request an in-force illustration. In this case, it didn't surprise me that the in-force illustration projected that the policy would lapse down the road just when they would need either the cash values or death benefit. The problem with the universal life policy is that the cost of insurance, provided through the annual renewable term insurance, is going up every year together with other costs in the policy. Unless they are willing to contribute more premium dollars when those costs are greater than the projected net return on the investment choices from the variable side of the policy, the policy will likely lapse.

So, in this case, it would probably make sense to 1035 the net cash surrender value into a better designed policy. However, nothing is ever easy, and in this case the policy also has surrender charges for two more policy years. Consequently, they have to decide if they should wait the two years to avoid the surrender penalty, hoping the stock market does not go south, or bite the bullet and move forward. I know what I would do, because they have no control over the market. But they have to make that decision, not me.

So, in this case, I have spent countless hours analyzing their situation at no cost to them (and yes, that included a comprehensive interview about their current financial condition and the preparation of their personal financial statement), and I am probably a couple of years away from having them as clients. My point is that this is okay because they know and I know that I am most concerned about what is best for them.

This is how I approach all of my prospective clients and I hope I get the opportunity to do the same for you. At the end of the day all I have is my integrity. It is very important to me that I keep it.

About Bruce

Bruce Spencer is a financial advisor with more than 40 years of experience in the financial services industry. He was born in Toledo, Ohio, and grew up in the Midwest. He graduated with honors from the University of Toledo, School of Business Administration, with majors in both finance and accounting. He served four years honorably in the U.S. Air Force.

Bruce then worked for two different trust companies in Ohio and Colorado. His pioneering work in the employee benefits record keeping area for the United Bank of Denver landed him a job in Atlanta, Georgia, heading up an employee benefits record keeping firm whose customers were major Fortune 500 companies.

He accepted an offer in 1978 to become the marketing vice president for an up-and-coming employee benefits record keeping firm in Sacramento, California. During his tenure, he saw the firm's client base grow from a few hundred to more than 13,000 clients. He developed strategic relationships with CPAs and tax attorneys that continue today.

In 1989, he was offered the position of executive vice president to head up the employee benefit record keeping division of Lexington Plan Administrators. He accepted the offer because it came not only with the challenge to turn the company around, but also to expand his securities and financial planning training. There, he had the good fortune to work with another fellow Midwesterner who was a CFP, CPA and tax attorney and was the executive vice president of the marketing division. They hit it off well, jointly helped many clients, and in 1995, left to start their own financial planning services firm.

On April 7, 1997, Bruce's beautiful wife, Bonnie, suffered a major stroke. This life-changing event required him to change the way he delivers services to clients and prospective clients, and because of time constraints, to become more of a specialist. This is why he now asks his clients to come to his home office or work with him virtually and why he decided to become a Bank On Yourself ™ certified advisor. By offering clients his knowledge, integrity and genuine concern, he has earned a reputation as a knowledgeable, trustworthy advisor and friend who knows how to think "outside the box." He teaches individuals, families and businesses how to "Bank on Themselves," which allows them to take advantage of one of the most important concepts in modern macroeconomics: the velocity of money. If they follow the plan he prepares for them, they ultimately will not have to pay interest and finance charges to any banking system other than their own, which means they will be making the profits the banks, finance, credit card and mortgage companies have been making off them. The resulting increase in wealth will eventually become their source of a passive tax-free stream of retirement income for life.

Contact Bruce at (916) 984-9974 with any questions you may have regarding your insurance or financial planning. He is happy to give you his professional experience on a personal level. Put his experience to work for you.

CHAPTER 3

FINDING TRUTH THROUGH ADVERSITY

BY CAROL BENNINK

Propaganda and indoctrination have a powerful influence on our lives. Yet most of us live out our lives completely unaware of these powerful influences. One of American's master manipulators, Edward Bernays, writes in *Propaganda* (1928):

> The conscious and intelligent manipulation of the organized habits and opinions of the masses is an important element in [a] democratic society. Those who manipulate this unseen mechanism of society constitute an invisible government which is the true ruling power of our country. We are governed, our minds are molded, our tastes formed, our ideas suggested, largely by men we have never heard of. This is a logical result of the way in which our democratic society is organized. Vast numbers of human beings must cooperate in this manner if they are to live together as a smoothly functioning society ... In almost every act of our daily lives, whether in the sphere of politics or business, in our social conduct or our ethical thinking, we are dominated by the relatively small number of persons ... who understand the mental processes and social patterns of the masses. It is they who pull the wires which control the public mind

Bernays was considered America's number one marketer during the 1920s through the 1950s. Among other things, he is credited with liberating women to smoke, making disposable cups and plates a growing industry (Dixie Cup), and making bacon a staple for breakfast in the American home, helping the pork industry. He was very well-versed in the psychology of "herd mentality" in human beings. His uncle and mentor was Sigmund Feud.

This should not come as a shock to you and me. We have seen this before. Many times during this century, there have been master manipulators who used indoctrination. Some used it in the name of progress, while others used it for true evil. Adolf Hitler once said, "How fortunate for governments that the people they administer don't think." This is how entire generations can be manipulated and indoctrinated.

So are we somehow cocooned from manipulation and propaganda today? No, certainly not. I believe that we continue to live in a world full of lies and propaganda. We need to be searching constantly for the truth. Truth is absolute; black and white.

It is often not until we encounter pain, devastation and darkness that we begin to really question what is important and what is truth. When we are brought to our knees in prayer and perhaps the only sounds we can make are groans, then we may see what's truly important in life and what is not important.

I plunged into my darkness when my 14-year-old daughter died suddenly and unexpectedly.

I had just given notice to Philip Morris and accepted the position of assistant general warehouse manager at Costco, a company I respected and with whom I was proud to be affiliated. My world was looking up. I believed that this position with Costco was a direct answer to a prayer.

Then, in the 10 days between leaving my job at Philip Morris and accepting the job at Costco, my beautiful 14-year-old daughter, Jessica, was diagnosed with leukemia and died. Out of absolutely nowhere, my world fell apart. In less than two weeks, I experienced one of the highest professional moments of my life, and the lowest personal moment of my life. She went septic after receiving her first chemotherapy shot. They sent us home. Jessica cooked the family dinner that night. The next morning she was back in the hospital on life support. She died the next day of massive organ failure.

We buried Jessica on October 14, and I started at Costco on October 30.

I worked for one year before deciding to step away from my work responsibilities at Costco to take care of my other two children and husband. Someone needed to be home to "ground" this family. A meal needed to be on the table. We were a family of walking zombies. I quit a great job with a great company. Ultimately, it is not what happens to us that defines who we are, but rather what we do with what happens to us in life that matters.

Once I stopped working, the grieving process officially started for me. I knew that pain, darkness and sorrow would be my new best friends for a while. If you want to reach the sunrise in the fastest way possible, which way would you head? Would you go east or west? You would need to head east. You must plunge into the darkness first to meet and greet the sunrise. Otherwise, you will find yourself chasing the sunrise and never catching up. That's what I did.

We all know that struggle, adversity or even great pressure helps refine us. This is seen every day in nature; ordinary coal transforms into precious, beautiful diamonds under great pressure, decay metamorphoses into oil, and forests are reborn after fires. I believe that loss and grief help the soul grow larger. I believe this jolt to realty truly gets your clarity and focus laser sharp on what's really important in life.

In looking back, our family enjoyed a rare kind of simplicity and freedom that we may never know again. We were just "doing life" daily; nothing more, nothing less. This may have been a grace disguised. I began to find truth through my adversity.

My story is not unique. Many families have experienced the loss of a child and must pick up the pieces of the puzzle and figure out how to put the new picture puzzle together with a piece missing. For 14 years, we were fortunate to have an amazing young woman in our lives. Through God, I know Jessica would always be with me. I also knew that, one day, I would be with her again.

"What's next? Back to reality.

The market is crashing. Unemployment is skyrocketing. Real estate prices are falling. Many people are losing their homes. Everyone seems to know someone who has lost their home to a short sale or foreclosure or job loss. It is a "new norm" for all of us. This is not the best time to re-enter the job market for a middle-aged female. My heart was screaming to my head not to take another W-2 job again. But what was I going to do? I still needed to earn a living and help support my family.

It was time to reinvent myself and get busy moving forward with my life. I decided to attend a real estate investing class. I learned at the class about something they called the "infinite banking concept." This was the day that I first learned about this amazing financial strategy; this "Bank On Yourself" concept. This was a game changing day for me; a day that I will always remember.

They talked about a way to recapture the interest that we give away to banks and credit card companies throughout our lifetime. He explained how the average person spends more on interest on cars and credit card debt than they will ever be able to save. The instructor quoted a man named Nelson Nash who was said to be responsible for helping bring this financial concept mainstream.

One of the concepts the instructor demonstrated had to do with the three different ways in which most of us purchase a car. We can take out a loan, pay cash or lease. Then he showed us a new way to purchase a car, through a turbo-charged participating whole life policy.

My jaw dropped open. How can this be? You could borrow your own money from yourself, but your money still grows like you did not borrow it.

But wait, it gets better. When you take a loan from a whole life insurance policy from certain mutual companies, your policy can continue to grow as though you haven't borrowed anything. Not to mention that the income from a life insurance product can be tax-free, by taking a combination of dividend withdrawals and loans against your cash value. Income from a life insurance product could be a great way to plan for retirement. Income received from a life insurance product would not reduce your social security benefits.

I was amazed that I had never heard about this before. Heck, I was educated. I had an MBA. I had worked for Fortune 100 firms for more than 20 years. I was an avid reader. How did I miss this?

Why did I believe the old "buy term and invest the difference" model?

Years ago, professional pension managers managed our parents' retirement accounts. Since the 1970s, the average American worker has taken on the responsibility that a professional pension manager once held. It was intended to allow taxpayers a break on taxes on deferred income.

Millions of Americans started to pour their retirement savings into the stock market. I started fully funding my first 401(k) in the 1980s, after graduating from college. I remember playing with my calculator and the "writing on the wall" looked amazing! I was on track to becoming a multi-millionaire by the time I reached the age of 45. I believed what I was told, hook, line and sinker. Why would I not? I became a savings machine. I would sacrifice fun, eating out, clothes and such, so I could save as much as I could in my 401(k).

Then, everything came crashing down (the first time). The first crash in 1987 didn't hurt me too badly. I was still in the game. I kept on saving. How little did I understand demographics, not to mention propaganda. "Keep on saving!" I did not question it, I just did it. I got swept up in the tech bubble and lost a bunch. Then I lost more in the crash of 2008. That's when I got out of the market.

At 45 years of age, I was nowhere near becoming a multi-millionaire, as I had calculated several years earlier. Remember my motto, "Keep on saving"? When I returned home later that night, I did two things. First, I back-tested my investments. I found that had I started a life insurance policy in the 1980s, rather than a 401(k), I would be better off today. During the last two boom and bust cycles, I had lost over 34 percent of the value of my 401(k). A person simply does not rebound from losses like that. I never rebounded. Not to mention brokerage fees that are never disclosed.

The second thing I did was to sit down at my computer and type "Mr. Nelson Nash" into Google. It must have been my lucky day. I learned that in two days, Nash was going to be at a conference 700 miles away from our home. I tossed my husband, Sjef, into the car, and off to Tennessee we went. Economists from all over the country were there. These were smart people. My eyes were now glued opened. I could not believe how blind I had been in the past. I felt as if I had been indoctrinated by our very own public schools, media and institutions.

43

You and I were taught to buy term and invest the difference, and that buying whole life insurance is a rip-off. What I have come to understand is that it is not a rip-off, especially the way that the folks at Bank On Yourself design their policies. They keep the whole life portion at the lowest possible amount, and turbo-charge the policy to build cash value fast. This will take effort on your part to re-educate yourself and shift your paradigm, as it did for me.

I believe that we all do not always know the truth. We are told what "they" what us to hear and believe. This process of indoctrination starts in school and continues with the help of our institutions and media. Sometimes we never learn the truth.

Did you know that qualified plans, such as 401(k)'s and IRAs, are under tax law, and that these tax laws that govern our qualified plans can change at any time? Have you been listening to the news lately? Did you know that life insurance is governed by contract law?

I believe it is God's gift to me that I found this wonderful group of people at Bank On Yourself. I met the designated "Godfather" of this concept, Nelson Nash, and he got me fired up. One of my passions in life is to share and educate as many people as possible about this amazing financial strategy. My company, Life's Financial Reserves, teaches people how to "bank on themselves." Many in my industry believe, as I do, that if just 10 percent of the total population of the United States started to fire their bankers, and start to "bank on themselves," that we could save our country. The reason for this is that we would no longer be slaves to the present system created by the Federal Reserve. We would, for the first time, be in control of our own money and future. Think about it for a moment. How many people do you know who have been able to retire in a comfortable manner because their qualified retirement plans performed the way they were supposed to? How many millionaires do you know?

I challenge you to think and get educated with regard to this concept. As Will Rogers once said, "The problem in America isn't so much what people don't know; the problem is what people think they know that just ain't so."

Charles Schultz, the creator of "Peanuts," once said, "In the book of life, the answers aren't in the back." It is imperative that you educate yourself and keep an open mind to this paradigm shift. We give too much control away in our lives. Then we spend too much time feeling out of control and helpless. Take your control back. Think.

About Carol

Carol Bennink is currently an authorized advisor with Bank On Yourself. Carol's company, Life's Financial Reserves, teaches people how to "bank on themselves." She believes that that through this business, she is doing one small part in building a better America, one person at a time. In addition to her life insurance business, Carol and her husband, Sjef, invest in apartment buildings and other affordable housing opportunities.

Carol has had a successful career with three great companies: Costo, Philip Morris, and Kraft Foods. In a 20-year span, she held various positions of responsibility and management, leading in sales and meeting budgets at every turn. Carol always prided herself in understanding how to work best with people while obtaining the company's goals and objectives.

Carol received national awards for sales and leadership, and had a proven sales track record that earned her multiple accolades. Her last W-2 job was with Costco, where she held the position of assistant general warehouse manager. Two weeks before taking this job, her 14-year-old daughter, Jessica, died suddenly and unexpectedly. She chose to start with Costco anyway, spending one year with the company before making the difficult decision to leave Costco, a company which she greatly admired, to support her grieving family at home.

Carol was born and raised in the Los Angeles area. Her undergraduate degree is from Humboldt State University, where the redwoods meet the ocean. Carol earned her MBA from California State University Fresno. When she met her husband, Sjef, they moved to Michigan, and lived in Clarkston, a beautiful suburb of Detroit, for 10 years.

Carol is a health nut and avid runner. She will tell you that she has been running since 1971 and that she still runs, only much slower. Her favorite things are hiking, camping, hanging out with her kids and family, reading and serving others.

Carol now lives with her husband, Sjef, in Lee's Summit, Missouri. She is most proud of her three children, Natalie, Lucas, and Jessica, who they lost to complications from the treatment of leukemia. "She is in heaven, and we will see her again in heaven." After losing Jessica, Carol started a ministry to serve families who have lost kids.

If you would like to learn more, please email Carol at:
Carol@LifesFinancialReserves.com

CHAPTER 4

COLLEGE PLANNING FOR THE MIDDLE AND UPPER-MIDDLE CLASS

BY CHIP WITTROCK

There is a struggling socioeconomic group in our country. This is the overlooked middle and upper-middle class. They have been the most stricken by the latest economic struggles our country has gone through. Most are hardworking, ethical and involved individuals. They are living paycheck to paycheck and have seen their retirement plans plummet. You might know someone in this situation. I certainly do. Most are overworked and over-obligated, but they still want the best for their children. Many are parents of high school students preparing for college and they have no idea how they will be able to pay for the ever-increasing tuitions. This group is also the least qualified for federal financial student aid, yet they pay the most into the system.

There are plenty of charitable organizations helping low income people, who actually need the least help because they qualify for the most federal student aid. There is not one nonprofit college planning group focused on this middle class demographic. I have coined this dilemma "the middle class gap."

Everything I do is in an effort to reach this group, one by one, to help them get their children to the right college at the best price for them, and equally as important, help these students get through college in a timely manner and go into the workforce prepared, passionate and ready to realize their dreams. Sounds like a logical and desired outcome, right? But, that is not what is happening today. Many students are going to the wrong colleges for them with no direction, and most are not graduating at all, or if they do, it's taking five or six years to get a 4-year degree. Then they are leaving college stressed out, starting their careers off in debt, and are defeated before they ever get a chance to start. My mission is to impact this situation with dominance, helping those who want to see our country return to the educational and economic powerhouse it should be and helping them become recipients of the right education for them without breaking the bank.

The traditional resources, advice and planning that families have relied on has let us down. Parents of college bound students just do not know what they do not know. But they have grown to rely on and believe in traditional advice, which has gotten us into the state that we are in today: almost half of the kids are dropping out of college before they finish, loaded with student loan debt and no degree, and the majority are planning to move back home after graduation. Not what we want for our children, right?

Another real tragedy is that parents want to help their kids through college, so they roll up their sleeves and sometimes don't save as much for retirement as they could or should because they are trying to save for college in traditional savings plans and are serving two masters. They are allocating some of their financial resources to college funding and some of it to retirement. What happens for so many people is that they end up not doing a good job on either one. They do not have enough saved when their child turns 18 and heads off to college nor do they have enough saved for retirement. Ultimately, though, these parents do help their kids go to college by creating yet another master for themselves by adding more financial liability in the form of PLUS Loans, taking equity out of their house or beating up their already under-funded retirement plan.

To get the word out about what works in college planning and what does not, I often meet with guidance counselors and help them with their college planning events by speaking to the parents and students on behalf of the counseling department. I'm asked to speak about the essential things that the counselors are not able to help them with, like financial planning for college and pre-FAFSA (Free Application for Federal Student Aid) techniques that the counselors cannot or do not talk about. Recently, I was speaking at a counselor association convention in Arizona. One of the participants shared with me that counselors across the United States are responsible for an average of 540 students each. Knowing this, would you agree that counselors today are overworked and overextended? Yet what I see on a regular basis is that counselors are asked to do too much and are relied upon in an unrealistic manner by families of college bound students.

Most families rely heavily on their high school guidance counselors to give them all of the necessary information to plan for college. This is one of the biggest mistakes in college planning. Another mistake that families make when planning for college is where they save money. I am sure that you have heard of 529 Plans, Coverdell IRAs, UTMAs and UGMAs, brokerage accounts and even traditional savings accounts. These are all traditional places people save for college. Did you know that every one of these savings vehicles actually causes most people to pay more for college than someone who was saving the same amount in a Bank On Yourself plan? Yes, these traditional savings plans can actually hurt you when you are filling out the FAFSA. This is because the FAFSA formula puts assets into two categories. The first is assessed assets, which include all of the traditional places people typically save for college. These actually count against you for financial aid purposes. The second asset group is nonassessed assets, which include plans like Bank On Yourself and some other insurance-based assets, such as annuities.

Let's take a look at a traditional planning scenario to see what happens and why it is an expensive and financially inefficient way to save for college. In this example, you are going to save $10,000 for college. You've got to put the money somewhere, so let's say you put it in a 529 plan. Well, for starters, when you fill out the FAFSA and show that you have $10,000 in a 529 plan, which is an assessed asset, then your expected family contribution (the minimum out- of-pocket expense you will have for college) will be increased by 5.65 percent, which is $565 higher than if you had saved in a nonassessed asset. But now, you do have this money saved, so the first year of college you write a tuition check for $10,000 from your 529 plan and your balance is…zero! It's gone. Not for a little while; it is gone forever. That is the traditional route.

That doesn't sound good, does it? OK, then, let's say you decide to go the nontraditional route and you roll up your sleeves and you put

$10,000 into your Bank On Yourself plan, which is also your retirement savings place. In this scenario, your expected family contribution does not go up because your Bank On Yourself plan is a nonassessed asset. When your child goes off to college, you take a loan from your Bank On Yourself plan to pay for it. Now ... read this carefully, because you don't see this every day ... while the money is out paying for tuition, you are still earning interest on the entire amount you have in the Bank On Yourself plan, as if there were no loan. If it's not enough that you are still earning interest on all the money in your plan – now, instead of paying other financial institutions for the loan, you pay back yourself. And, ultimately, these become your retirement dollars. And the kicker is ... when you write those checks, who controls the $10,000? Is it the university? Is it a bank? Is it a credit card company? Or is it you? It's you! And, when that sinks in, it changes everything for you. There is not a better way to save for college and retirement.

I used it as an easy example, but we all know that $10,000 is not going to cover the cost of college. So, let's say that it is going to cost $100,000 to put your child through college and you start saving as soon as they are born. There are two ways to go about it: the traditional way or the nontraditional way. You could save $100,000 in a 529 plan or some other traditional college saving vehicle and then when you spend the money, it's gone.

A Bank On Yourself plan, on the other hand, allows you to recapture the cost of college. For example, if you saved $75,000 in a Bank On Yourself plan, you could take a loan for $25,000 for your child's first year of college. Then, with just a little more financial effort than it took for you to put the $25,000 in the 529 because you pay the insurance company some interest, you would have three years to pay yourself and get the money back into your Bank On Yourself plan, recapturing the cost of the first year of college ... and then it's there for the fourth year of college. Remember who controls the cash when the check you write clears? It's not the university, or anyone else ... it is you. Do this for four years of college expenses and you have just significantly improved your financial picture. You are having to save less and still accomplishing your goals of paying for college and retirement.

Think about this: You have three kids and you are going to save $100,000 for their college in a traditional manner. That is $300,000. Very few people have even saved $300,000 for retirement, yet traditional college planning tells you to put that money into something over 18 short years and then spend it all? Poof! That is mind boggling. It doesn't make any sense.

Now, if we look at a Bank On Yourself type plan, what are you doing? You are driving dollars into a place that you are ultimately going to use for income when you hit retirement, but can use it for college along the way. No matter what savings vehicle you choose, when you first start saving for college you are most likely younger, have kids at home, are incurring debt, and are in the "acquisition stage." But, by the time your kids head off to college, you are older, your debt is paid down and you're making more income. You are in a much better financial situation than when you started planning. This is the time most people put more money toward retirement.

Since you used a Bank On Yourself plan, you are going to use the same savings effort to save for college, but you will be recapturing that money spent on college and putting it back into your plan for your retirement dollars. You have consolidated your resources and you are serving only one master…you!

I recently worked with a family on the east coast who saved for college in the traditional manner. One of their children is starting college this year. After looking at their asset allocation, we moved some of the money from their brokerage account into a single premium whole life policy (the same type of chassis that is used for Bank On Yourself plans) and we made a few other strategic moves, reducing their expected family contribution by more than $14,000 this school year. This also qualified them for more than $5,000 in Pell Grants (money they get, but do not have to pay back). This change will affect them for the next 15 years since they have more children preparing to enter college. And, going forward, we will be able to save them even more by converting their future savings strategy from 529 plans to a Bank On Yourself plan.

Please be advised: All financial advisors do not know how to properly plan for college. You need to make sure you are working with an experienced college planning advisor. Money is a big factor in planning for college and knowing the ins and outs could save you thousands of dollars, sometimes without restructuring assets. For example, another one of my clients who is a medical specialist has a child going to a prestigious private university. When we met, he was going to pay more than $40,000 per year for his child's education. Without changing any of his assets, but by filling out the financial aid form correctly, we helped him send his child to her dream college for just over $8,000 per year. It pays to work with experience.

As I said, money is a big factor in planning for college and there is much more to it. Students today cannot afford to go to school undecided. That in itself is a recipe for frustration, debt and disappointment. Your student needs to find their passion, pick a major that will put them in a career that resonates with that passion, and then find the best fit school for them at the right price for you.

One last point. Although high school makes your student eligible for college it does not always prepare them for academic success in college, so a comprehensive study skills program is a must. And, while your students are working hard to obtain the best GPA possible in high school, they need to remember to study just as hard for the SAT/ACT college entrance exams. Taking the PSAT or a weekend crash course and thinking this is the best or sufficient preparation can be a costly mistake. The only apples-to-apples comparison a college or university has to differentiate between your child and another potential student are these exams. Doing well on the SAT/ACT can be the determining factor in whether your child gets into a specific college or not and at the same time can really make a big difference in what kind of financial package (price) the college will offer.

I know all of this can sound very overwhelming, but don't worry: There are proven tools available to you that you may not be aware of, even though they have been around for decades. Those who have had the good fortune of seeking them out have reaped great benefits from them. They are superior to the tools and resources that you can get from your high school guidance counselor or from any of the nonprofit companies that give free help. Remember: college is a 40-year decision, not a 4-year decision. Please do not rely on traditional planning. You can rely on the experts and your child's future will have the best chance of being the one you both dreamed about and you won't have to drain your retirement fund to do it.

—Best Success and God Bless Chip Wittrock

About Chip

Chip has helped clients with their financial futures for more than 25 years. He started out in the insurance industry, moved to securities-based investments, then returned to the safety and certainty of insurance based products for both himself and his clients. Chip says, "In securities, I found no 'security' in the very real opportunity to lose my hard-earned money in stocks and mutual funds. Years ago when I found Bank On Yourself, I realized I had found a 'secure' home for my money, as well as for the money that my clients wanted to keep safe."

While working with his Bank On Yourself clients, Chip recognized a horrific trend: hundreds of parents and college-bound grads buried with college debt by following traditional advice. This debt load for most families was second only to their home mortgage. So he began helping families arrange their finances to take advantage of the special allowances on financial aid forms, much like an accountant helps with available tax deductions.

When his daughter was entering college, he arranged his own financial affairs properly but relied on traditional resources from the high school for other college planning needs. Chip says that after following that guidance he felt like he made "every mistake in the book" and soon found that this was the norm. Changing majors, feeling unprepared and frustrated, going to the wrong college along with saving in the wrong place, were all things happening to the majority of students.

Chip knew this could be prevented with proper guidance and advice. So he struck out to find help…but he could not find what he needed. As a maverick in everything he does, he set out on a mission to create a college planning company with no hidden agenda. Along with being an authorized Bank On Yourself advisor, he is the cofounder of College Prep Mastery LLC, the only online full-service college planning company. He helps students find:

- their passion
- a major and career that resonates with that passion
- the colleges that are the best fit for the student
- the ultimate way to study once in college

He compares colleges side-by-side so parents can see which schools will actually cost the least in their unique situation (because everyone is treated differently). He does all of this and gives families advice on how to get the most financial aid possible before they fill out financial aid forms.

Chip found the top companies so students will be well-prepared for the SAT/ACT and parents will not apply for financial aid without help. He does this for his clients and for himself since he and his wife are still raising their own college-bound high school student and did not want to make the same mistakes twice.

If you are looking for more information about Chip, check him out at www. collegeprepmastery.com. Or you can find him on a golf course with his family anywhere near his Scottsdale home.

CHAPTER 5

MANAGING RISK ONE BUCKET AT A TIME

BY CHRIS MORRIS

When I was growing up, I lived next door to my grandfather, Dee, who was a builder. I dated a beautiful girl named Jennifer, whose dad was a wealthy builder, and one of my good friends, Steve, was the son of perhaps the wealthiest builder in Maryland in the 1970s. I didn't have to wonder why they were so wealthy and Dee wasn't. They told me their secret was borrowing from banks, so I took this secret to Dee.

Well, Dee wasn't impressed. He told me that banks make you bankrupt. He told me the real secret was to take the profit from the house you built and sold, put half of it into a savings account, and use the rest to live on until you built the next house.

Not realizing the importance of his advice, I went away to college, and when I returned the next summer, I decided to call on Jennifer. So I went down the street and knocked on her door. Some strange woman answered and I asked, "Are you the maid?" She looked miffed. It turned out Jennifer's dad had gone bankrupt while I was at college. I couldn't believe it.

When I got home, Dee explained, "Chris, all of the builders went bankrupt except for me. They borrowed from banks and the 1970s recession hit. Now you know why you should never borrow from banks. They loan when you don't need the money and take it from you when you do. And don't knock on Steve's home because his dad went bankrupt too."

That's when Dee told me his story. He had been a builder in the 1920s and 1930s. He borrowed money from a bank to help finance the construction of houses. When he couldn't sell the houses he'd built, he discovered he couldn't pay the bank back, so like most people during the Great Depression, he went bankrupt.

When Dee died years later, just a day shy of 100, his birthday party became a celebration of his life. I remember several people telling me what a fine man he was and how they respected him for becoming successful after all he'd gone through. Dee, whose family lived on chickens and vegetables that he grew in his backyard, left millions to his children, and he invented how to become your own banker years before Nelson Nash wrote *Becoming Your Own Banker*.

You see, gaining wealth has more to do with financial discipline than with anything else. It was Dee's ability to save and not borrow from banks that allowed him to accumulate wealth. And now that I'm older, I can see only one improvement that could be made to Dee's methodology, and that is his investment formula.

When Dee was growing his savings, he only used CDs. Not the worst way to save, because they are "safe." You'll always get your money back, as long as the government doesn't go bankrupt, but it doesn't help accumulate wealth like other strategies. One strategy is Bank On Yourself®, but I'm going to take this one step further: risk management.

It may not seem like it, but Dee managed risk by not borrowing from banks to build houses. Dee limited possible overexposure to the real estate market by not building houses that he couldn't pay for outright and he only spent half the sale proceeds of a house on building more houses. If he built a house he couldn't sell, then he had to wait. Once the house sold, he built a new one to replace the old one. This system effectively cut his spending on real estate when that market was drying up and increased his spending on real estate when that market was booming. Wouldn't it be nice if we had such an easy guide to investing in other markets?

Dee did not understand the full ramifications of what he was doing, or his other investments would have mimicked his investment in homes. CDs are great things, but they aren't risk-free. Just as in the real estate market, they have a market and all markets have risk. For CDs, most of the risk concerns purchasing power. So once your CD matures, you want it to have grown enough to keep up with inflation so that you have at least as much spending power as you gave up to invest in the CD. CD rates rarely keep up with inflation before tax and their growth is taxable, and therein lays the risks of owning CDs.

CDs need to mature before money can be used. If Dee knew about Bank On Yourself® whole life insurance that grows without taxes, pays dividends, and is friendly to loans, his money would have been readily available to build new homes. Instead, he often had to wait for CDs to mature. The Bank On Yourself® policy also has the advantage of growing without taxes. You can borrow the money without taxes and when you die it goes to heirs without income taxes and without probate.

On the other hand, putting all of your money in high tech stocks in 2000 is the other extreme of risk. There, the upside potential could be great, but the downside risk could wipe out a fortune built over a lifetime in a few short months.

The markets do not move in straight directions, and success when investing can often be boiled down to an exercise in risk management more than an exercise in stock or bond picking. That's why William O'Neil, one of the ten best traders in American history, defined success in investing as being right 6 out of 10 times, as long as you kept your losses to a minimum.

In the 1950s, a mathematician named Harry Markowitz tried to quantify market risks in a book titled *Portfolio Selection*. This theory tried to optimize returns by considering the risk tolerance of an investor. The result of this mathematical treatise was the creation of a new field in finance taught at business schools called "modern portfolio theory," and later called "asset allocation."

Here is a simple explanation of how it works. If an investor invests 100 percent of their money in bonds, bonds have a standard deviation (quantified risk) of 12. The higher the standard deviation, the greater the risk. Large cap stocks, such as those listed on the S&P 500, have a standard deviation of 18, which is 50 percent riskier than bonds.

The average return of all bonds over the last 100 years is 5 percent per year. The average return of the S&P 500 over the last 100 years is 11 percent per year. One would assume the average return of a portfolio that was half stocks and half bonds would be 7.5 percent. And that is correct. The average return is 7.5 percent.

Now consider the standard deviation (quantified risk). One would expect it to be the average of the two standard deviations or 15 for the portfolio. But Markowitz found it was 12. So a portfolio that contains 50 percent stocks and 50 percent bonds amazingly has the same risk of a portfolio containing 100 percent bonds, but has a 2.5 percent higher return.

The reason the risk stayed the same was due to the correlation coefficient, which is a fancy term for the measure of how close bond returns correspond to stock returns. Since stocks and bonds aren't highly correlated, it works out more often than not that when stocks rise, bonds fall, and vice versa. The result is risk reduction to the overall portfolio. The reason is risk management: Gains in one asset class (bonds) offset losses in the other (stocks), and vice versa.

By adding other classes, such as commodities, real estate, international stocks, absolute return funds, international bonds, REITs, limited partnerships, venture capital and futures contracts, to name a few, one can manage risk. Each class has a unique average return, standard deviation and correlation coefficient that one can use to optimize a portfolio by one's standard deviation (or quantified risk), such as 10. The balance of classes is used to get the highest return possible, given that risk. And, while this is much more complex than my grandfather Dee's management of overexposure to debt, this is still risk management.

Markowitz, his student, Sharpe, and another professor named Miller received Nobel Prizes in Economics in 1990 for their work, and now every business school in America teaches asset allocation as the best way to invest. This theory has morphed into more complex theories as the science has progressed through articles published in the *Journal of Portfolio Management* and the *Journal of Investing*.

Today, universities, such as Harvard and Yale, use these theories to manage their endowment funds. The results over a 20-year period have been astounding. Harvard and Yale's money managers beat every mutual fund manager in America over the same 20-year period. In fact, their returns were 15.5 percent per year at Harvard and 16.1 percent per year at Yale from 1984 to 2004* when the S&P 500s average return was a mere 10.6 percent a year. No mutual fund manager came close.

One of the inherent problems with the modern portfolio theory is the assumption that the investor is an institution, such as a bank, not a person. Thus, the theory assumes that the investor (the institution) will stay fully invested forever and never take large distributions like an individual would in retirement. So here's a real life problem:

> John and Amy retire in 2007. They have $1 million. Their financial advisor tells them the Dow Jones Industrial Average has an average return of 10 percent per year. John and Amy realize 10 percent of $1 million is $100,000, and they can take that out and not touch principal, so they invest all of their money in the Dow Jones Industrial Average and begin taking $100,000 per year. Using the ending value of the Dow Jones Industrial Average from Oct. 31, 2007 to Oct. 31, 2012, their assets decline from $1 million to $337,525 net of distributions.

> If John and Amy panic when the market drops and sell 100 percent of their stocks after the market bottoms out around February 2009 and buy bonds yielding 5 percent but continue taking $100,000 per year in distributions, we estimate they would run out of money by February 2013.

Over the long-term, the market may grow at 10 percent per year, but short-term drops with distributions can wipeout a lifetime of savings. Since Markowitz's theory deals with minimal distributions from institutions, such as insurance companies and banks, they really did not foresee the need to plan for large portfolio distributions.

In an attempt to deal with his clients' need for distributions and still manage risk, Ray Lucia, CFP, wrote a book titled *Buckets of Money: How to Retire in Comfort and Safety*. His theory has a simple solution to the problem above.

Ray studied the markets in the United States and concluded that we never had a market, since the creation of the U.S. markets, where the general markets made no gains for more than 14 years, even during the Civil War and the Great Depression. So Ray created the Three Bucket Theory, which allocates seven years of investment income needed to one of two buckets with the rest of the investment money in bucket three:

Bucket 1: Years 0-7, Investments that have little or no principal at risk

Bucket 2: Years 8-14, Investments that can lose some principal

Bucket 3: Years 15+, Investments that can lose a lot of principal

Using modern portfolio theory and Ray's Three Bucket Theory, we help our clients manage their risk. We run computer models to determine their asset allocation based on their risk profile. The model mathematically recommends different classes for each client to achieve the highest return for their risk. For example:

Cash equivalents	0.94%
"Safer Investments"	70.00%
Long-term govt. bonds	2.10%
Corporate bonds	2.89%
Small value stocks	3.53%
Real estate	6.27%
Commodities	5.21%
Limited partnerships	0.86%
International stocks	1.91%
International bonds	4.27%
Emerging equities	.02%
Total	**100%**

After the computer quantified Paul and Marcy's risk or standard deviation at 11.19, it then generated an asset allocation to get the clients an average return of 8.52 percent. The return of a Bank On Yourself® policy alone is not so robust, but it plays the role of managing risk in this portfolio.

.

Here's how we broke up the preceding assets into three buckets:

	Bucket 1	Bucket 2	Bucket 3
Cash equivalents	0.94%		
Long-term govt. bonds			2.10 %
Corporate bonds			2.89%
Small value stocks			3.53% (a)
Bank On Yourself® policy	35.00%	30.00%	5.00%
Real estate		6.27%	
Commodities			5.21%
Limited partnerships		0.86%	
International stocks			1.91% (a)
International bonds			4.27%
Emerging equities	_____	_____	2.02% (a)
Total	**35.94%**	**37.13%**	**26.93%**

Sum of (a) = 7.46%

Each year, Paul and Marcy spend one-seventh of Bucket 1. At the end of each year, we move enough money from Bucket 2 to Bucket 1 to keep a seven-year supply of funds in Bucket 1. We also move enough money from Bucket 3 to Bucket 2 to keep a seven-year supply of funds in Bucket 2. And the growth in Buckets 2 and 3 provides enough money to keep Bucket 1 fully funded.

Notice how the Bank On Yourself® policy is broken up into the three different buckets representing how it helped fund retirement for this couple. Bucket 1 needs a seven-year supply of money for the client to live on without principal risk and Bank On Yourself® provides that, along with more money for the other buckets.

Almost all the cash value is created by redirecting interest that would have been paid to creditors, but Paul redirected it to himself for retirement using the Bank On Yourself® methodology. Even more important, they couldn't retire without having saved the interest others paid to creditors.

This money came to Paul through discipline to never borrow from creditors again. We find Bank On Yourself® policies can add hundreds to thousands to more than a million dollars to someone's assets in a lifetime, simply by redirecting interest they would have paid to others back to themselves.

Now consider John and Amy, who invested their $1 million in the Dow Jones Industrial Average. Imagine they were like Paul and Marcy and only had 7.46 percent of their money in stocks as the (a)s indicate in the previous example. Stocks dropped more than 50 percent from 2007 to 2009. What was Paul and Marcy's actual loss? Well, if you take 7.46 percent and divide it by two, their loss is 3.73 percent. How panicked do you think Paul and Marcy were compared to John and Amy? Even better, the Bank On Yourself® policy did not lose any value during the market correction and actually added money to their portfolio to offset the stocks' losses.

Since Paul and Marcy won't need the money in stocks for 15 years, the market will recover long before they have to sell. Knowing this helps everyone sleep soundly at night, even when the markets unravel.

EPILOGUE

Based on conversations with hundreds of financial advisors in America, Canada, England, New Zealand and Australia, we have never met one financial advisor who offers "tactical asset allocation" as a method of investing for their individual clients.

One of the skills to be a successful "tactical asset allocator" is the ability to time markets. William O'Neil, one of the best traders in American history, said, "It takes three years as a full-time money manager before a person can successfully master market timing." It is so difficult to teach market timing that few people even admit it can be done. The lay press is replete with pundits who say no one can time the markets. Yet it is a minimum requirement that a person must master before they can perform "tactical asset allocation," or in William O'Neil's words, "…

---

* "The Money Game," by Marcia Vickers, Oct. 3, 2005, Fortune magazine

before they can become professional traders." So it is highly unlikely that the investment techniques used at Harvard and Yale will be available to most investors.

Doing the mathematical calculations needed to perform either "strategic" or "tactical asset allocation" manually requires weeks per investor per year to rebalance their portfolios annually. Since the average investment advisor has over 1,000 clients, such a method is too time-consuming to use. Fortunately, there is software published for financial advisors that does the complex calculations needed to perform "strategic asset allocation" in hours instead of weeks. This software is too expensive and too complex for most individuals to use, but there are numerous financial advisors that use "strategic asset allocation" as their method for money management. *"Strategic asset allocation" is acceptable and can be combined with the models above, although the returns are typically lower than they are with "tactical asset allocation."*

On the other hand, professional money managers who work for insurance companies use "tactical asset allocation" for managing their company's money. Institutions demand that their professional money managers use "tactical asset allocation" because it is the best way to invest. This is one reason for buying a Bank On Yourself® policy. Professional money managers who work for insurance companies use "tactical asset allocation" and should be able to get higher returns than other investment methodologies. The fees in insurance policies are high. But the client gets the life insurance they badly need and the tax benefits of life insurance. Plus, they should benefit from the higher returns of "tactical asset allocation" because mutual insurance companies pay profits back to their policy holders through dividends.

We have done comprehensive written financial plans for hundreds of individuals. To date, not one client (who was not already financially independent) had an adequate amount of life insurance. Considering this, along with the fact that most of our clients and the general public need a tax-advantaged method to save money, Bank on Yourself® is a great alternative to most other investments.

Many of our clients are maximizing their 401(k) and IRA investment contributions. But according to their financial plan, they need to save more money each year to achieve their goals. One solution to continue receiving some form of tax deferral is to use an insurance policy, whether that is a Bank On Yourself policy or some other form of insurance, such as an annuity.

It is the combination of all these points that makes Bank On Yourself® a wonderful solution to the complex problem of retirement planning. Again, not everyone should have a Bank On Yourself policy. It is one solution of many. But it is extremely compelling for a variety of reasons, and in general, we feel this is a fabulous foundation for building a successful financial future, especially for young people.

Clearly the best way to achieve all your goals is to find a professional financial advisor who can combine a Bank On Yourself® policy with the Nobel Prize-winning investment methodology called "asset allocation."

About Chris

Chris Morris started at a Big 8 accounting firm, and went into industry where he held positions ranging from planning manager to assistant secretary and treasurer and chief financial officer for several large corporations in Georgia. He was also president of two divisions of companies. He took four companies public. During that time period, he also managed money for three insurance companies and ran a hedge fund. In 1990, Chris started a CPA practice, Chris Morris & Associates, PC. Subsequently he created a financial planning company known as CMA Financial Services.

CMA Financial Services' mission is to serve and work for the client. We offer "tactical asset allocation" and the three bucket system as part of our services. Our comprehensive financial services also include: money management, estate planning, insurance, tax preparation and tax planning. Our firm was founded on the highest ethical standards and puts every client's success first. Our goal is not to sell but to help our clients achieve their goals for reasons that are important to them. Aligning our clients' goals with their most deeply-held values allows us to guide them on a path that ensures their future success and happiness.

CMA is unique because we use a team of professionals who work together to guide our clients through the world's financial challenges. Most people have to seek out and hire a certified financial planner, money manager, insurance specialists, attorneys and tax professionals separately. They then have to meet with them individually, extract the advice and piece that advice together themselves, in hopes of finding a path that will help them achieve financial success. These same people often wind up frustrated when the uncoordinated advice of their professionals, who don't meet together, doesn't work and their path takes a turn for the worst.

We guide our clients along the path to achieving their goals for reasons that are important to them. We bring this team together to offer comprehensive, coordinated and consolidated advice to each client. Our professionals span a wide range of financial services and include all of the professions listed previously. We believe the best way to ensure that our clients achieve their goals is to have these financial professionals meet and recommend client action as a team instead of individually. The team also must see our clients' future success as paramount. The better the quality of our services, the greater will be the success of our clients. The greatest reward we receive is when our clients achieve all of their goals for reasons that are important to them.

For more information about CMA, call (770) 493-7578 or visit www.cmawizards.com.

CHAPTER 6

DISCOVER YOUR OWN PERSONAL FINANCING SYSTEM IN YOUR 40s AND BEYOND

BY DALE MOFFITT

My story most likely is not much different than that of millions of Canadians. I was raised in an average middle class household. Money was tight but I never felt like I missed out on anything of significance. My parents worked hard to ensure that we had the basic necessities, and more. Like most, I suspect, I never received any financial education from my parents or at school, for that matter. Once I entered the workforce, I was too busy making money to have time to be directly involved in my personal investments. I gladly handed my money over to financial advisors, then crossed my fingers and hoped that they would make a return on my principal or at least not lose my principal.

At the time, I did not realize that there is a mentality to money, and my mentality was very poor. I made a lot of money in my 20s, 30s and 40s, but because I did not respect money, it did not respect me back and it did not work very hard for me. My portfolio was heavily invested in RRSPs and mutual funds, and I had no control over its eventual outcome in the volatile markets. I had entrusted my money to others who I thought could do a better job than me but who in the end were not as concerned about the safety and security of my financial future as I was, or should have been.

67

After the market crashes of 2000 and 2008, I realized in my late 40s that I had to change the financial road I was travelling on. I needed to reduce the volatility and risk while simultaneously increasing the safety and security of where my money was residing. I also needed to have access to my money in a hurry in emergencies or for special investment opportunities. My only problem was, I did not have a clue how to do this. I kept hearing that I must "stay the course" in the markets and invest and chase a rate of return for the long term. Sadly, this game plan has not worked out for me or for millions of other Canadians. I just knew there had to be a better way.

Life presents us with many financial, emotional and health-related ups and downs. We have been trained to accept all the risks in life with no guarantees in return. Often we are not in control of many things in our lives at all.

Then I discovered that it does not have to be this way. I was contacted by an acquaintance who spoke about a book that he had read that changed his whole way of financial thinking. I was skeptical, but I inquired about the book. He said it was called *Bank On Yourself* by Pamela Yellen. He had piqued my interest as I view myself as a free thinker and someone who is willing to explore the possibility that there may be a better way of doing things financially that currently I was unaware of. I ordered the book and once it arrived, I read it. Then I read it again. This Bank On Yourself concept used a specially designed dividend-paying whole life policy from a mutual life insurance company to create wealth in a safe and secure way that would give me control and access to my money at the same time. It consisted of a living benefit and a death benefit all in one package. The insurance was the vehicle and the cash value within the policy was the financial engine.

Although it seemed too good to be true, I was very intrigued. I became so consumed with this Bank On Yourself concept that at the age of 50, I started a complete career change and became licensed in the insurance industry. If I had never heard about this concept to create wealth safely and securely, then there had to be thousands, possibly millions of other Canadians who were also unaware of it.

Years earlier, I had graduated from university with a teaching degree, but I chose not to pursue that career path. Somehow I felt that my life was meant to come full circle. I proceeded to learn everything I could about this concept. I read all the applicable books and completed the extensive training. My goal was to be a financial educator on the Bank On Yourself concept and be a messenger to reach as many Canadians as I possibly could with this wonderful financial tool. Once they were armed with this new message and concept, then hopefully they would implement it to enhance their lives as well.

My new career path has become very personally rewarding. Helping one family at a time discover how to take back control of their finances in a safe way that also gives them access to their money when life happens. It provides them with peace of mind and a good night's sleep.

If you find yourself in midlife and feeling helpless or lost in the financial world, there is hope, if you have an open mind and a willingness to learn. There will be some effort and commitment required to change the financial road that you may be currently on, but it is worth it. You will also have to deconstruct your current financial thinking about money, investing and chasing a rate of return in the volatile markets, but once achieved you will discover your financial freedom. Then you can become a messenger to your children, family and friends to help them achieve safety, security and control with their finances. But beware in that others will try to dismiss you and what you have learned. They will insist that you do not break free from the herd that they are travelling in. They believe that if everyone is doing the same thing then there is security in numbers. I relate it to the blind leading the blind.

Once you discover how to recapture the interest on everything you finance, instead of giving it away to others, you must implement it with an authorized advisor who can properly structure your banking system for maximum performance. Every banking system is different for each individual or business. What can you use your banking system for? Anything you want! Emergency funds, vacations, vehicle purchases, down payment on a home, education, wedding expenses, capital expansion for your business, retirement and a legacy for your charities or loved ones, plus more. You cannot be denied a loan from your own bank. No credit checks or extensive paperwork is required, just easy, flexible and quick access to your money. We must respect ourselves, however, and pay back the loan to our own bank, resulting in a safe creation of wealth that can be a valuable and much-needed source of eventual retirement income.

If we are in poor personal health, we do not have to be the person insured. We can create a banking system on an insurable interest such as a spouse, child, grandchild or business partner. As a result, we are never too old to have our own banking system to start to recapture the financial control that has been missing in our lives. A tax-advantaged, whole life, dividend- paying insurance policy is guaranteed to grow by contract and is creditor-protected and also provides a death benefit to our loved ones.

As a parent, it is never too early to start a banking system for our children, as they have the luxury of time, growth and compounding to create a lot of safe, controlled, predictable wealth to enhance their lives and eventual retirement. As the owner and payer of your child's policy, you control every aspect and can decide when in the future you would like to hand over the policy to your child to use as their primary financing tool, which will help supplement their eventual retirement.

Similarly, grandparents can vastly improve the lives of their grandchildren by setting up a banking system for them. Grandparents remain the owners and payers of the policies and can use the policies for their own financing needs and to supplement their retirement. When the time is right, they hand over the policy to the parent or the child. For families, this cycle can become perpetuated throughout the generations.

I have clients in their 50s, whom I'll call Bill and Mary, who wanted to do something very special for their two grandsons: Chris, age four, and Kyle, age six. They were considering an RESP for each grandchild but were concerned about the possible restrictions, especially if they did not end up going to a university or college. Bill and Mary attended one of my financial information sessions that I regularly hold. They were intrigued and met with me a couple of days later to find out more on the subject. They stated to me that this concept seemed too good to be true. I replied that I indeed had felt the exact same way when I was first told about it. I said to just keep an open mind and be willing to learn something new.

Bill then asked me why the insurance company should be a mutual company versus a stock company, and what exactly is the difference. I explained that a stock company is owned by shareholders, and stock companies sometimes have to make short- term decisions to appease their shareholders. Mutual companies, on the other hand, are owned by us, the policy holders, and a life insurance policy is a long-term process so they do not have to make those short-term investment decisions and can avoid the volatile markets chasing a rate of return.

Mary had a question, as well. She asked me if an insurance company is at high risk of becoming insolvent. I told her that insurance companies are audited on a very regular basis, which is a great safety feature for the policyholder. I told them that as a policyholder, they are protected in part by an industry-sponsored nonprofit consumer organization, as well.

Both Bill and Mary seemed satisfied with the answers to their questions. They were very excited to be setting up lifelong financing systems that would most certainly enhance the lives of their grandsons. As we were preparing to complete the applications for Chris and Kyle, Bill asked if I could explain how it was possible to take a loan from your own bank but have your money grow as if it were never touched. I explained that the long-term game plan and objective was to have our money remain in our own bank for as many years as possible so it could safely and predictably work hard for us, growing and compounding at the same time. I then explained that to achieve this, they would use their money as collateral and take a loan from the life insurance company's general fund, which is a huge pool of money used in part as their operating fund. Then they would pay back the loan at a predetermined rate to the insurance company on their own terms. They could decide for how many months they wanted to pay the loan back and even how much the total monthly payment would be that they could afford to pay back. If they fell ill or lost their jobs, they could even suspend the loan payments. I also explained that they could never be refused a loan from their own bank and that there were no credit checks, approval processes or complicated documents to fill out. Just quick and easy access to their money when they needed or wanted it. They had incredible flexibility.

Slowly but surely, Bill and Mary got all their questions answered to their satisfaction and chose to set up a whole life banking system for each grandson. They remained the owner and payers of the policies and could take out policy loans at their leisure.

In the financial information sessions I conduct, I always say that we should secure permanent whole life insurance on our children as soon as possible. I go on to say that it is much less expensive when they are younger and that we never know when our children could become uninsurable or disabled. I ran into Bill and Mary a few months after they had purchased the policies on their grandchildren and they told me that Chris had been diagnosed with autism. Bill said that it was comforting to know that coverage was put in place much earlier. Then, last August, their oldest grandson Kyle suffered a collapsed lung and spent considerable time recovering in the hospital. Again, Bill and Mary felt comfort knowing that insurance coverage had been attained much earlier. As long as the premium payments are being made regularly, the insurance coverage on the two grandchildren cannot be taken away.

Since then, both Bill and Mary have taken out policy loans from the policies for various reasons and purposes. Years down the road, Bill and Mary will hand off the policies to Chris and Kyle, who will be adults. They will use their whole life banking systems for their life-long financing needs and as an emergency fund.

Business owners of any size can use this tax-advantaged concept of self-financing to create wealth safely and securely. If we can self-finance both personally and in our self-employed business, we can multi-task our money and keep more of it in our own pockets where it belongs to enhance our lives and our retirement. It is crucial that our money resides within our own bank to truly become a win-win situation for a financially enhanced future.

My clients almost always say, "I wish I had known about this 20 years ago." I reply, "I wish I had as well." My wish and hope for you is that you thoroughly and completely discover this wonderful financial tool as soon as possible. It is never too late to start. Seek out a competent, well-trained, authorized advisor. Ask questions and learn as much as you can about this concept. You are never too old to change your financial path. It is possible to create wealth in a safe and secure way that gives you control and access to your money at the same time. The peace of mind that this financial tool will provide you is well worth the effort.

There is no charge or obligation to see what this powerful financial tool can do for you and your family. Knowledge is power. We all have the power within us to take control of our financial futures, and to enhance our lives, our retirement and the lives of our loved ones. Having the courage to be a leader and a free thinker is crucial. Taking your first step towards that financial freedom is essential.

Good luck and all the best!

About Dale

Dale Moffitt is a trusted advisor-life insurance broker with the MacDev Financial Group. He is recognized as one of the top experts in Canada on how to create wealth in a safe and secure way that gives you control and access to your money when you need it.

Dale is a highly organized, self-motivated and goal-oriented financial professional. He seeks to educate and help others to achieve fulfilled, balanced lives and to protect families from the uncertainties that may arise in life.

Dale's goal with his clients is to create safe and secure life insurance and financial solutions through education, mutual trust and respect. Dale regularly conducts presentations and information sessions on this wealth-generating concept, which empowers Canadians to take control of their financial futures.

For more information, visit www.macdevfinancial.com, email dale@macdevfinancial.com, or call (403) 872-7135.

CHAPTER 7

FINDING A SAFE PLACE FOR YOUR MONEY

BY FRED LEWIS, CLU, CHFC

I grew up in a family where life insurance was the family business. In fact, I'm a third-generation insurance professional. My grandfather began his career by owning a general store when he was in his twenties in the early 1900s. He began selling life insurance part-time in 1911 at the age of 28. The general store burned to the ground in 1914 and he accepted an offer to go full-time in the life insurance business and moved to another city to start his own agency. He sold masses of whole-life insurance from 1914 until his retirement in 1948 at age 65.

When the stock market crashed from 1929 to 1932, my grandfather didn't get very many calls from clients because most of his policyholders didn't own stocks at that time. In 1933, however, he began to get a lot of calls when more than 9,000 banks defaulted in the country. Every bank in his town went under except for two. He was relieved and thankful that he could tell his policyholders that the cash values in their policies were safely protected in the general account of the insurance company. Throughout the depression of the 1930s, the insurance companies remained strong because they held their assets primarily in investment-grade corporate bonds with companies that were able to remain investment-grade during those severe market conditions. In fact there were more than a few of my grandfather's clients who were able to borrow on their cash values to meet critical expenses after losing money due to bank failures.

My father joined my grandfather in the life insurance business in 1936 at age 30 and took over as general agent in 1948, when my grandfather retired. I joined my father in the business in 1964 and took over as general agent in 1975 when my father went into semi-retirement at age 69. He remained active with his clients until 1992 at age 86, when he fully retired due to failing eyesight.

My father and I both obtained our securities licenses in 1972 to be able to offer a full range of financial products to our clients. That year, the Dow Jones Industrial Average (DJIA) closed over the 1,000 mark for the first time in history. Two years later, in 1974, the DJIA had fallen to 577 and we were asking ourselves, "Is this anywhere we want to put our client's money?" It took 10 years for the DJIA to stay consistently over 1,000 again and, needless to say, we didn't recommend stocks in those years.

Along with life insurance, I began to put clients into the stock market during the 1980s and 1990s with tremendous results. As we approached the 2000s, many of my clients were arriving at a dangerously high percentage of their total net worth in the stock market due to gains, and I began to reduce their exposure by moving money into safer alternatives. Also, at that time I began to be concerned that the stock market might be heading for another drop like the one we went through from 1972 to 1974. At its peak in 2000, the DJIA got up to 11,722.98, and by the fall of 2002 it had fallen to 7,286.27. During that time I recommended that my clients get out of the stock market and I sold off the remaining securities business to another stock broker in the fall of 2002.

HISTORICAL CYCLES OF THE STOCK MARKET

After experiencing a couple of market cycles during my career, I began to investigate the various forces that cause movements in the stock market. I found that during the 1930s, cycles or wave patterns were discovered that have been repetitive throughout the history of the financial markets. About once a century, it was observed, there has been a huge run-up to a topping process that has always ended in a severe collapse.

The first collapse occurred when the price of tulip bulbs peaked in Europe in 1637. The price of one bulb rose to exceed the annual salary of skilled craftsmen by 8 to 10 times! The price then fell to near worthless and the whole process became known as "Tulipomania."

The next one involved stocks on the London Exchange from 1720 to 1722 and was known as the "South Sea Bubble." At that time, stocks had risen to unbelievable levels and collapsed back to where they started in just two short years. The next topping process occurred in the U.S. stock market when it topped in 1835 and fell precipitously back to where it started by 1842.

The fourth collapse occurred from 1929 to 1932 and is known by almost everyone as the Great Depression. The DJIA came into being on May 26, 1896, closing at 40.94. It soon dropped to 28.66 on August 7, 1896, and then rose to 381.17 by September 3, 1929 (+1,230%). During the next 34 months, it cascaded in the familiar pattern back down to 41.22 by July 8, 1932 (-89%), where it had started more than 36 years earlier. This time it took more than 22 years to get back over 381 on November 23, 1954. Recall, that in my third year in the securities business, the DJIA fell to 577 in 1974, which is less than 200 points from its peak of 381 in 1929 ... 45 years earlier!

From the bottom on December 6, 1974 of 577.60, the DJIA zoomed up to 14,164.53 by October 9, 2007 (+2,352%). Seventeen months later, on March 9, 2009, it had fallen to 6,547.05 (-53.8%). Now, it's back over the 14,000 level again and the next step in the recurring pattern is likely to take it down through the 6,500 level it was at in March 2009. Those who closely follow these patterns are looking for a bottom in the DJIA sometime in mid-2016 and some forecasts have the DJIA below 3,000 at that time. I hope it doesn't happen, but based on the foregoing history of the markets, there is a high enough degree of uncertainty that I recommend avoiding stocks altogether for now.

FINDING A SAFE PLACE FOR MONEY TO GROW

This brings up the main purpose of this chapter: "If my money isn't in the stock market, where can I put it to avoid a disaster and still get a decent return along with some tax advantages?" A very important principle I share with my clients is what I call the SRT strategy: Safety, Return and Taxes. What the strategy delivers first of all is safety, then an increasing return, and finally, a reduction in taxes. All three of these components must be carefully considered when making investment choices.

Throughout the history of the financial markets, the only safe place to be, under all market conditions, has been investment-grade corporate bonds with major corporations who can and will stay investment-grade under all market conditions. Interestingly, the majority of the assets of major life insurance companies are held in investment-grade corporate bonds and this explains why, since the 1840s, insurance companies have been viewed as safe harbors for money. Major life insurance companies have developed the knack over the years of buying the bonds of corporations that can and will stay viable under all market conditions. Furthermore, since they generally hold the bonds to maturity, they don't realize losses in case of rising interest rates. By owning these bonds indirectly through the life insurance policy, you have both safety and liquidity.

There are two main products offered by major life insurance companies that can hold your assets: dividend-paying whole-life insurance and fixed-indexed annuities. I've left out any form of universal life since it is, in my opinion, inferior to whole-life. I discovered that there are only a handful of life insurance companies that offer features on these products that also make it possible to have a decent return along with the tax advantages unique to these products. There are features some companies have built into their modern products to keep your values liquid and available for investments or financing your lifestyle and major purchases. I also consider it to be the safest, most efficient and reliable way to provide for retirement income.

I believe the best strategy to adopt at this point in the history of the market is to be on the safe side and stay out of the market. Keep your money in cash and the products of major life insurance companies. I hope I am wrong and that nothing dramatic happens to the market, but the likelihood is great enough that no one should expose themselves to this amount of risk. How would you feel if you experienced a decrease in the value of your assets of 50 percent or more due to another market correction? How long would it take you to get back to even and how old would you be then? Compare that to how you would feel if you didn't have to worry about a downturn and you were still able to achieve a decent return on your money. There are specific life insurance plans that can help you accomplish that goal.

THE HISTORY OF LIFE INSURANCE

Life insurance has played a significant role in people's lives for centuries and it has never become obsolete. The history of life insurance is a long one, dating all the way back to the Roman Empire in 100 B.C. After the Roman Empire fell, life insurance didn't reappear until 1662 in London. In this country, it wasn't until 1760 that some form of life insurance was available.

The only product available in the early years was term life insurance, which only pays a claim at the time of the death of the insured. Whole-life, on the other hand, builds cash value to provide a substantial living benefit. With term life insurance, many complaints came in due to the insured having to pay higher and higher premiums as they survived and were growing older. Unlike fire insurance where premiums stay fairly level due to the risk remaining fairly level, the risk in a life insurance policy increases with age. Thus, the insurance company had no choice but to increase premiums on existing policies.

By using the law of large numbers, insurance companies can determine how much to charge each insured based on tables compiled from actual death rate statistics that are known as mortality tables. The field of study that makes these calculations is known as actuarial science and the people schooled in this science are called actuaries. In addition to increased risk and cost due to increasing mortality rates, there is one more risk that the actuaries have to factor in to remain solvent. It is known as anti-selection or adverse-selection and is a phenomenon that occurs as a group of insured individuals, that comprise a block of business, progress down the corridor of time.

Here's what happens. As the years go by and the premiums increase for the policies, the healthy insureds tend to discontinue their policies at a greater rate than do the unhealthy insureds. This causes a higher rate of mortality as a given group of policies age and therefore results in a higher percentage of death claims than would be the case if all the insureds kept their policies. This additional cost has to be added to the remaining insureds each year, resulting in exorbitant premiums as the remaining group ages.

In the 1860s, the actuaries went to the drawing board to design a way to mitigate these outcomes. What they came up with is what we now know as whole-life insurance, whereby an insured can pay a level premium for life. To accomplish this, the actuaries schedule in overcharges in the early years to build a reserve against increasing mortality costs as the years go by. To combat the risk of anti- or adverse-selection, they also build in enough overcharge so the entire death benefit can be taken by the insured if he or she survives to a specified age. Therefore, there is an increasing incentive for you to keep your policy regardless of your health so the insurance company can build in lower mortality costs and you have a more efficient vehicle to build cash reserves for your future.

WHOLE-LIFE INSURANCE WITH PAID-UP ADDITIONS RIDERS AND NONDIRECT RECOGNITION DIVIDENDS

The whole-life policies that I recommend are a modern, updated version of the original design that are, in fact, quite rare in the industry. These special dividend-paying, whole-life policies are only offered by a handful of companies and include features that most insurance agents don't even know about. The two main features of these up-to-date policies are: 1) paid-up additions riders and 2) nondirect-recognition dividends. These features make it possible for you to build equity quickly in your policy where you can have a cash value available that is greater than your total outlay in less than 10 years. The annual return, after your policy gets up and running in the first few years, is in the 3.5 to 4.5 percent range. This annual return is net of all costs and expenses and, based on current income tax law, is net of income taxes. If you compare what rate of pretax return you would need to get to beat your policy's after-tax return you would need pre-tax returns in the 4.5 to 8.5 percent range, depending on your tax bracket. The average client would be overjoyed with a 3.5 to 4.5 percent net return over the last 10 to 15 years.

A paid-up additions rider makes it possible to pay in extra money in addition to the base premium and almost this entire extra amount goes directly to your cash value each year. Very few companies offer this feature.

Nondirect-recognition dividends are a feature that will enable you to borrow on the cash values of your whole-life insurance policy without reducing the annual dividend you receive. This is like "having your cake and eating it too." The insurance company does not "recognize" that you have a loan when they pay you the dividend. Again, very few companies offer this feature.

QUALIFYING FOR LIFE INSURANCE

You qualify for life insurance and annuities on two levels. The first level is good health and is the main consideration for life insurance. The second level is financial suitability. Buying whole-life insurance with accumulating cash values involves a long-term threshold and therefore you must take into consideration the factor of suitability. Once you have passed the health underwriting and financial suitability requirements, you can arrive at the maximum amount you can comfortably place into your policy.

ACHIEVING FINANCIAL FREEDOM

Below are the steps I recommend you follow to achieve stress-free financial freedom:

1. Get up to speed with the safe money concepts of Bank On Yourself.

2. Move any risk-based assets to safety.

3. Go through the medical underwriting and financial suitability process.

4. Determine the maximum amount of lump sum and annual outlays you can qualify for and comfortably set aside.

5. Have your advisor get the life insurance and annuities issued and begin making payments.

6. Start waking up every morning with the understanding that you are safely in control of your growing finances and are enjoying some income tax advantages.

7. Have your advisor regularly review and update your financial program to address any changes that occur.

I encourage you to join the Bank On Yourself revolution. Fire your banker, bypass Wall Street and take control of your own financial future.

About Fred

Fred Lewis, CLU, ChFC, LUTCF, is an outstanding professional in the financial services industry with more than 30 years experience in insurance and securities as a chartered life underwriter (CLU), chartered financial consultant (ChFC), and life underwriter training council fellow (LUTCF), holding an intermediary insurance license in numerous states. Over the years Fred has helped hundreds of clients achieve their financial goals. As a sought-after speaker, he has spoken at numerous financial services industry events, local service organizations and seminars. Additionally, he has been featured on television and numerous radio programs as an expert financial advisor.

Fred completed his undergraduate work through the Wisconsin University system; finishing up at the American College, Bryn Mawr, Pennsylvania. He attained life and qualifying membership status in the Million Dollar Round Table and was a member of the prestigious Court of the Table. He is a current member in good standing of the Society of Financial Services Professionals and also currently serves on the board of the local branch of the National Association of Insurance and Financial Advisors (NAIFA). He received the distinguished service award from both his local branch of NAIFA and from one of his primary insurance companies. He is active in his church, family, community and profession, having served as a member and officer on many organizations, boards and committees.

Fred is a U.S. Army Vietnam veteran and lives in Wisconsin with his wife of more than 40 years, Jan, their three children and two grandchildren. His pastimes include family activities, Bible study, traveling, reading, writing, speaking, oldies music and muscle cars.

CHAPTER 8

MOVING UP TO PRO BALL: My Story

BY GEORGE FAATZ

What if the new VP of Marketing for a start-up, multilevel marketing company, owned by Christian Broadcasting Network founder Dr. Pat Robertson, is diagnosed with a rare form of leukemia within several months of starting the job? What if just when you get the vitamin line going, and the skin care line from Israel going, and company growth is like a rocket, you learn that it's more than a sore throat and a couple nosebleeds? What if you are travelling all over the country hosting meetings on weekends, and you are eating vitamins like M&Ms? What if you eat an orchard of apples, gallons and gallons of carrot juice and green barley drink and the blood counts stay dangerously low? What if you still feel good and have a year-round "carrot juice tan" but the blood counts won't budge? What if you figure out that you are not in control?

No matter how hard I worked at it, no matter that I was a pure raw food vegetarian (well almost pure), I learned there are some things you cannot control. Almost three years into the battle just described, I stepped off the "I can do it, I am a workaholic" train ride and turned my heart toward my home and my family. I decided to start a one-man general contracting business. At least I'd be home every afternoon. My kids were young and I needed my family. After a six-year battle ending with one long dose of chemotherapy, I was declared back to normal in all my blood counts. And I said, "Thank God I am strong and healthy today."

My name is George Faatz and I am 62 years old. Today, I can still thank God that I am strong and healthy. I am still married to my first and only wife. I have three adult children and I have a dream.

THE PROBLEM

Despite a wonderful marriage, great kids and a great credit score, I suffered for years with a nagging and ever-increasing debt. Not because we took extravagant vacations, not because I'm a big game hunter, but just living our lives with the usual water heater replacement, transmission issues, orthodontist payments, and especially nongroup health care costs. It was a debt load that I could not control.

I have always seen myself as a businessman who challenged the status quo. I have always wanted to make things better for myself and for the average Joe. I wanted to be on the cutting edge of innovation, doing something new with something old, something to make things better. I had an exciting and unusual career path to reflect that, but I also had this ever- present, ever-growing debt. I had high hopes for saving some money in the stock market. Twice, I was on the way to what I thought was a decent stock portfolio. But in the dotcom bubble, and again in 2008, my savings dropped like a stone, and I didn't know what to do. I remember asking my financial guru if I should just sell everything and buy some gold or something. He told me to my face that I was silly to even think about gold; I was nowhere near big enough for gold to be in my portfolio, and that actually I was earning about a 7 to 8 percent average rate of return. I lost more than half of my money.

Robert Kennedy once said, "Tragedy is a tool for the living to gain wisdom, not a guide by which to live." Someone else said, "Figures don't lie, but liars figure," and I'm just saying . . . Do you think it might happen again? I hope it doesn't happen again to you.

THE LIGHT TURNS ON

About that time, my good friend, and very successful Norfolk real estate investor, Andy McFie, told me he wanted me to meet his brother Tom, coming to visit from Oregon, with Ray Poteet from Kansas. They were going to talk about Nelson Nash's Infinite Banking Concept. I had never heard of Infinite Banking, or of any financial wizards from Kansas except, of course, the Great Oz. If Andy thought it was a good idea, I wanted to know more.

Right from the start it was stuff about banking that I had never heard. The "volume and velocity" of interest, how bankers rated certain insurance policies as tier 1 assets, about IRS Code 7702, and how whole-life insurance just smoked term insurance. They peppered the seminar with compelling and practical examples. I started thinking…well, I admit it was more like drifting than thinking, the banker, the banker kept going through my mind, and then it hit me. I remembered the parable of the talents.

But before I get into the details, I have to tell you: I happen to be a Christian. Now don't worry, I'm not going to have an altar call. In fact, why even mention it? Because the Bible has a lot to say about growing your money, and I'm going to share a few lines from one parable with you. So if you have a problem with that, here is your chance to turn to another chapter. I promise I won't hold what you believe against you if you will coexist with me. If you are sticking with me, then let's get started.

As the parable of the talents goes, the Master gave one man five talents, which he doubled; and he gave another man two, which he doubled as well. The Master said, "Well done, my faithful servant" and told them, "You have been faithful with little; now you shall be given much."

The final servant got one talent, which he buried. The master called him a wicked, lazy servant. Taking back the talent and giving it to the rich one, he said, "You could have at least put it with the banker so I would have earned interest." Put it with the banker, the banker, the banker. Still drifting I realized I was feeling uncomfortable, pondering the parable.

What if I were called on that day to explain myself? I would have less to show than the lazy servant. I had lost more than half of my talents in the stock market, and worse than that, I had an even bigger negative bag of talents known as debt.

I had to find out what bankers knew, and find out fast. In the next few hours I learned that bankers do not invest, they loan; that the volume of interest is more important than the rate, and when they reloan interest payments, it is called is velocity. I learned that the average American earns between $1 million and $2 million in a lifetime, of which taxes in one form or another consume about 28 percent. Of his after tax income, the average American spends between 30 to 35 percent on interest and financing costs to sustain his lifestyle. He saves less than 5 percent. So without getting too personal, ask yourself how you can pay 35 percent in interest and fees, and think you are going to retire on the interest you earn from your 5 percent savings?

With Bank On Yourself, you will learn banking strategies that have been hidden in plain sight for centuries. Strategies that grow "talents" without the unnecessary risk of investing. In just over three years of working with what I call my private family financing system, my wife and I learned to recycle our way out of Visa debt, car payments, business credit and so forth, while making the same payments we would have paid to our creditors. We recycled our equity and recaptured the interest we would have paid to others. Thank God we are financially strong and healthy today.

THE RULES OF ENGAGEMENT

A wise man once said that if you think about it, everyone is really in two businesses: the one you are in and banking. You are either making money with whatever money you have or losing it to someone who understands its inherent opportunity. Recapturing the 30 to 35 percent interest you are currently giving to the bankers is the first of the secrets which are hiding in plain sight.

You might ask if it's just like what Dave Ramsey says about paying first one debt and then adding that payment to the next debt and snowballing your payments. The simple answer is no.

A well-executed Dave Ramsey plan can be a thing of beauty, much like watching a championship football team. The trouble is you are watching high school championship ball. I'm not challenging his plays; they are simple and obviously work. But Dave Ramsey's plans have an upside and a downside. When you only pay cash, you do avoid paying interest on your expenses, but you also avoid earning interest on your savings. Like high school football, there are only so many plays to run. Dave's system does not use the full power of compound interest to your advantage. And that's just not playing pro ball.

How much do interest do you earn when you pay cash and empty your savings account? What about the lost opportunity costs of earning interest on your savings? Check my arithmetic. You can borrow $10,000 for two years at 6 percent, and it costs you about $637 in interest. If you save $10,000 for two years at 4 percent interest, you earn about $816. With this simple example, if you can save at 4 percent and borrow at 6 percent for two years, you are almost $200 ahead, but you also violated one of Dave Ramsey's basic rules.

His way works, if you want to play high school football. If you can follow my arithmetic, you know that blowing your savings to pay cash is not always the best strategy. With Bank On Yourself, you move up to pro ball. Bankers use interest coming and going. You should, too.

With a properly designed Bank On Yourself system, you take full advantage of the tax code, have guaranteed growth, and enjoy extraordinary liquidity and control. There is no loss of equity regardless of the performance of the stock market and you create an intergenerational legacy unmatched by any other system or program. Did I say, "You get to go to Disneyland?"

MY ROLL-OUT

We used $10,000 from savings to buy the first specially designed participating whole-life policy for my wife. Because of the unique design characteristics, we were immediately able to borrow about $6,500 from the available cash value, and pay off my 21 percent Home D credit card. We were paying about $575 every month, so we made exactly the same deposit back to our policy. I call it our private family financing system. In eight months, we had $4,600 back in available cash value. We borrowed $4,200 to pay off my wife's car. We had been making $210 payments to the credit union, so we acted like honest borrowers/bankers, and deposited that amount back into our system. Simple arithmetic tells you that we were now depositing $785 per month back into our account. We kept getting our equity back, simply by making the same payments we were used to.

Do you see that by acting like honest borrowers/bankers we were recycling our equity and recapturing the interest we would have paid to others? We spent the $6,500 over again. In another few months we had the money back to spend again. That's not high school football, my friend, that's what the Bank On Yourself system is all about. It's not magic, it's arithmetic.

Finally, specific insurance policies have been developed that allow regular families to take advantage of strategies that were previously only available to wealthy people. Never before have these powerful tools been available for the average American. These systems work for you no matter what size policy you start with. As I said, I have always been attracted to new ways to solve old problems. I'm a problem solver, not a problem maker.

As I saw the system work for my family, I became so excited that I decided to study for the state examination for insurance. I passed the exam and then began the journey to qualify for the Bank On Yourself authorized advisor team. I knew I wanted to work with the most successful organization in the country. With more than 200 authorized advisors who meet the strictest guidelines of knowledge and integrity, you can be confident you are playing professional ball.

YES, I AM TALKING TO YOU

I have always been willing to challenge the status quo. I teach people to establish their own private family financing system. I teach them to Bank On Yourself, and become financially set for life without taking unnecessary risk in the stock market. I care about the average Joe.

Today my wife and I own our own private family financing system with three branches. So far, our children own two more. Today I am proud to be an authorized Bank On Yourself advisor. I will help you with step-by-step details, the rules of engagement if you will, for regaining control of your checkbook and dominating your debt. I like to call it "Your Family's 3- to 5-Year Plan" to financial security. We are not competing with your stock broker or financial advisor. He probably has never heard of Bank On Yourself, or the infinite banking concept anyway. We are competing with your Visa card, your car payment, your education loans, all your financing needs. And that's just the beginning. In time, we'll compete with your home mortgage, too. Again, ask yourself how you can lose 30 to 35 percent of your income to interest and fees for lifestyle, house payments, car payments and such, and expect to retire on the gain from a 5 percent savings program.

Let me caution you: keep your own counsel as you research this concept. It is not for everyone. There are probably 7 billion people on the planet, and about 6.99 billion of them are really good at identifying the problem without any actual research to back up their conventional opinion. They never ask the questions that I hope you are asking right now. This is something special, something counter-intuitive. If you think you are hearing the truth in these many chapters, dig in. Read more. Go to the Bankyonyourself.com website. Ask questions, and don't take answers from people who already know all about something, before they know anything.

I told you, I have a dream…I care about the average Joe. I do not care about the status quo. I have a dream to help average Americans establish their own private family financing system. I help them regain control of their checkbook and dominate their financing needs. I teach them strategies that were once reserved for the wealthy. I'll help you learn to Bank On Yourself and become financially set for life, too, without unnecessary risk. The path to the truth is narrow; the road to conventional wisdom is wide and well-traveled. Bank On Yourself provides light for your financial journey. Yes, I am talking to you; it's as simple as that.

About George

George Faatz, a 25-year resident of Virginia, is a small businessman and entrepreneur who has been involved with many cutting-edge concepts and ideas. From pioneering ecologically innovative business ventures to undertaking handicapped accessible residential remodeling, George has a wide range of business experience. When evaluating a new business opportunity, George always asks, "Who benefits? Who can this help? Is this project good for all the parties involved? Does the project represent the highest integrity and intent?" George has a history of volunteering in his community, civic league and church men's ministry.

George's message for his clients is that you can get control of your debt; you can get control of your checkbook. Using simple financial strategies that were once only available to the wealthy, you can learn to Bank On Yourself, and become financially set for life.

George's question for you is simple: "Are you willing to take a fresh look at how you manage your finances and discover how to 'recycle your equity and recapture the interest' you are currently paying others?" George teaches you how to regain control of your checkbook, and create an intergenerational legacy for your family.

CHAPTER 9

ANCIENT SECRETS: What the Bible Reveals About Money Management

BY GLEN OAKS

"My people are destroyed from lack of knowledge."
~ Hosea 4:6

There are more Bibles in print than any other book in history. In the Bible, there are more than 2,000 scriptures related to money. Jesus said more about work, possessions and money than any other subject while on this earth.

So why am I saying that these are secrets? I believe many who read the Bible are looking for spiritual answers and don't use it as a manual for living every aspect of their lives. Of course, the Bible can transform someone's life with spiritual truths but God's word instructs us in every area of our lives. It provides knowledge applicable to our lives for today, including how to use all of the talents and resources (money, etc.) that God has allowed us to have. I will point out just a few examples in the following pages.

DEBT AND SERVITUDE

One of the biggest obstacles to financial security is debt. Proverbs 22:7 says, "The rich rule over the poor, and the borrower is slave to the lender." Another verse, Romans 13:8, warns us "Let no debt remain outstanding." When we are in debt, we are in a position of servitude to the lender. We are sacrificing the future to pay for a lifestyle we cannot afford.

I have observed over the years what financial security looks and feels like. My first several years as an insurance agent were quite lean. Soon after I got up in the morning I had to figure out how I was going to make enough money to pay the bills we had. I knew God was going to take care of my needs but I was concerned about finding out how and when.

Today, days and weeks go by that I don't even think about money. Because I have been following the advice from the scriptures, the best I know how, I have financial security. So one indication of how financially secure you are is to ask yourself, how soon in my day do I start thinking about money and how I am going to make ends meet?

If the stress of money issues, especially debt, is keeping you up at night, then you know you are out of balance. Either you have made or are making mistakes with your finances or you are lacking faith in God that He will take care of your basic needs (Matthew 6:25-34).

AMERICANS AND DEBT

So here is where we as Americans are. The average American is spending 34.5 percent of their income to service debt. With Uncle Sam demanding another 15 to 35 percent of our income, no wonder we cannot get ahead. Even if we save 5 percent of our income for retirement and even if we could earn a 10 percent return on that fund, it is still like taking one step forward and taking two steps back.

The media in our country is more powerful than ever and advertisements are telling us that we deserve and can afford more than what we need. And we can have it today! If we fall victim to these pressures, we lose the present value of the money spent, as well as the interest on that money. We must also consider the interest we could have gained had we not made the purchase at all. Let's look at the true cost of interest in the chart that follows.

If you keep just a $5,000 balance on one or more credit cards at 18 percent interest, Figure 1 shows what the consequences look like:

YEARS	10	20	30
Amount You Pay to Creditors	$9,858	$19,716	$29,575
Potential Earnings Lost (6% interest)	$12,994	$36,264	$77,937
Earnings for Creditor	$25,235	$177,829	$1,100,560

(Figure 1)

$77,000 of potential lost over 30 years. That will buy a small house in my neck of the woods.

Even if we are reading God's word daily, the messages we hear the rest of the day are loud and enticing. Every day I am confronted with trying to help people to save for the future and delaying gratification as they are being bombarded with messages such as, "Sign here and you can drive this new car today." It's a constant battle. I feel like I am battling for my clients' future. I know if they live within their means now, they will have a better lifestyle later.

HOW BANKS ENSNARE YOU

Banks have gotten more aggressive in their advertising. Besides sending me credit card offers almost daily they are including blank checks in their statements. They encourage me to use the checks to go on vacation or buy a boat or remodel my house. I am amazed at what they are allowed to say in some of their advertisements. For example, I was in my credit union the other day and a sign in the manager's office said, "Save money while going to college." As I was contemplating how a credit union could do that, I read the rest of the sign. It went on to say, "By getting a student loan." Now how does getting a loan "save" money? Even if the student paid off the loan right after graduating so he wouldn't have to pay any interest, it still wouldn't "save" him any money!

When banks tell us we can afford something today, people think the bank should know; they are in the money business. What banks know is how much money they can make if they can convince us to live above our means ($1.1 million in Figure 1.).

The opposite of going into debt is saving money. It is an easy formula: Spend less than you make. Not that easy to live out with all the temptations we have in life today. Studies have shown that the more TV we watch, the more we spend. The more time spent on the Internet, the more we spend, and of course, the more we look at catalogs or "window shop" at the mall, the more money we will spend. Think of how many times you have gone to the mall shopping for one or two things and come home with six bags of stuff you didn't know you "needed" when you left home.

Proverbs 21:20 says, "The wise man saves for the future, but the foolish man spends whatever he gets." Driving your car for 2 to 3 years after

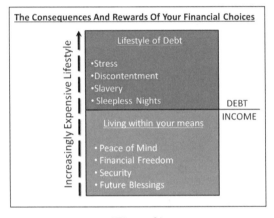

(Figure 2)

you have paid off the loan is not the normal thing to do today. Doing that a few times, though, may allow you to buy cars with cash eventually, or better yet, use your private reserve fund as collateral to purchase your cars and other major things. Let me tell you that it is well worth it. Living within your means now allows you to have a better lifestyle later, which means better sleep because you have peace about your finances. The opposite of slavery is freedom.

THE POWER OF COMPOUNDING YOUR MONEY

Let's look at the power of compound interest working in our favor instead for the banks.

If Matt saved $3,000 per year for just 10 years in an account that paid him 6 percent every year, in 30 years his account would be worth

$134,427. If Cyndi waited 10 years to start, but put the $3,000 per year into her account for 20 year at 6 percent interest also, her account would be worth $116,978. Cyndi would have contributed $60,000 compared to Matt's $30,000, twice as much, but because of the power of compound interest over several years he would have almost $18,000 more in his account.

How much and how long you save are the two most important elements in determining how much of a nest egg you can accumulate. Chasing better rates of return could lead to disaster. Proverbs 21:5 says, "The plans of the diligent lead to profit as surely as haste leads to poverty." The example above shows how important it is to start on this path early. If you haven't started yet, now is the time to start. You can do it!

So what does the Bible say about saving money? Well, in 1 Timothy, Chapter 5, it says that we should provide for our households. I believe this means to save so we will not be dependent on the government or other sources later in life. And what about providing for the next generation? Life insurance is designed for that purpose (more about this later). With whole-life insurance, you can take care of the next generation and have access to your money for yourself when needed; whether it is for repairs of the house or cars, or medical bills. It is always nice to have a few months income saved.

One of the great things about this method of saving money is that the money is liquid enough to help out in these times. It is also available for opportunities that may present themselves. I just recently had an opportunity to make a short-term investment with an excellent return. I was able to participate because my money was liquid and not tied up in some tax qualified plan or a hard asset that I would have had to sell.

RETIREMENT, IN A BIBLICAL SENSE

As far as saving for retirement, the Bible does not say much about it. Retirement is a fairly new phenomenon. In my practice I see more and more people leaving their full-time employment in their mid- to late-60s to take consulting jobs or work per diem, etc. Some of this is driven by inflation and the loss of pensions. I like the idea of being able to put in fewer hours in the office over the years to spend more time doing volunteer work (yes, some on the golf course and some with the grandkids). I have seen many people being fulfilled by doing this. The idea of quitting your job to lie around the house and pool or garden seems to be fading away. I think that is a good thing. By following financial principles in the Bible that goal may be more attainable. God has a purpose for you no matter what your age. Our goal should be to have enough financial freedom to be able to pursue His purpose.

The Bible tells us to train our children (Proverbs 22:6). All parents make mistakes when raising children, and I am not an exception by any means. One area that did work out was the lessons I gave my children about handling money. When they were 13, they were given their own money to budget. My wife and I laid down some ground rules, like they had to save 10 percent and tithe 10 percent to the church. The rest of their money was theirs to spend as they wished. We bought some necessities that they might have tried to go without, but for the most part they had to buy the clothes they wanted to wear and budget for the recreational things they wanted to do. Learning from their own mistakes proved to be more valuable than my wife and I telling them what to do or not to do with their money. As adults, they have both been very good at making the money that they get go a long way. I have been blessed by applying God's principles in my life and it is an added blessing to see that continue with them.

YOUR LEGACY ON EARTH

Scripture tells us that our life on earth is short; a vapor in the wind. The mortality rate has been the same forever, one death per person per lifetime. One of the things I like about helping people plan for the future is planning their legacy. I can only remember one man who did not care about leaving a legacy of bills and chaos. After one meeting with him I never saw him again. I hope he has changed his views since then. Unless you could care less like this man claimed, the legacy you leave behind matters. In 1 Timothy, Chapter 6, it says that we brought nothing into this world and we will take nothing out of this world with us. This is true; there are no trailers full of stuff behind hearses carrying things that will go with us into eternity.

So we will leave everything we own. One of the great things about life insurance is that it is the only vehicle that can make sure that what you want to happen will happen. I believe that if you have children who display good attitudes toward money, work and possessions, you should feel good about helping them on their journey by blessing them with a good amount of income tax-free death benefit. If, on the other hand, they have not established good habits in these areas, you have a couple of choices. You could leave the life insurance proceeds to a charitable organization that you love and trust. You can be responsible for allowing this organization to spread goodwill in whatever form that may be.

Another choice you have if you don't feel your heirs will be responsible with the windfall is to set up a trust or trusts through an attorney. There are numerous ways to have proceeds held until certain criteria are met by your heirs. In this way you may be teaching them God's principles even after your death.

FINAL WORDS

In concluding this chapter, I want to point out that the concepts mentioned here and in the other chapters of this book are in alignment with God's inspired word (in my opinion). To use the concepts of bank on yourself, infinite banking or the private reserve strategy (different names for the same strategy), you must live on less than you make. Put money in a position that allows it to grow with little-to-no risk. This strategy also allows your money to be accessible, have tax advantages, and guarantee an outcome that you desire, even if you die.

To sum it up, I will end with a promise from the Old Testament, in Deuteronomy 28:1-2: "If you diligently obey the Lord, your God, being careful to do all His commandments which I command you today, the Lord, your God, will set you high above all nations of the earth. All these blessings will come upon you ..." Verse 12 pronounces the last of many blessings: "You shall lend to many nations, but you shall not borrow."

I pray that this book may help many people experience the blessing of being debt-free and financially secure. I also pray that leaders in our nation would realize that applying these "secrets" would bring more of God's blessings upon our land.

About Glen

Glen Oaks began his career in the insurance and financial services field in 1981. From the beginning, he sought top-quality training in all aspects of life and health insurance and related topics. He obtained his Fellow designation from the Life Underwriters Training Counsel (LUTC). He is a member of the National Association of Insurance and Financial Advisors (NAIFA). Today, he continues to attend workshops and educational classes related to his field.

In 2010, Glen joined the Wealth and Wisdom Institute, which is a growing number of professionals from across the country who are deeply concerned about the direction this country is headed and the financial impact it is having. In 2011, Glen qualified to be an authorized advisor for Pamela Yellen's organization, Bank On Yourself.

Glen enjoys teaching people how money works in their lives. He aspires to be known as someone who can help people get from where they are to where they want to be financially. Many times this comes about by capturing money they are transferring away from themselves and growing it in tax-favored accounts for their future. He believes people can achieve their financial goals without taking unnecessary risk. He uses his training and tools to help people get on the right track.

Glen and his staff are available to speak at your organization or your business on the challenges people face in today's financial world. He offers educational events from 20 to 90 minutes in length. These events reveal the strategies that lead to financial success.

Glen founded Financial Security Management Agency Inc. in 1986 as an independent agency where agents can shop for the best product(s) that meet their client's needs. The agency represents several top-rated insurance carriers that provide those products. The goal of the agency is to provide peace of mind through safe money options and financial security by using the right strategies and products.

The agency website is www.fsmagency.com, where there are educational materials available to help people realize their financial goals.

CHAPTER 10

BUILDING WEALTH WITHOUT RISK

BY JIM CONRAD

I was 47 years old, and I had just been laid off from my career job of 24 years. This was not what I had planned or envisioned when I graduated from college with an engineering degree. Financially, I had done what all the "experts" told me to do: Put as much you can into a 401(k) retirement account with your employer, especially if they match your contributions (which they did). In addition, my wife and I led a pretty frugal life; we saved money every month, and I had invested our savings in stocks and mutual funds.

After rolling over my 401(k) account into a variable annuity (diversified among various mutual fund asset classes, of course), I participated in the final stages of the biggest bull market run in history. I switched careers, capitalizing on my MBA degree with a finance specialty, and started working with friends and referrals on financial services and planning. Just as I was getting started in this new career, I lost over half the value of my retirement savings in the market crash of 2001. Needless to say, this roller-coaster stock market ride was an eye-opener for me as a fairly new financial services professional, and I vowed that I would find a way to avoid all future stock market crashes, both for me and for my clients. This led me to look closely at life insurance and annuities because they have guarantees, and, if designed properly, they do not lose value when the market goes down.

Before the next stock market and financial system collapse in 2008, I had started my own Bank On Yourself policies, I began working with Pamela Yellen and her MasterMind group of advisors, and I stopped offering anything other than insurance products to my clients.

My passion is helping people, just like you, build wealth without risk, have access to their savings without losing guaranteed growth, and achieve financial peace of mind. When you work with me as your Bank On Yourself coach, you can rest assured that I am going to take the time to understand your financial goals and dreams, and I will work with you on a plan to fund a Bank On Yourself-type whole-life insurance policy that will last as long as you do. You'll be able to forget about the stomach-churning ups and downs of the real estate and stock markets. You will know how much your policy will be worth, at a minimum, next year and every year for the rest of your life. The only thing you can do is make it better by paying as much premium as you can and by financing your purchases through your policy's loan privilege. I like to say that a properly designed Bank On Yourself policy gets better every year, and there is nothing you can do about it!

So, since Bank On Yourself has so many advantages that it blows away every other financial strategy, why wouldn't everybody want to have a Bank On Yourself plan? Well, beyond the fact that some people just won't look at anything different, I have found there are others who are convinced that there is a "magic" investment out there that only rich insiders know about. They think there is a conspiracy that keeps it from them, and they are determined to discover the secret. This magic investment has fabulous features: something like 10 percent per year gains, guaranteed by God, that are completely tax-free. I say that these people are gripped by the Magic Investment Conspiracy Syndrome. They will talk to me about Bank On Yourself, and as soon as they realize that Bank On Yourself is not a magic investment, they become disinterested, and they move on to the next possibility.

In reality, if there were a better plan for building wealth than Bank On Yourself, somebody would have won the "$100,000 Challenge" that BankOnYourself.com has been offering to the world for more than five years…and I would be an advisor for that plan and doing that for myself! But, as I discovered after more than 30 years of searching, there is no better financial strategy in existence than Bank On Yourself; that is, dividend-paying whole-life insurance from a great mutual life company …and there is nobody who can do a better job helping you put Bank On Yourself to work for you and your family than me.

In more than seven years as a Bank On Yourself authorized advisor, I have interviewed hundreds of prospective Bank On Yourself clients. The vast majority of them have told me that their top financial concern is having enough retirement income. Why do you suppose that is? I thought we have all been encouraged, because of the tax deduction, to put money into government-controlled retirement plans, such as 401(k) and 403(b) plans, IRAs and SEPs. How could so many people be worried about having enough retirement savings, especially if their employers are giving them matching contributions?

Could it be that these government-controlled plans are all invested at risk? Could it be that, like I did, everybody is experiencing devastating losses when the financial markets crash, which they have done twice in the last 12 years? Could it be that hard-working people, just like you and me, have trusted the financial advice they have been getting from Wall Street, not knowing that the risks are simply insurmountable for most people?

It doesn't have to be this way. When I first heard about Bank On Yourself, I was very skeptical about it. After all, everything in which I had ever invested had lost money at one time or another. It sounded too good to be true…there had to be a catch. What was it? Being an engineer for so many years, I started to analyze Bank On Yourself to find out how it really worked…and you know what? The more I learned about it, the better it looked! This had never happened to me before in more than 30 years of investing. In fact, after all the years that I have been Banking On Myself and coaching my clients, it's still looking better. I still find new ways to help my clients benefit from their Bank On Yourself plans. Together with Pamela Yellen and our MasterMind group of advisors, I am always learning about new strategies by seeing what others are doing with their policies.

I am a problem solver. I have been a problem solver all my life…it's what I do. It is why I studied engineering. I look at every challenge as a problem with a solution. When you work with me, you can count on me delivering a rock-solid plan that will last as long as you do. If you are committed to making Bank On Yourself work for you, I am committed to being your Bank On Yourself Coach for as long as you want me to be. You see, desire and perseverance are far more critical to making Bank On Yourself work for you than anything else. If you have considerable savings, that's great…we can protect them from losses and, very likely, income taxes. If you have to begin a Bank On Yourself plan by committing part of your monthly cash flow, we can make that work, too, and in a few years, you will be saying goodbye to credit cards and finance companies. I haven't met anyone yet who I couldn't help— if they wanted to be helped. I can only help people who want to be helped—people who are committed to funding their Bank On Yourself plan to the maximum, using their cash value for financing their major purchases, and eliminating banks, finance companies, and government-controlled plans from their lives.

If you are somebody who is tired of getting beaten down every time you think you are winning the money game … if you are tired of wondering if you're ever going to be able to quit worrying about your savings and enjoy life … if you are finished believing the myths that the big money guys on Wall Street are selling … like this one: "Just put your money in good mutual funds every month, and the market always goes up over the long run" …or this one: "Max out your 401(k) contributions because you will have a lower tax rate in retirement" …then Bank On Yourself is probably what you have been looking for.

What can you expect when you work with me? First, I will ask you to read the *New York Times* best-selling book, *Bank On Yourself* by Pamela Yellen, prior to our first meeting. (Since I work with clients all over the country, I can only meet with you via phone and Internet. I have found, in more than seven years of meeting with prospective clients, that this mode works extremely well. You are in front of your computer in your own home or office, while I have access to, and can show you, anything in my vast file of Bank On Yourself information.)

After you have had time to read the book (I call this "Bank On Yourself 101"), we will meet via the phone and Internet. In that first meeting, my objective is to answer all of your questions about Bank On Yourself by showing you the details about how the concept works—information that is not in the book. (I call this meeting "Bank On Yourself 201 and 301.") During our next meeting, I will take as much time as necessary to learn about your financial goals and dreams, your financial balance sheet, your current life insurance coverage, and everything else that I will need to produce your personalized Bank On Yourself solution. As I said, I solve problems, and your Bank On Yourself plan will be a unique solution, based on your unique financial picture.

For our third meeting, I will show you the details of the unique Bank On Yourself plan I have designed for you. You will know how much cash value your plan will have when you start to take passive, potentially tax-free income, how and when you will be able to pay off debts or fund college expenses for your children, when you could pay off your mortgage, and much more. Once you see the projected results of your Bank On Yourself plan, you will be amazed that you will immediately start to have a more peaceful feeling about your financial future. Of course, whether or not you decide to proceed with applying for a Bank On Yourself-type life insurance policy will be up to you, but the most common response from people upon seeing their Solution is, "I wish I had started this kind of plan years ago."

Lest you think that I have a standard plan for everybody I choose to work with, I want you to know that I work out every single Bank On Yourself plan from scratch. Not only is this the case because everybody's financial situation is different, but I take this responsibility very seriously. Therefore, I need to know every detail about the plans I recommend. How can I coach you on using your Bank On Yourself plan most effectively over the years if I don't know exactly what went into the design of the plan in the first place? In addition, and most importantly, I have already done all of this for myself. You will not be committing to anything that I do not practice myself—and that includes moving my old 401(k) account funds into my Bank On Yourself policies.

Several months ago, after I had helped another new client start her first Bank On Yourself policy, I received the following note from her:

Jim, thank you for everything you have done to help me understand all of this! I could not have done it without you. Your prompt yet patient follow-up has made a dream come true for my financial future. Thank you for your integrity—that's very important to me and I can see it is with you. Here's to many years of future red sailboats…

The sailboat comment in her note refers to one of the visual aids that I created to help new or prospective clients understand how a Bank On Yourself-type policy is designed and structured for long-term success. My original "Sailboat Diagram" (I use a red pen for emphasis) is just one of many visual aids that I use to describe, in detail, how a Bank On Yourself plan works – from policy design, to the advantages of using your own capital for financing…from my unique "Dollar Diagram" (which proves that there is no such thing as paying too much premium), to a description of how the insurance company operates, how they can guarantee you anything, and much more.

A while back, I received this note from one of my most committed clients:

Jim, I checked my policy values this morning and the drop-in premium has become available. We would like to take the second loan for $11,000. We can up the monthly loan payment of another $100 per month. We are paying off a timeshare and have paid off the credit cards. We are hoping once the model home in our neighborhood closes on Wednesday we will be able to start the process of refinancing our first mortgage to get a much lower rate. Since we have paid off so much in the last few weeks, our credit scores should go up considerably, and that will help us get the rate as low as possible! We are so excited that Bank On Yourself is working for us exactly as advertised!

Bank On Yourself has brought financial peace of mind to thousands of Americans, including me and my wife. We own six Bank On Yourself-type policies so far. After banking on ourselves for about seven years, my wife and I have enough capital in our policies that we can self-finance anything we can afford to purchase. We no longer need banks or finance companies. It is a terrific feeling and a great place to be.

I would like to help you reach that same place! Call me at (704) 260-0470.

About Jim

Jim Conrad, president of Conrad Financial Services, has helped more than 200 clients grow their wealth without the risk, worry or volatility of stocks, real estate, and other investments; achieve financial security; and reach their short- and long-term personal and financial goals and dreams.

Jim has put his clients on track to building more than $100 million of additional wealth they would most likely not have had otherwise, through safe, proven financial strategies. That's why his clients think of him as their "secret weapon," helping them build and safeguard their wealth.

One of only 200 life insurance agents in the country who have successfully completed the rigorous training program and continuing education required to become Bank On Yourself Authorized, Jim has been a financial services professional for over 11 years. Jim holds a Masters degree in business administration and finance from Lewis University, and he is also a member of the Society of Certified Senior Advisors (CSA)®.

Jim and his wife, Deb, both grew up in the Chicago area. Near the end of 2007, they relocated to Concord, North Carolina, from Decatur, Alabama, where they had resided for 17 years. They have two adult children, and they are the proud grandparents of a 4-year-old grandson and a baby granddaughter. When Jim is not helping his clients, you may find him relaxing with Deb, working in the yard, or reading nonfiction, mostly conservative writers and history. He also has a passion for genealogy and has traced some branches of his family tree back to the 1600s.

To provide his clients the level of service he believes they expect and deserve, Jim only takes on a limited number of new clients each year who are committed to achieving lifetime financial security.

Jim Conrad MBA, CSA
Bank On Yourself® Authorized Advisor
Conrad Financial Services • 1040 Hearth Lane SW • Concord, NC 28025
Phone: (704) 260-0470• 1Email: jim@conradfinancial.us
Insurance Licensed in North Carolina and 15 Other States

Web Page: www.conradfinancial.us 4-Digit Code: JC35

CHAPTER 11

NOT ALL LIFE INSURANCE POLICIES ARE CREATED EQUAL

BY JOE OVERFIELD

Although I didn't realize it at the time, my financial life was deeply impacted in 2001 by a conversation I had with a friend. John came to me to discuss a plan to help secure my financial future. At the time I was working in the telecommunications industry and was doing quite well. The future looked very bright and I was excited to be involved in the work sector that I loved. John told me that since I was making good money I really needed to look at the concept he was suggesting. After John's presentation, I kind of laughed and said, "John, this is insurance. What are you trying to sell me?" After all, the telecom business was taking off and my company's stock was going through the roof. I knew that telecom was where I should be putting my money. But, much to my chagrin at the time, I followed John's suggestion and only because he was my close friend. That day I became John's client even though I thought the plan was dubious at best. I really wasn't sold on the concept. Little did I know that only a couple of years later I would find out how important this decision was to my financial well-being.

Some months after my discussion with John, the telecom company I worked for, much to my astonishment, went bankrupt. I was suddenly out of a job and without a regular pay check. When an opportunity was made available to me to follow my boss to another company in the same industry, naturally, I jumped at the chance. The new job gave me a renewed sense of security and a regular pay check. We were there only six months before that company went bankrupt. As you can imagine, these job loss experiences began to create a significant financial hardship. After the first job loss I quickly ran through my emergency fund. After the second job loss, my emergency fund was already depleted and I had no other resources from which to draw. I had funneled most of my investment money into the stock of the first company because it was doing so well. Of course, when the company went into bankruptcy, the stock went to zero and so did a very significant part of my financial portfolio.

A LIGHT BULB GOES ON

It was at this point in my life I came to the realization that my friend John was a very insightful individual. It occurred to me that I did have another resource from which to draw. The plan John set me up with became my financial lifeline at a very crucial time. That which I had initially had doubts about was now the source that would give me financial stability until I was able to find a new job. I was able to borrow money from the policy John sold me and keep myself going until I could get back on my feet. I could pay back the loan at my own pace, whenever I wanted. There wasn't a set payment schedule. It was entirely up to me. But, what was so amazing about this plan was that it kept growing even though I had taken money out of it. I was even earning interest and dividends on the money I borrowed—I couldn't believe it. This was completely different than anything I had ever seen. That's when the proverbial light bulb came on for me. What I once considered questionable, I now saw as a very effective and powerful financial strategy.

That experience changed my life and even set me on a different career path. Today, I own five different policies set up in a similar fashion. I don't think there is anyone who believes in this concept more than me. Because of the benefit I derived from this concept and my deep conviction of its importance to anyone's financial future, I made a career change in 2008 and now I teach other people how they can also receive the same benefit. I share my story with everyone and I even show people my personal policies so they can see the interest and dividend growth. I want them to understand this is very real and that they also can benefit from this concept. I show them the illustration that I was given in my first policy and the policy values that were forecasted in the illustration.

Then I show them my actual policy values. Even though I've taken money out, put money back and even still have a loan on the policy, they can see that the true value is still there and it is right on target as it was forecasted.

DEMYSTIFYING THE WHOLE-LIFE POLICY CONCEPT

If a person is willing to open their mind and listen, they can see how this plan works. The most difficult part is to get people to set aside any preconceived notions and open their mind to the uniqueness of the concept. When John initially shared this concept with me, I had certain preconceived ideas that caused me to listen with a great deal of reluctance. My initial thought was, "This is just a whole-life insurance policy."

Let me ask you, what do you know about whole-life insurance? Most people say something like, "I don't know much about it" or "I've always heard that it's not a good investment" or "It's expensive insurance." In my experience, about 70 percent of the people I talk with think that it's not a good investment. It may surprise you to know that I agree that traditional whole-life insurance is not a good investment. It's expensive insurance and the cash value inside that policy grows very slowly. However, what I teach people is something very different. I use the shell of a whole-life policy, but I design it very differently than a traditional plan. What I share with my clients is not traditional whole-life insurance. The Bank On Yourself (BOY) whole-life policy is much different in many ways.

What people usually say they know about whole-life insurance is most often what they have heard about it. Let's talk about the realities of a traditional whole-life policy. At one time people would buy whole-life insurance because they needed or wanted permanent insurance. They wanted life insurance, at a level premium, for the rest of their lives, so they paid for it. The cash value inside the plan was minimal, but the intention was to have the insurance and if they earned a little cash value along the way they considered that better than nothing. The cost of insurance was expensive because it was expected to cover you for the rest of your life.

Over the years, insurance buyers evolved to believe that you should buy term insurance and invest the difference in mutual funds or in a stock portfolio that would give you a substantial rate of return. If the market is doing well and you're making 10 percent or more every year, that's not a bad strategy. The problem is that the market has not performed as many of those investors anticipated. In many cases, people who subscribed to this philosophy are hitting their 50s and 60s now and their term policies are expiring. They may have not earned the money they expected to earn over the accumulation phase of their life and they now still have a mortgage, have credit card bills and other expenses they didn't anticipate 20 or 30 years earlier when they purchased their term policy. Many of them find they still have a need for life insurance, but because they are older now, the premiums are very expensive, and in some cases, unaffordable.

THE BANK ON YOURSELF DIFFERENCE

The Bank On Yourself strategy I recommend to my clients uses a whole-life policy, but it is much different than traditional whole-life insurance and it also addresses the issues that are raised with term life insurance that were described earlier. I want you to think of this as an investment strategy, not as an insurance policy. Rather than determining how much life insurance you need, you should determine how much cash value you need, what it's for and when you will need it. For example, if you want to save money for retirement, that is a long-term strategy that fits well with this concept. You will want to think of the Bank On Yourself strategy as a long-term investment plan for your retirement that allows you to access it along the way without penalties.

If you tell a traditional insurance agent you can afford, for example, $500 a month to purchase an insurance policy, that insurance agent is going to sell you $500 a month of insurance. In the first year you will have no cash value. In 15 years you may have accumulated $5,000 in cash value, but the death benefit is still the same as it was when you originally purchased the policy. That's how the traditional life insurance plan works. A Bank On Yourself whole-life policy is much different. Using the same $500 as in the previous example, a Bank On Yourself policy may be set up with $250 a month worth of insurance and the other $250 may be put in a "level paid up additions rider" (LPUA). That rider will accelerate the growth of your cash value and your death benefit in the policy. So, using this example, at the end of the first year you would have paid in $6,000, but instead of having no cash value, you will have approximately $3,000 in cash value that you can start using. Additionally, your death benefit has also grown to be larger than when you first started.

Now, you might ask, "If I put $6,000 in the policy in the first year, but it's only worth $3,000 after the first year, how is this a good investment?" I would say, the only downside to this plan is that it does take time to grow. It may take six to 10 years for your cash value to equal what you've contributed. Remember, if this is a long-term strategy the first 10 years should not matter as long as you can access your funds. However, once you get to that point, your cash value will continue to grow every year and your death benefit also grows exponentially. You have started off with $150,000 in life insurance, but in 10 years that may have grown to $300,000 in life insurance. So, the older you get, your death benefit is also getting bigger.

A LONG-TERM INVESTMENT STRATEGY

You don't want to do the Bank On Yourself plan as a short-term strategy of five or six years. You need to look at it as a long-term strategy. You need to look at this as a strategy of 10 years or more. If you do a comparative analysis between the Bank On Yourself strategy and a traditional market strategy of investing, you will find that you will be significantly further ahead with the Bank On Yourself strategy.

Another advantage to the Bank On Yourself plan is that your money will continue to grow even if you borrow money from the plan. For example, if you had $30,000 in your account and you borrowed $20,000 to purchase a vehicle, the cash value left is $10,000. But you will still receive interest and dividends as if you still had $30,000 in the account. Because you are earning interest and dividends on money that technically isn't in your account, it makes a significant difference in the accumulation of your cash value, providing you with a larger retirement account.

Compare that to your 401(k) or any other personal account you may own. If you are in retirement and you withdraw $20,000 from your 401(k), the amount of money on which you are earning interest drops accordingly. In comparison, in a Bank On Yourself account, you would continue to be paid interest and dividends on that amount. You could have $300,000 in your Bank On Yourself account and $450,000 in your

401(k) and take out the same amount of money each year from each account, and the Bank On Yourself account will last longer than the 401(k) account. Additionally, you can take money out of your Bank On Yourself account income tax-free so you get the full value of the money. You can't take money out of your 401(k) on a tax-free basis.

The BOY strategy is flexible in many ways. A policy can be structured to have less death benefit and more cash value. This is especially helpful when dealing with people who are older or those who may have health issues that would prevent them from qualifying for preferred insurance rates. The biggest difference is not necessarily how old a person is, but how many years will they be able to contribute to the policy.

A DIFFERENT RETIREMENT OPTION

There is also a single premium policy option for those individuals already in their retirement years. Many clients have a lump sum of money sitting in a savings account and don't want to put those dollars at risk. This plan allows them to put that money in a policy and within two years their cash value is worth more than what they initially deposited and their death benefit is a lot higher. This gives those individuals better growth opportunity than having their money sitting in a savings account, they have no risk and they are able to pass the death benefit on to their heirs on an income tax-free basis. It becomes a fantastic way to move money on to your heirs on a tax-advantaged basis.

I have a client who has a significant amount of money in a savings account. He didn't use the money, but he wanted it to be protected in case he ever would need it and also so he could pass it on to his heirs. We discussed creating a single premium policy for him. However, because of health reasons, he is uninsurable. So, we took two Bank On Yourself policies out on each of his children and he pays the premium every year. He is the owner of the policies, retains all the money within the policy, and is the only one who can access the money if he should need or want to use it. At any time he can assign ownership to his children if he desires. If he assigns ownership to his children, they can simply let the cash value continue to grow, they can choose to continue to pay premiums on the policies, or they can simply begin taking cash out of the policy. If the current policy owner passes away, his children, the insured, then automatically become the policy owners.

TRY IT FOR YOURSELF

Bank on Yourself is a very unique strategy and not just any insurance agent can provide you with this type of policy. The agent must be certified as an authorized Bank on Yourself advisor. Every Bank On Yourself policy must be written by a nondirect recognition mutual company that also has all the specific features required for your policy to work properly. There are a lot of mutual companies that are direct recognition companies and quite a few that are nonrecognition companies, but there are only a handful of nondirect recognition companies that also have the features necessary to make the BOY strategy most effective. I strongly recommend that if you want to be certain your plan will work properly, you should work specifically with a Bank On Yourself authorized advisor.

About Joe

Joe Overfield, senior vice president of the Financial Planning Division, is a Bank On Yourself Authorized Advisor, with a B.A. in organizational communications from The Ohio State University. Joe is one of only 200 advisors in the country who is trained to correctly design the type of policies used for Bank On Yourself. Joe has been the guest speaker at a several Fortune 500 companies and nonprofits to discuss wealth accumulation and safe money. In addition to becoming an Advisor, Joe has been using the Bank On Yourself concept himself since 2004 and he is proud to share with his own clients how they, too, can provide a secure future for themselves and their families. Joe lives in Ohio, with his wife and two daughters.

What Joe says about Bank On Yourself: "I continue to find new reasons to be thankful for all the benefits the Bank On Yourself concept has offered me. During a previous financial downturn, I was able to borrow money "tax free" from my Bank On Yourself plan and have since paid myself back, plus interest! If someone would ask me if I have any regrets for investing in this program, my answer would be yes. I regret that I did not start investing in the Bank On Yourself system sooner!"

To learn more about Joe, go to www.eaglefinancialsolutions.com.

CHAPTER 12

IMAGINE... A ROAD TO FUTURE SECURITY THROUGH STRATEGIC COLLEGE PLANNING

BY JOHN J. LENNON

With a name like John Lennon, I can't help but become an immediate conversation piece for everyone I meet. When I'm booking trips, travel agents take a pause. When store clerks see my credit card, they ask about Yoko, Paul and Ringo. Or they ask me to sing a few bars from "Imagine." Once they learn more about me, they wonder how a musical lad from Liverpool became a college financial planner and tax advisor in Pottstown, Pennsylvania. Once all that is out of the way, I tell them that there is a major difference between myself and my legendary namesake: I played guitar as a kid and later in high school learned the trumpet. The other John supposedly took up trumpet as a kid before becoming a guitarist.

Just as the Beatles' sound evolved throughout the '60s, my career has taken some interesting turns. In 1988, I began working in the financial and criminal investigation fields as an agent for the U.S. government, assigned to a well-traveled team that resolved certain congressional inquiries. I then made the transition to private industry, moving from a fast-paced whirlwind to a slower lifestyle—but during that time I realized how much I really wanted to help people. I worked in other financial fields and then opened my own tax and accounting firm, Lennon Financial, catering to individuals and small business owners.

MY JOURNEY INTO COLLEGE PLANNING

My shift into the world of college planning and the launch of my now primary business, The College Planning Center, started very unexpectedly. One of my tax clients had twin boys who were applying to college and asked me to help them fill out the forms while I was doing their personal return. One of the last steps in the college app process is filling out the Free Application for Federal Student Aid (FAFSA), which helps colleges and universities determine a student's eligibility for financial aid, including the Pell Grant, Stafford loans and Federal Work-Study. Colleges often offer applicants help filling out these forms, but this might be like asking the IRS to do your taxes!

While continuing my tax business, I spent two years researching the college funding process and learned some amazing things about the way different schools deal with applicants for aid. One thing I learned from my research is not only how much I didn't know about this complicated process, but how much applicants and tax/financial advisors think they know about it but don't. From talking to my clients and other families I met, I realized that the most common problem is that most had no idea how to pay for college. I wanted to help them figure out how to come up with this money and plan for these expenses. I think the turning point was when my research showed me that most people were paying more to send their kids to college than they paid for their last home.

EASING THEIR ANXIETY

In an effort to serve these anxious parents better, I continued to do research and soon developed extensive knowledge about the college financial aid system, benefiting our clients with advice and strategies that most parents don't think about or have access to when saving for and paying for college. Since 2001, the College Planning Center has helped more than 1,000 families pay for college and navigate the financial aid process. Our mission is simple: We approach financial aid from the parents' perspective, as we seek to arm them with as much information as possible to make informed fiscal decisions when preparing and paying for the often overwhelming cost of a college education.

Realizing the value of getting out and educating people—and hopefully earning their trust as clients—I began conducting educational workshops to outline the many ways, largely unknown to the average parent and advisor, to make college as affordable as possible. As I detail on our website (www.collegeplanningofpa.com), my focus is to help the family:

1. Prepare for the significant out-of-pocket expenses to get all their kids through college.

2. Find strategies to insure they will get out of debt.

3. Supplement their retirement.

4. Minimize their tax burden.

5. Develop a contingency plan, should something happen to one of the parents.

I remember one particular family that finally came, at the beckoning of friends, to my workshop. They were having a hard time getting started because they were so anxious and confused. The dad was turning 70 and had a senior in high school, plus triplets who were juniors. He was overwhelmed, thinking he might never retire. He came in all hunched over, but his ears perked up as I explained how EFC works. EFC is the expected family contribution number that represents the minimum amount a family will pay for one year of college. He realized that it was actually to his benefit to have more kids in college at the same time. Most people assume that the college retail price is what you pay and they could not be more mistaken.

THERE'S NO MAGICAL MYSTERY TOUR—IT'S ABOUT KNOWING THE FACTS

In the workshop I explain the basics of financial aid, the difference between merit aid (academic, athletic, artistic scholarships) and need-based aid, which breaks down to what I call "green stuff/positive" (scholarships and grants) and "red stuff/negative" (loans and work-study). In addition to explaining how assets are calculated (between 529s, Coverdell Accounts, Roth IRAs and children's UGMA/UTMA accounts), I get down to the basics of working out a magic number.

Let's say it's going to take the average family 20 years for the planning and paying phase of sending their children to college, then end up completely out of debt. When is the best time to start? When your oldest is a senior in high school or when they are in second grade? It's all up to you, but the truth is that starting too late just pushes retirement out.

I call it the magic number lightheartedly because people often think that they will stumble upon a magic solution. So they pay the ultimate procrastination penalty. One couple in my workshop informed me their son was in eighth grade and asked, "It's probably too soon for me to begin getting help with this process, right?" Of course not! It's no different than retirement planning, if you know years in advance that you plan to retire at a certain age, is that going to change? Most come to us when their kids are in their early high school years, but I actually encourage people with young children to start a lot sooner.

Beyond adjusting their mindsets about the timeline, we teach them about how schools sometimes count things against you, including the money the prospective student has in his or her college fund accounts that were established in childhood. Sometimes there is a penalty for having a savings account in the kid's name. It's also important that they know it can be illegal to move those assets incorrectly so as to avoid the schools finding out about them. We try to give them stories of different families and what difficulties they may encounter. Like those who were proud of their son working throughout high school to pay for college—only to realize that the school's financial aid office penalized him for earning too much. We offer tips about what amount of income is reasonable and won't be penalized.

We also show them the expenses beyond tuition and fees, including books, transportation and housing. This all-inclusive number is officially referred to as the COA (cost of attendance). They also learn how to interpret certain results that can be baffling at first. Once they see a side-by- side comparison of two schools, they realize it's not always simply about the retail price—and that can be very good news for them.

Another key is learning how to take on the right loans and avoid the wrong ones. I particularly steer them away from PLUS Loans with a fixed interest rate just under 8 percent. Colleges often recommend these to parents who don't know the hidden costs, high interest rates, points and stacking nature of these, where a family qualifies for freshman year but they later, unfortunately, realize this is going to get way out of control.

THE 3 MOST COMMON MISTAKES PARENTS MAKE WHEN APPLYING FOR FINANCIAL AID

What if every parent in America who wanted to send his or her son or daughter to the college or university of their choice knew how to avoid the big mistakes? How much money could they save that could later be applied to their retirement and future financial security? I've broken down the most common missteps that parents make:

Mistake #1: Thinking that it doesn't matter where I keep my money; it's all counted in the same way

Nothing could be farther from the truth. Where you keep your money could mean the difference between you getting $10,000 in financial aid or getting nothing. For example, money in the child's name is weighted much more heavily than money in the parent's name. If you don't know how to legally and ethically position your money properly for purposes of financial aid, you could end up losing thousands in your financial aid package.

Mistake #2: Assuming all schools are created equal and will be able to give you the same amounts of money

All schools are not created equal and will not be able to give you the same financial aid package. Some schools are well-endowed and get a lot of money from alumni and corporations. These schools have more money to give out and are generally able to meet most or all of a student's financial need. Other schools, like state universities, get little or no private funds and rely solely on state and federal funds to help fill a student's need at their school. In many cases, these schools leave students short and give them less money than they are potentially eligible to receive. It could actually end up costing you more to send your child to a "cheaper" school if they don't have the money to meet your need.

Mistake #3: Assuming that waiting until January or later of your child's senior year of high school to start working on your college financial aid planning will do no harm

Since financial aid is based on your previous year's income and assets, it is imperative to start your planning as soon as possible before January of your child's senior year. If you want to set up your income and assets legally so you can maximize your eligibility for financial aid, you must start working on this, at least, one year in advance—preferably in the year before your child's junior year of high school. The longer you wait and the closer it gets to your child's senior year, the tougher it gets to set up your most advantageous financial picture without creating a red flag for the colleges and universities. It is also important for you to know what your "Expected Family Contribution" is so you can start saving for it. And, you should also know which schools could give you the best packages before you start visiting and applying to them. My advice: If you haven't started planning, do it now!

SIMPLE WAYS TO GET THE MAXIMUM FINANCIAL AID FOR YOUR CHILD'S EDUCATION

So you're the parent of a college-bound high school junior. While enjoying your summer, you should make some time for the following:

1. Start visiting colleges and universities to which your child is interested in applying.

2. Have your child take a good test preparation course to get a better SAT score.

3. Start looking for private scholarships.

4. Start setting up your income, assets and personal finances to get the maximum amount of money from each school.

And most important…

5. Don't procrastinate…because the financial aid your child will be awarded is based on the current tax year.

3 CONCEPTS PARENTS FAIL TO CONSIDER WHEN APPLYING FOR FINANCIAL AID

Concept #1: For the purposes of filling out financial aid forms, certain assets will be considered "included assets" while others will be "unincluded assets."

Reality: Certain assets are counted much more heavily in the financial aid formulas than others. For example, savings accounts, CDs, stocks and bonds are all included and asked about on the federal financial aid form, known as the Free Application for Federal Student Aid (FAFSA). It does not, however, ask about retirement accounts, annuities or life insurance anywhere on that same form.

Concept #2: Thinking that "My CPA or tax preparer is qualified to fill out my financial aid forms, so I'll let him/her do it" may actually hurt your eligibility for financial aid.

Reality: Unfortunately, CPAs and tax preparers are experts at tax planning and preparation—not financial aid planning. For example, a CPA or tax preparer might suggest that you put some or all of your assets in your child's name to save money on taxes. While this advice is well-meaning, it will usually kill most or all of your chances of getting financial aid. Also, CPAs and tax preparers are not trained in filling out financial aid forms. In many cases, they will unknowingly fill out these forms improperly and these "minor" mistakes will bump your financial aid forms out of line.

Concept #3: Going through the financial aid process by yourself because it's "cheaper" may actually cost you more when it's all said and done.

Reality: If you are thinking that it will be cheaper to go through the financial aid process alone, the colleges and federal government are going to love you. This misconception allows them to keep control over the process instead of you, the parent, understanding how the process works. It always amazes me that people will readily use a doctor when they get sick or a lawyer when they get sued, but suddenly when they are going to send their child to college and spend between $30,000 and $60,000 per year, parents want to save themselves a couple of dollars and do it themselves.

The analogy I like to use about this whole process is one that connects to the travel industry. If you're planning a trip by either going online or talking to a travel agent, you're going to research the best way to pay for things. When you get on that plane, you're looking around, wondering whether everyone paid the same amount for that ticket as you did—and, of course, you realize that's not the case, even if you booked everything on the same day using the same parameters. As with any other aspect of financial planning, it's best to get a professional's advice when you're approaching this daunting process so you don't get deeper in debt than you ever intended to be. It would be a real shame to pay too much for college, after all.

About John

John J. Lennon grew up in the Delaware Valley, just outside Philadelphia, Pennsylvania. He found a passion for helping others and entrepreneurship at a young age. This passion led him to become an Eagle Scout, something fewer than 7 percent of all Boy Scouts achieve. Transcending his passion for helping others into community outreach, John has served more than 10 years with several fire companies near his hometown. He currently resides in Boyertown, Pennsylvania, with his wife, Shari, and enjoys traveling, exploring and volunteering.

Shortly after graduating from the University of Dayton with a Bachelor of Science degree, John began his career in the financial and criminal investigation fields. He specialized in accounting and criminal justice, and started working as an agent for the government. Located in the Philadelphia and Washington, D.C. areas, he was assigned to special teams that resolved congressional inquiries while working for the Office of the Inspector General.

Making the transition to private industry, John continued to hone his skills in the financial industry and found his true calling; to open his own office. And in 2001, John opened the College Planning Center, now headquartered in Pottstown, Pennsylvania, to address the overwhelming need to educate parents on the college process and successfully get all of their kids through college (in the most timely manner).

John has researched and developed an extensive knowledge base about the college financial aid system, allowing him to best serve his clients by giving advice and strategies that most parents don't think about or have access to when saving for and paying for college. More information about the College Planning Center is available at www.collegeplanningofpa.com.

CHAPTER 13

WHAT IS THE BIGGEST FINANCIAL SECRET TO SUCCESS?

BY JOHN A. MONTOYA

The number one symptom of all physical ailments is stress. In financial terms, the major cause of financial stress is uncertainty. This uncertainty is created because we are either misinformed or uninformed when it comes to managing our money. While we have a multitude of financial options, we lack the financial education to safely navigate us through life. The end result, as you'll discover by reading further, is the banker's gain and a lifetime of opportunity loss for you and your family.

The purpose of this book is to fill in a much needed gap of financial education you won't find in the mainstream press or from your traditional Wall Street financial advisor. As a Bank On Yourself Authorized Advisor, I learned the hard way that the conventional financial advice I had received my entire life is the reason why I struggled to consistently grow my net worth despite making a good living. Having access to some of the largest financial institutions in the world and formalized training did little to help. This is because I was drinking the same Kool-Aid as everyone else.

Thankfully everything changed when I began to unlearn the folly that is traditional financial planning. The reason is simple. Everything I had learned about money benefited the banks and Wall Street. Naturally nothing changed when I went to work for them. It was only when I learned how the banking and financial systems worked that my financial life came into focus.

I am grateful to Pamela Yellen for writing her best-selling book and the Bank On Yourself nation of advisors for taking me under their wing in 2009. It was in that year I asked to become an Authorized Advisor and was accepted into the program by Pamela. I also need to thank Mr. R. Nelson Nash, author of *Becoming Your Own Banker*, who called me up out of the blue in 2007 to answer my silly questions about the concept. I know my questions were silly now because I had yet to fully grasp the bigger picture. I was concerned about the little things. Mr. Nash set me straight right away. He told me in his calm, southern drawl, "Son, you're majoring in the minors!" The words were simple yet profound.

Nelson has taught thousands of people over the years that how they think makes all the difference in the world. At the age of 82, he currently shows no signs of slowing down, so why should I? I have the great blessing to be able to reach people on a very human and sincere level to help them solve one of life's greatest mysteries: the black box secret on how to eliminate traditional banks (usury) and Wall Street (uncertainty) from their life forever!

Before I share what I've learned with you, I think it's important to agree on a few things: Our public school education system doesn't teach anything on the subject of money, and bankers/advisors on Wall Street do far more recommending than educating. If that's fair enough to agree on, let's agree on just one more thing: You probably need to become better educated about how the traditional banking system works. Do I have your agreement? If so, let's continue.

For all practical purposes, accumulating wealth is a series of trial and errors. We don't even realize that there is a system that profits from our mistakes. As a result, we're all essentially pawns in this chess match that is our modern day financial system. It's a system that pits the uninformed against the behemoths of the banking and investing world. It's little wonder why everyday common people fail to get ahead while banks and investment firms own the tallest buildings in the best locations in every town across the country.

The inequity of our financial system was never taught at any of the schools I attended. There wasn't even an entry-level course at my university, which at the time cost $20,000 a year just to attend. So much for a liberal arts institution of higher learning providing a well-rounded education. Perhaps even worse, the financial industry offers no formal training on the history of money.

The only history most people know are associated with their 401(k) statements, and as most people have learned, the stock market is filled with too many ups and downs to be able to comfortably rely on it as the main source of wealth building. Sadly, this type of mainstream thinking serves as conventional wisdom for any modern day wealth-building plan. (Google Frontline's "The Retirement Gamble" for an eye-opening documentary.)

It finally dawned on me through my own trial and errors that the conventional financial wisdom most Americans use is severely flawed. I realized the consequence of following the mainstream financial plan is a lifetime of opportunity costs most people never recover from. This is because the holes in a traditional financial plan are never truly closed. They are papered over with new money. The only way to overcome losses is to keep throwing more money at the problem. It's a flawed and broken system to say the least.

Much like you, prior to learning and applying the Bank On Yourself system, I had no reason to question what the banks and financial institutions were recommending. After all, they all recommend the same model, the only difference being the hope of a better rate of return. What's the definition of insanity? Doing the same thing and expecting different results! We've been unwittingly trained by Wall Street to seek higher rates of return, as if that's the solution! It's a clever sleight of hand to disguise the real problem: the lack of control of our money.

My epiphany finally happened when I discovered what banks do with their money and what they recommend for their clients are polar opposites. Banks don't invest their reserves in mutual funds or government-qualified accounts! The mental hold on my money that the traditional financial model had was finally breaking.

So this financial discovery begged a question: Where do the majority of banks and financial institutions put their reserves? Would you believe that most banks keep a large portion of their Tier 1 assets (this is a financial asset class that has be ultra-safe and ultra-liquid) in permanent life insurance? In fact, they buy so much of it that the Federal Reserve puts a limit on just how much of it they can buy. Life insurance companies give it a special name because banks buy so much of it each year. It's called bank-owned life insurance, or BOLI, for short.

The common person like you and me buy what's called dividend-paying whole life insurance contracts. I should also note that corporations are also large purchasers of permanent life insurance. Their contracts are called COLI, or corporate-owned life insurance. Ever wonder how corporate executives retire with golden parachutes? Now you know.

Although the Dave Ramseys and Suze Ormans of the world would have you believe dividend-paying whole-life insurance policies are the worst place you can put money, they don't understand how a properly designed whole-life contract can include a special cash-building rider to turbo-charge the growth in the early years. It should be obvious that when banks and corporations are putting large amounts of their capital in life insurance contracts, it's because there are very good reasons to do so. (For a fascinating and very detailed read on this subject, I highly recommend picking up a copy of *The Pirates of Manhattan*, by Barry James Dyke. Mr. Dyke's book is financially enlightening as the *Bank On Yourself* and *Becoming Your Own Banker* books.)

The beauty of what Bank On Yourself teaches is that everything you need to protect and grow your wealth already exists. There is no need to put yourself and your family in harm's way by taking unnecessary risks. The specific type of life insurance contracts that Bank On Yourself advisors use have actually existed for over 160 years. You just have to know they exist! As I mentioned, you won't learn about it in school, and your banks and Wall Street planners hope you never find out. Why all the hush?

Imagine if you had a whole life insurance contract set up by your bank (which they can offer you, but I doubt they ever have). Ask yourself what would happen if banks were no longer the primary option for your need to borrow money in the form of a loan? You would bypass the banks and borrow against the collateral in your own whole life contract instead. No more bank loan applications, credit score checks or job verifications. You would have access to all your capital as you needed with no questions asked. No more bank control over your financial life!

And wait...it gets better.

The cash values in your life insurance contract receive preferential treatment under section 7702 and the modified endowment rules under section 7702A of the Internal Revenue Code. This means you can grow and access the money tax-free like a Roth IRA, except on much better terms. You get liquidity without penalties before age 59½, and you aren't limited by an arbitrary cap on your contributions, which are decided by Congress. Ultra-wealthy people use the IRS tax code to their advantage. You should, too!

Furthermore, by using the cash values in a properly structured dividend-paying whole life policy, in the form of a policy loan, you have the ability to grow your net worth uninterrupted for the rest of your life. This is because you are never actually withdrawing the money from the contract. When a loan is taken, your cash values stay intact. You are actually borrowing against your cash value asset. As such, the life insurance company will continue to pay your guaranteed contractual increases and dividends (not guaranteed) because you never actually removed your own money.

Do you realize what happens each time you deposit money in your banking account and then remove it? The bank stops paying you interest, of course. This will never happen with your Bank On Yourself plan. Can you visualize what happens to your lifetime net worth when you eliminate the interruption of compounding growth?

Without a Bank On Yourself system, the amount of money transferred from your net worth to the traditional banking system is staggering. For nearly all my clients, the opportunity cost is in the $100,000's. All this money is transferred unknowingly and unnecessarily because the banks control your money.

So what if you could eliminate these wealth transfers? What if you could keep your money working for you as if you never touched it? Does that sound like a financial system that would interest you?

That's what Bank On Yourself is all about. The strategy is about moving away from the traditional banking system that has controlled your money all these years and, unbeknownst to you, has kept you from accumulating the net worth you should rightfully have. It's a system that provides a contractual guarantee on the growth of your money, which is something no Wall Street designed plan can duplicate.

Let's examine a traditional banking system so you can understand why.

These are the three steps in the traditional banking system that banks use to create wealth for themselves:

1. Your bank leverages your money to create new loans for borrowers. (Additional uses of the same dollar.)

2. The cash flow received from the newly created loans increases the bank's capital base, which allows them to create even more loans for additional borrowers. (More opportunities for profit.)

3. They repeat the process again and again.

By implementing a Bank On Yourself plan, you will have the ability to replicate the same three steps as your current traditional banking system. The Bank On Yourself plan will create:

1. *Leverage:* You have multiple uses with the same dollar.

2. *Cash flow:* As you pay the life insurance company back on loans taken, you increase the capital in your policies available for new loans. Additional payments create additional capital for greater accumulation and future use.

3. *Velocity of money:* You have the ability to repeat steps 1 and 2 repeatedly.

Having a financial system you own and control gives you the ability to reverse the flow of money back to your personal economy instead of into the traditional banking system where it's outside your control. By eliminating the opportunity costs on the use of your money, your money is always increasing in value for the rest of your life. It solves the dilemma of having to constantly interrupt the growth of your money when you spend it or invest it anywhere else.

Now I'm not saying all your money should be in life insurance contracts, but I hope you realize that money must reside somewhere. Doesn't it make sense to warehouse your money in an ultra-safe and ultra-liquid vehicle that is outside the control of bankers, where it can receive tax-favored treatment and grow uninterrupted for the rest of your life? Did I mention that you also get a death benefit to protect your loved ones? No savings account, mutual fund, or 401(k)-type of retirement vehicle does all these things.

This is the secret bankers hope you never discover. The reason why is simple. They want you in the dark about how money works so they can continue to profit from your need to rely on them for all your banking functions (saving and borrowing). Contrary to what you mostly like to think, the most important of these functions is the borrowing function because it is the one that interrupts the growth of your money in the traditional banking system. The solution is having the right type of system, and that's what Bank On Yourself accomplishes.

While the Bank On Yourself plan is not a get-rich-quick scheme, the results are worth having. The sooner you begin implementing a Bank On Yourself plan, the quicker you'll get where you want to go financially.

As an Authorized Advisor of the Bank On Yourself strategy, I believe it is the safest and most predictable way to grow your wealth without any luck, skill or guesswork. If my words haven't resonated with you, perhaps a testimonial from one of my clients will:

"I do find it very intriguing your approach to improving others' lives with financial education and options for relief. We are so ingrained with the current financial system to follow along, not think for yourself or not break from the mold—not to mention the large gap in the education system that does not include financial or health education. It is easier to be a lemming, just not necessarily the best bet. It's refreshing to find someone talking about alternative solutions instead of the same conventional advice—and Wall Street hype, which can be an exhausting roller coaster ride."

—Kelly V., Alamo, California

About John

John A. Montoya, founder of JLM Wealth Strategies and co-founder of LifeTrust Financial Group, began his career in financial services in 1998 and is one of only 200 financial advisors in the country who has successfully completed the training program required to become a Bank On Yourself Authorized Advisor. John holds a bachelor's degree from the University of San Diego and is the proud father of three children. In his free time, he volunteers for the Society of Financial Awareness, a nationwide 501(c)3 nonprofit educational speakers bureau to end financial illiteracy across America and is active coaching and playing soccer.

CHAPTER 14

HOW TO FREE YOURSELF FROM THE SLAVERY OF DEBT

BY JOHN J. SHEDENHELM

"The issue which has swept down the centuries and which will have to be fought sooner or later is the people versus the banks."
~Lord Acton, writer, politician, historian

Nearly a decade ago, I was introduced to an astonishing idea. An idea that dramatically changed my life and the life of hundreds of my clients. That idea is…"How well you manage debt will be the single largest factor for the success or failure of your overall financial well-being."

This idea might seem obvious. But let me assure you it's not. Instead, most people are focused on one thing:"How can I get a higher rate of return on my savings and investments?"

Admit it, you probably fall into this camp. I know I did.

This all changed for me nearly a decade ago, when I was introduced to *How to Become Your Own Banker*, by Nelson Nash. This book instantly changed my life. It was as if an invisible hand reached out from the pages of the book and slapped me in the face and shook me from my current and limiting mindset.

At the time, it was the only book that dared to tell the truth the way people actually used and controlled their money. In the book, Nelson explained what big banks do to create wealth and how individuals could use those same techniques to make themselves wealthy. He states that on the average, American family's pay more than 30 percent of their monthly income on principle and interest related to car, mortgage and credit card debts—a number that matched most of my own clientele.

This reality about debt hit home like a Mack truck. In the financial planning world up until that time, we would never address the debt and liability column. We wrongly assumed that our clients would take care of their debts themselves, so we left those details to them and focused solely on their growing portfolios. I would talk to my clients about the need to save for their children's college or their own retirement. They might mention that their car payments, credit card debt and mortgage could be obstacles, but I would switch topics and ask when they thought they would next receive an increase in pay or be able to pay off those debts, without getting into much-needed specifics. Two years later, I would talk to them again about it, only to find out nothing had changed.

CRUNCHING SOME TOUGH NUMBERS

Nelson's book was a wake-up call for all of us. He said that all of us have money in four places. Our income comes in and goes out into ...

1. Federal and state taxes

2. The lifestyle we have

3. Our debt

4. Our savings

That's it. Those are the only four places that our income can flow into.

As little as three to four years ago, the savings rate in this country was nearly zero percent and virtually everyone was maxed out. Because banks stopped lending as much after the last crash, people had to learn to save to make down payments, resulting in a 5 percent uptick in average savings over the past few years.

The basic numbers stack up this way: Out of 100 percent of your income, if 20 percent goes to taxes, 20 to 40 percent to pay your debts and 30 percent to maintain your lifestyle that leaves only 5 percent or less for savings. Most people don't want to cut back on the lifestyle to save a little more, and student loans have overtaken credit card debt as the largest cause of debt in America.

So the challenge became if we can help clients get rid of 30 percent of their debt, we can facilitate more savings. This is such a simple idea, yet hardly anyone does it.

So Pamela Yellen convinced Nelson to teach financial advisers around the country how this works, and via her investigation of more than 450 savings and retirement planning strategies and vehicles, she began learning and implementing the Bank On Yourself concept. She wrote a book on this concept in 2009, about our clients and what this idea has done since to change the lives of so many families.

INTRODUCING BANK ON YOURSELF

It's now been more than nine years since we introduced the Bank On Yourself concept to our clients, and it's by far the best financial strategy we've ever introduced. It is a guaranteed way to grow their savings, without the nail-biting ups and downs of the stock and real estate markets. It also lets you become your own source of financing and reduce or eliminate the control banks and financial institutions have over you.

Today, more than 500,000 Americans of all ages, incomes and backgrounds use Bank On Yourself to reach a wide variety of personal and financial goals and dreams. Not one of them lost a single penny in their plans when the markets crashed. In fact, their plans have continued to grow—safely and predictably.

Our mission at Eagle Financial Solutions, which is based in Columbus, Ohio, is all about helping free our clients from the slavery of debt. We want to help them grow their wealth with little-to-no-risk and retire in comfort with zero reliance on Social Security.

Bank On Yourself furthers our mission by helping our clients pocket the interest they would otherwise pay to financial institutions, take control of the debt-cycle through wise personal financing, and grow their wealth steadily and consistently, without the risk and volatility of the stock market.

Just before telling prospective clients about Bank On Yourself, we ask them a simple question: *"Should you position your future in the equities markets where you have little control, have high risk and can only hope to get the returns as planned?"*

They usually say no, and then we introduce Bank On Yourself by saying there are alternatives that should be considered that offer guarantees, liquidity, flexibility and consistent growth.

HOW IT WORKS...AND HOW IT CAN HELP YOU

So what is the Bank On Yourself Method? Bank On Yourself uses a turbo-charged variation of a financial asset that has increased in value during every single market crash and in every period of economic boom and bust for more than 160 years. It's called dividend-paying whole-life insurance.

But this is not the kind of whole-life policy most advisors and experts talk about. With this little-known variation, you don't have to die to "win." Bank On Yourself requires a dividend-paying whole-life policy with some features added on to it that few financial advisors currently understand. A large portion of your premium goes into a rider that significantly super-charges the growth of your money in the policy and reduces the commission the agent receives by 50-to-70 percent. The growth of these plans is both guaranteed and predictable.

Bank On Yourself uses this unique and flexible vehicle to accomplish many different financial goals throughout a person's lifetime:

- In your youth...Bank On Yourself can be used for college expenses, purchasing cars, even financing a home.

- In middle age...Bank On Yourself is great for financing large purchases, from cars to home improvements to family vacations. It can also be used to reduce and/or pay off debts, or even pay off your existing mortgage.

It can also be an amazing tool for business owners—if you purchase or finance any type of equipment or property for a business, this strategy could benefit you in ways that you would never even have imagined.

And in your senior years...Bank On Yourself is absolutely one of the best methods for building retirement income that will last you the rest of your life, and can also be used for medical expenses, vacations and travel, and final expenses, when it comes time.

But it doesn't end there...after you pass away, your Bank On Yourself plan can live on after you as a legacy to your family, or go to support a charity of your choice.

Okay, it sounds great, right? So what's the catch? Well, as with anything, there are a few caveats:

1. **This is not a "get-rich-quick" strategy.** It will take some time, and it will take some discipline. Anyone interested in building true long-term wealth understands that nothing comes for free—you will always have to invest some money as well as time, in order to achieve true long-term growth. Those who have done so in a Bank On Yourself plan will reap the benefits many times over.

2. **This is not a business opportunity, a job or any other type of work.** In fact, you really don't have to do anything at all, other than discipline yourself and stick to your plan. This has nothing to do with multilevel marketing, pyramids, recruiting or anything like that.

3. **For some people, it's the easiest thing in the world;** for others, it is such a major paradigm shift that it may take some time and discipline to master.

4. **If you learn and practice this strategy well, you will never look at money or finances in the same way ever again!**

What's fascinating is that this proven strategy has existed for more than 100 years, but most people—including even most financial advisors and CPAs—know nothing about it. Some of the unique benefits provided by the use of this concept to manage and grow your wealth include:

Benefit #1: Consistent growth

Benefit #2: Protection of your wealth from stock market and real estate market fluctuations

Benefit #3: The ability to finance large purchases through your policy, and recapture the interest you would otherwise have paid to a bank

Benefit #4: Permanent elimination of credit card debt

Benefit #5: May protect your wealth from lawsuits, government entities, and other potential threats

Benefit #6: Liquid access to your money whenever you need it

Benefit #7: Tax-free retirement income benefits

WHY DEBT DOES MATTER

I recently met with one of my clients whom when I first met them several years ago had credit card balances of more than $70,000 at an interest rate of more than 20 percent. Like most people, it was very easy to get addicted to the credit and before you know it, wham! No one plans to rack up debt but I have seen many people with good incomes fall into this trap. They had not conquered Parkinson's Law ... more on this a little later.

I, too, have learned a hard lesson about credit card debt and the dangers of it. We have to create new habits and what we did with this client is they were paying more than $3,000 a month to pay down their credit cards. They were tired of being in this mess and they were open to change. We helped them start a Bank On Yourself policy for $1,500 a month and the other $1,500 a month was their *minimum* payments on their cards that they kept paying.

As cash built up in the policy, they have been able to borrow from it systematically and pay off large chunks of the credit card debt. The Bank On Yourself policy has allowed them to pay off more than $50,000 of the credit card debt in four years. But it gets better ...

Once they are done with all the credit cards and pay back the loans to their Bank On Yourself policy with the $1,500 a month that was being paid to the banks, then we can start a second Bank On Yourself policy for the family for another $1,500 a month.

At age 65, their two policies will have a projected total cash value of more than $883,000, and a death benefit of more than $2.283 million that may pass income tax-free to their heirs or charity of their choice. Should they have a long-term care illness, they will have more than $300,000 that they can use for this purpose.

This is the amount of money that would have gone to the banks had they not had the courage to change their paradigm. Do you think they are happy with these results? Do you think they feel good about their future?

Nelson Nash, my friend and the author who first educated me about the Bank On Yourself concept, told me a long time ago that if you and your clients cannot whip Parkinson's Law, then you will not win the financial game. What this means is working into retirement years, cutting back on your lifestyle, sending your kids to a lesser college or no college at all. Read Nelson's book for more clarification as it is only a few pages. Basically Parkinson's Law means as your income rises your expenses rise right along with it.

For those of you who are saying to yourself, "Well, I don't have credit card debt so that does not apply to me," you might be feeling pretty good but you probably have the same problem. I know people who don't have a lot of credit card debt but are still spending most or all of their money on their lifestyle choices: cars, homes, food and drink, entertainment, vacations, etc. Parkinson's Law applies to you, too.

I see many people who have good resources or income but are spending more than they are saving. The effect is that you will have to work longer and you will not be able to do the things financially in the future that you want to do.

I hear all the time from people things like, "I don't know where all the money goes." It is no wonder because we are becoming a cashless society and families are not accounting for their money. We help our clients with a cash flow analysis to determine what the family can save above their fixed expenses. At that point the families can start paying themselves first so they can whip Parkinson's Law for good.

BREAKING THE CHAINS

I'm driven to do this because the debt hanging over our countries and so many individual families' heads means that we are living in slavery. I like being able to give my clients economic freedom and choice.

I was in debt myself. And when I paid off my credit cars there was this amazing sense of accomplishment and a feeling of well being because I was not in bondage to anyone else.

The numbers never made sense to me. A bank will pay you 1 percent interest on your savings account but if you need to borrow money they'll charge you 3 to 7 percent, depending on your credit score. And if you get a card from them, it's 10 to 20 percent interest. How does that inequity make you feel?

A lot of people are skeptical about changing their thinking on this system and I hear it all the time: This is all they know. And this has led to us becoming a society of "gotta have it now, will pay it later."

Just a few generations ago, we paid cash for cars. But the banking industry is so big now that financing is the norm and the individual debt crisis keeps growing because people now finance everything from computers to furniture.

Another tough stat is the fact that in countries like Japan and China, workers save a minimum of 20 percent of their income, and we only average the 5 percent I mentioned. It doesn't take a rocket scientist to know that the person who saves 20 percent can ultimately buy more assets than the other. Collectively, that's why we have become weaker economically as a nation.

Fortunately there is a way out…it's all about believing that you can Bank On Yourself. In fact, here is how Bank On Yourself has impacted the life of just one of our hundreds of clients:

"Discovering the Bank On Yourself concept has changed my life! When I met John, I was drowning in debt, had no savings, and had no plan for the future. I felt my financial situation was hopeless.

About John

John J. Shedenhelm, CEO of Eagle Financial Solutions, has been in the financial services industry for more than 22 years, and is one of only 200 financial advisors in the country who has successfully completed the rigorous training program and continuing education required to become a Bank On Yourself® authorized advisor. John holds a bachelor of arts degree in business management from Kent State University.

John decided to change his financial philosophy after he and his clients lost money in the stock market during the technology bubble crash during the early 2000s. It was the best financial move he ever made to utilize the Bank On Yourself® concept starting in 2003 for his clients especially since the stock market crashed again in 2008. Since 2003 John has helped more than 400 families protect and grow their money with little or no risk.

John is active in youth sports, serving as a coach for many years. John lives in Pickerington, Ohio, with his wife, Maryanne, and their two children, Cameron and Hunter.

What John says about Bank On Yourself: "Personally, I love the fact that Bank On Yourself will allow me to become consumer debt-free forever. It is also satisfying to know we'll also be able to become our own source of financing for our business expenses, which is phenomenal. I also love knowing that I am helping my clients feel a sense of control, empowerment and freedom by eliminating the banks and consumer debt from their lives, and reaping the long-term benefits of tax-free, guaranteed growth on their money."

For more information go to www.eaglefinancialsolutions.com.

CHAPTER 15

THE TALE OF THREE DENTISTS:
How to Fund Expenses
With Tax-Favored Money

BY JULIE GRANT

This is the tale of three dentists: Dr. Abbott, Dr. Baker and Dr. Connelly. All three are well-trained in the most advanced techniques of dentistry. They each graduated from a leading dental school and all three understand the importance of providing patient-friendly care in a welcoming environment.

Each wants to expand his dental practice to offer more services to his patients and to handle more patients each day. They also want to enhance their patients' experience while adding value to their practices and improving their bottom line.

Dr. Abbott, Dr. Baker and Dr. Connelly are ambitious and have important goals to accomplish. At 35 years of age, each believes he has plenty of time to accomplish what he wants to do in his career while also achieving a pleasing work-life balance. However, each dentist has a different way of thinking about money—a different financial paradigm that guides his choices about paying for his office renovations. Each man's financial paradigm will ultimately determine the financial success of his practice and, to a large extent, his financial success in life.

Let's find out more about the dentists and why they each embrace a particular paradigm.

- Dr. Abbott is goofy with family and friends. He likes to joke with his patients and enjoys playing occasional pranks on his staff. He is spontaneous and fun to be around, but doesn't plan far ahead.

- Dr. Baker is affable, kind and forward-looking. He minored in music as an undergraduate and plays clarinet in a local jazz band. He is a frugal man who saves a portion of his income every month.

- Dr. Connelly is a history buff; he enjoys sharing obscure facts about the Civil War with his colleagues. He is a disciplined man who carefully plans both his personal and professional life.

THEIR RENOVATION COSTS

The cost of equipment to deliver excellent service and maintain high productivity in a dental office is considerable. Selecting the method to finance these costs has a strong influence on the financial performance of the practice and, therefore, the ability of each dentist to meet his financial obligations and enjoy his career and life style.

The renovation process begins with the design of a "state of the art" workstation to create space that will be efficient and attractive. With the assistance of their design teams, Dr. Abbott, Dr. Baker and Dr. Connelly select furnishings and equipment, including:

- Exam Chair $ 5,000

- Cabinetry $25,000

- Lighting $ 3,000

- Utility Cart and Tools $ 5,000

- X-Ray Station $45,000

- Patient Chair $ 500

- Patient and Staff Monitors $ 2,000

- Sink and Water Filter $ 7,000

- Ultrasonic Cleaners $ 6,000

- Bleaching Systems $ 7,000

The total cost per work station exceeds $100,000, and for a practice to be successful, each dentist should have at least three fully functioning stations so several patients can be progressing simultaneously through their procedures. In addition, the office will need reception, records and patient waiting areas; a rest area for employees; storage and sterilization areas; a restroom facility, and a private office for the dentist.

Although the cost is indeed high, the value to the practice is well worth it, as Dr. Abbott, Dr. Baker and Dr. Connelly all will be able to offer exceptional care, with safe conditions for both patients and staff. All three will realize higher productivity and professional satisfaction with commensurate profitability.

Dr. Abbott, Dr. Baker and Dr. Connelly each approach the project with a distinct financial paradigm. They will likely choose one of the following methods to pay for their renovations:

- Borrow from the bank

- Save from current cash flow

- Bank On Yourself: a new paradigm

THE FINANCIAL APPROACH: DR. ABBOTT

Dr. Abbott realizes he needs to update his practice to remain competitive. The catch is, he doesn't have money saved for such expenses. However, he does have good credit so he negotiates a loan with his local bank for $100,000 at 5 percent interest for five years. The terms seem reasonable, and Dr. Abbott understands that when he borrows from the bank, he is obligated to pay back the principal with interest. He will also incur lost opportunity costs (LOC), which represent the value of an alternative choice that must be forgone because of the particular choice that is made. Over the next five years, the money he pays for principal and interest cannot be used for any other purpose.

Although Dr. Abbott will acquire a great new workstation, his equipment and tools eventually will wear out, break down and become obsolete, so he will have to repeat the process several more times during his career. His costs for just this initial renovation will look like this:

- Loan Amount $100,000

- Loan Term   5 years

- Interest Rate   5%

Dr. Abbott will pay $1,887.12 in monthly installments. Over the five-year term, he will pay $13,287.40 in interest and a total of $113, 287 with principal and interest combined. Although Dr. Abbott is pleased with the renovation results, and his patients compliment him on the comfort and attractiveness of the new office, he wonders: Is there a better way to pay for future renovations?

THE FINANCIAL APPROACH: DR. BAKER

Let's see what the other funding options look like as Dr. Baker decides how to pay for his renovations. He is a saver and in anticipation of the renovation, every month for the past five years, he has saved $2,000 in a money market account to be used for the project. The numbers for Dr. Baker's method of financing look like this:

- Monthly Deposit $2,000

- Savings Term   5 years

- Accumulated Cash $125,101 at 1% growth

- Cost of Improvements $100,000

Keep in mind that Dr. Baker must pay taxes on the gain in the money market account, which reduces his net savings; however, for this exercise we will not consider the tax impact. He also realizes that he will need to continue saving every month to pay for future improvements and replacements as technology advances and equipment becomes obsolete. Like Dr. Abbott, Dr. Baker is pleased with the results of the renovation and his patients compliment him on the comfort and attractiveness of the new office, but he wonders: Is there a better way to pay for future renovations?

THE FINANCIAL APPROACH: DR. CONNELLY

Dr. Connelly has studied the challenges of saving in a low-interest rate environment. He understands the cost of borrowing to finance upgrades to his dental practice. And he realizes there are lost opportunity costs to every transaction. During his research, Dr. Connelly is introduced to an advisor who shows him a unique financing and savings method called "Bank On Yourself." From his Bank On Yourself authorized advisor, Dr. Connelly learns that a particular type of life insurance policy can be designed to maximize its capability to store wealth.

The type of policy best suited for this purpose is a participating whole-life insurance policy, underwritten by an insurance company offering a non-direct recognition policy. While the conventional practice with life insurance is to purchase the maximum amount of death benefit for the lowest premium, Dr. Connelly's Bank On Yourself authorized advisor shows him a way to maximize the cash value in his policy with minimum death benefit and minimum cost. A participating whole life policy provides the framework for a superior method of accumulating wealth with extremely low risk to principal. It offers higher returns than most other investments or savings alternatives, in addition to providing important tax advantages.

Dr. Connelly's Bank On Yourself authorized advisor has designed a policy with $2,000 monthly premium that will allow him to borrow $100,000 in five years to pay for the renovation. The participating whole life policy gives him ownership in the insurance company and he can receive a share of the company's profits in the form of dividends. He will receive full dividends even when he borrows from the policy, and furthermore, the policy is designed so he may either pay back the loan or have the loan deducted from the death benefit. Note that the monthly commitment of $2,000 is comparable for all three dentists. By purchasing the participating whole life policy, Dr. Connelly creates far more value for both his immediate and long-term goals than either Dr. Abbott or Dr. Baker. Using his participating Whole Life insurance policy to finance his renovations, Dr. Connelly is able to essentially recapture the cost of the renovations when he repays the loan and restores the equity in his life insurance policy.

Dr. Connelly's numbers for a single renovation look like this:

- Monthly Premium $ 2,091

- Initial Death Benefit $ 754,344

- 5-Year Cash Value $ 125,256

- 5-Year Death Benefit $1,120,849

- Cash for Remodel $ 100,000

- Loan Repayment $ 127,628 (5-year term)

- Loan Interest Rate 5%

Dr. Connelly may choose to fund his policy out of his cash flow for five years or so, and then let the policy values pay the premium. Or he may fund it every year throughout his working career. He has chosen to fund it to age 65, and the results are shown in the numbers below:

- Policy Cash Value at Age 70 $2,133,402

- Death Benefit at Age 70 $3,469,364

- Tax-Free Income Per Year $128,000 tax-free income per year (age 71-90)

- Total Tax-Free Income $2,560,000 from age 71 to 90

In a relatively short period of time, Dr. Connelly has established a method of financing all his major expenses, including future renovations. He has created a unique source of truly private financing using his Bank On Yourself program for multiple uses, multiple times. Dr. Connelly will actually increase his monthly cash flow while simultaneously creating tax-free income for retirement and a valuable safety net for his family in the event of his untimely death.

THE ADVANTAGES OF BANK ON YOURSELF

Bank On Yourself offers Dr. Connelly a number of distinct advantages that aren't possible with conventional savings and borrowing methods. Let me count the ways:

First, with Bank On Yourself, Dr. Connelly will earn contractually-guaranteed cash value that increases every year, regardless of what happens in the stock or real estate markets. In addition, although not guaranteed, he will almost certainly receive dividends. Once credited to the policy, cash value increases and dividends cannot be rescinded or reduced. They are permanently locked in and grow tax-free inside his policy.

Second, because his Bank On Yourself policy is underwritten through a mutual company, he has ownership in the insurance company and thus owns both sides of the ledger: He is the lender and the borrower. He can set the terms for the loan—the payment frequency and the payment amount. Thus, Dr. Connelly helps determine the rate of return for the policy. In addition, if he needs to skip payments for a period of time, he may do so without penalties.

Third, he can recapture and recycle the costs of all purchases, gaining more value each time the money circulates through the policy. In effect, he is spending and saving concurrently, creating more value with each cycle.

Fourth, because Dr. Connelly's Bank On Yourself policy is underwritten by a nondirect recognition insurance company, he can borrow to pay for the office renovation and his policy will continue earning full dividends as though he never borrowed a penny. Nondirect recognition insurance companies base dividends on an aggregate of all invested assets, including policy loans. Thus, the loan is an asset on the books of the insurance company and he is earning dividends on cash from the policy he has spent elsewhere.

Fifth, Dr. Connelly can borrow cash from the policy to pay for much more than his office renovations. He can also pay for college expenses (for his children and for himself); he can use the money to buy cars, boats and recreational vehicles; he can purchase real estate and invest in stocks and business enterprises; he can acquire another dental practice, and much more, all with cash from his Bank On Yourself policy. Interest on the loans may also be tax-deductible if the money is used for business expenses. (Consult with a qualified tax professional.)

Sixth, dividends grow tax-sheltered in the policy and may be taken as cash, with no taxes due (up to the cost basis, under current tax law).

Dividends may also be used to pay premiums. Or best of all, dividends may be used to purchase fully paid-up life insurance for which he never pays another premium, and which comes with guaranteed cash value and more dividends. By using the level paid-up additions (LPUA) rider, Dr. Connelly can grow his policy values in the most cost efficient, tax-advantaged way.

THE BEST APPROACH

Dr. Connelly has indeed found a better way to pay for his renovation and all of life's major purchases. And if he dies before he completes his life's mission, his family will receive a substantial death benefit, income tax-free, and his policy loans will be fully discharged. Dr. Connelly has found Bank On Yourself to be superior in all ways to the conventional methods of saving and borrowing through commercial banks. By using Bank On Yourself, Dr. Connelly can recapture the cost of the renovation back into his policy, including principal, interest and lost opportunity costs, while also saving for retirement and protecting against the hardships that a premature death would cause his family.

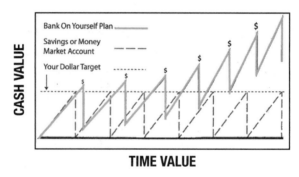

With conventional financing, once the check is written and the money is spent, there is no residual monetary value. With Bank On Yourself, the policy values continue to grow with dividends and guaranteed cash value increases. This is unlike any other financial instrument or system in the world where money is linear and cannot earn value after it is spent.

Dr. Connelly has included participating whole life insurance in his financial paradigm because he understands the basic principles of wealth:

- All wealth must reside some place

    o Stocks, bonds, mutual funds, annuities, life insurance

    o CDs, cash, collectibles

    o Real estate, business enterprise, intellectual property

- All wealth is subject to taxation at some time

    o Time of contribution or acquisition

    o Time of growth: income, interest, dividends, rents

    o Time of withdrawal, transfer, death

- All wealth incurs lost opportunity cost

    o What you could have earned by saving…instead of spending

    o What you could have enjoyed…had you spent the money instead of saving

Bank On Yourself positions the policy owner to take advantage of all three principles of wealth:

- The wealth resides in a low-risk, guaranteed growth, participating whole life policy, where it accumulates tax-deferred with immediate liquidity, and can be accessed with no taxes due, if done correctly.

- Upon death, the face amount transfers to the beneficiaries income tax-free.

The policy owner can save and spend his wealth concurrently.

Over time, the policy can become completely self-supporting (through dividend earnings), while simultaneously generating tax-free income for an entire lifetime!

YOUR OPPORTUNITY

How will your financial paradigm guide your decisions and pay for your opportunities? Contact a Bank On Yourself authorized advisor today to plan for a future with financial certainty. Everybody needs a place to store money, where it is safe and available when needed for opportunities as well as emergencies. Your life may depend on access to private money on your terms. With Bank On Yourself you own both sides of the ledger, you are both lender and borrower; you set the terms—how much money you want, when you want it and how you pay it back. You are in control!

About Julie

Julie Grant graduated from the University of Washington with bachelor and Master of Arts degrees in history. After completing college, she started her career in the insurance industry as an independent life and health insurance agent, specializing in disability income protection for physicians, dentists and attorneys. She received one of the first commission-only appointments in the industry from a national firm, earning top production rankings every year during her tenure with the firm.

To meet the expanding needs of her clients, Julie established her own agency, Insurance Research Associates, and incorporated in 1994. Under her leadership as president, the firm has appointments with more than 70 national carriers and many regional insurance associations and trusts. Julie has successfully managed and built the agency so it now serves more than a thousand clients. The guiding principles in building the agency have been to provide quality products, careful attention to detail and excellent service.

Since 2005, Julie has worked with the National Association of College Fund Advisors and has recently earned the Bank On Yourself certified advisor designation. For more than 25 years, she has been a member in good standing with the National and Washington Associations of Health Underwriters (NAHU and WAHU). She earned her registered health underwriter (RHU) designation in 1986.

In addition to insurance, Julie has a keen interest in real estate, dating back to her college years, during which time she worked on commercial and residential development projects in Washington state. She currently owns and manages commercial properties in the Puget Sound region; Fort Worth, Texas; and Winston Salem, North Carolina.

With a desire to make a difference in the community, Julie participated in the leadership program, Advance Bellevue, graduating with the class of 1995. She has served on several nonprofit boards and supported fund raising events for numerous charitable organizations, including Washington Women in Need (WWIN), Northwest Harvest and Emergency Feeding Program. Julie is an enthusiastic patron of the arts, providing financial support to Pacific Northwest Ballet; she also subscribes to Seattle Opera and frequently attends performances of the Seattle Symphony and other performing arts groups.

As founder and president of Insurance Research Associates, Inc, Julie has committed time and dedicated resources to be a client advocate. She has adhered to the principle of client satisfaction as the paramount focus in conducting business. Evaluation and selection of insurance programs is a complex, often baffling process, requiring both expert advice and a comprehensive view of the financial and insurance markets. Her goal is to simplify that process and help her clients manage risks, control costs and maximize their financial potential.

CHAPTER 16

START MY BANK ON YOURSELF PLAN OR GET OUT OF DEBT FIRST?

BY BEKKI HARPER

Do you know that 36 percent of take home pay is going to finance debt? Or, to put it another way, the average American is handing over 36 percent of his or her hard-earned money to financial institutions in the way of interest. Ouch. It grieves me to say that this is just the average; some are paying more. That means less than 64 percent of the average American's money is staying at home with them. When you consider the additional financial hit incurred with taxes, the average American is keeping less than 54 percent of their earned income to fund their lifestyle. Disgraceful!

If you're among the many Americans in debt, do you feel like you are trapped in quicksand and sinking fast? After reading the alarming statistics I just shared, you may feel like you will face a certain muddy death.

Stop! Would you like to know how others fixed this?

One attribute of Bank On Yourself is redirecting the money you are now giving to financial institutions, pulling yourself out of that quicksand and getting your money back to you, where it belongs.

Don't have debt?

You still want to read this chapter. You may learn something. You may be able to help a friend who is in need. You may Bank On Yourself, too!

Bank On Yourself is all about redirecting any and all money now going to financial institutions back to you!

My Quicksand Story

When the real estate bubble burst in 2006, I was buying, fixing and reselling houses on credit. You've seen the shows like "Flip This House," where you buy an ugly house, fix it and sell it. I was on a roll. Years earlier, my first deal brought in $64,000 and I thought real estate was my ticket to financial freedom. Until 2006, that is.

The Bottom Fell Out

Remember that $64,000 from my first transaction? I was that much in credit card debt and more, not to mention the mortgage responsibilities. Filling the retirement bucket or living on passive income had been my goal. Filling the deep hole I had dug for myself was my reality. I was looking at being in debt for the rest of my life.

When the bottom falls out, whether it is due to real estate losses, business failure, loss of a job, medical expenses or divorce, the numbers can go negative fast. And there you are, paying, paying, paying, just to fill a hole. Just to get back to zero. High interest rates are nipping at your heels and attacking your gut every 30 days. Those due dates keep showing up like dirty dishes.

Fast Action Required

While I was watching some of my closest investor friends crashing and burning, I was determined I was not going to be one of them. I had to get an MBA in winning the credit card game, pronto, or I was going to be another statistic. And somehow, even as upside down as I was, I had to put some money to work.

Out of the Quicksand and onto Solid Ground

How am I going to get out of this? How can I get out of debt when most of my payment is interest? How can I save any money? How can I get back on track financially? How can I ever retire? How can I invest money instead of giving it to the banks every month?

It comes down to having and implementing this plan:

1. Break out of debt and stop interest payments from eating away your power to obtain wealth.

2. Get savings and emergency funds working 24/7.

3. Get an increasing return that will continue to increase until your last breath.

Every dollar is an employee that works 24/7 for someone. Those employees don't complain, require vacations or take sick leave. The more of them you employ, the sooner you employ them, the better.

BANK ON YOURSELF, BUT STABILIZE FIRST

Stabilize 1, 2, 3

The first order of business was to look at everything I owed and the amount of interest I was paying. It was about as much fun as having a tooth pulled without Novocain, but it got me organized.

The second step was to get interest rates reduced as low as possible. I called every credit card company I owed and asked them to lower my interest rate and raise my credit limit. Some will say "yes" and some will say "no." I called every 3 to 6 months and asked again and again. I explain more about this in my article, "Strategies to Minimize the Interest You Pay While Eliminating Credit Card Companies From Your Life," available free on my website.

Third, I looked at every balance transfer that came along with a zero percent offer. It makes sense to pay a one-time transfer fee to enjoy 100 percent of your payment going to principal. Currently, Bank of America and Citi card give these offers the most liberally. Look for offers with the highest credit limit and the lowest interest rate after the zero percent offer expires. I kept this going and didn't pay interest for four years.

Here is your action plan:

1. **Get organized.** Make a list of every credit card, balance, interest rate, minimum payment and credit limit.

2. **Call the card companies.** You want two things: Lower your interest rate and increase your credit limit.

3. **Reduce your interest rate.** Look for zero percent balance transfer offers.

If these offers aren't coming in, employ these strategies and watch the tide turn. Some individuals, if their credit is too far gone, may need additional professional assistance.

Discipline is key. Getting another credit card, even with a zero percent balance transfer offer, isn't going to help if the mall sirens beckon you and drag you crashing onto sharper debt rocks.

Changes for the Better

With lower interest rates more of your money goes to principal and banks earn less money. When banks earn less money, you keep more money. Now we are getting the money flowing in the right direction. Minimum monthly payments come down, too, which equals an increased ability to obtain wealth.

Raising credit limits (the maximum amount that can be charged) indicates a lower percentage of your total available credit being used. Example: A $2,500 balance on a credit limit of $5,000 is 50 percent, while a $2,500 balance on a $10,000 limit is only 25 percent. This is why increasing your credit limits will be in your favor. Your credit score will improve and give you options, increasing your ability to obtain wealth.

Using balance transfers with zero percent offers, even for a limited time, enables you to pay down principal. Lower minimum payments and reduced debt increase your ability to obtain wealth.

Congratulations! Breaking out of debt and stopping interest payments from eating away your power to obtain wealth is underway.

Employ Wealth Rule Number 1

Wait for it. Wait for it. Pay yourself first. It is a saying you have probably heard before. That is why it is so easy to let it slip away. Setting aside money for your future makes sense, yet things that are easy to do are just as easy not to do. Most people don't know where to start, how much to pay themselves or where to put the money so it can make them wealthy.

Every dollar is an employee who works 24/7. The more of them you employ and the sooner you employ them, the better.

Maybe you are one of those people. Or maybe it's someone you know. It was me. So allow me to pave the way to solidarity. But first, proclaim a promise to yourself. Repeat after me: "I will pay myself first!"

Your Starting Number

A standard starting place is 10 percent of every dollar earned. Fifteen percent is even better and a must if you are over 50. This may be a stretch in the beginning, but it is essential to wealth and financial freedom.

Sustainability Vs. Instant Gratification

Determine where your money is currently going. Having control of your life is rewarding. The short-term gratification is typically what gets us into trouble in the first place.

Our culture is adapting more and more to accept $5 for a cup of coffee as normal when in reality a cup of home brew is still less than 50 cents. As Northcote Parkinson said in Nelson Nash's book, *Becoming Your Own Banker: Understanding Parkinson's Law*: "A luxury, once enjoyed, becomes a necessity." For a quick exercise in proving Parkinson's Law, leave your cell phone at home today. (Just kidding. We proved it, didn't we?)

One client of mine was spending $500 a month on Monster drinks at Circle K and had no clue why he was out of money before he was out of month. By all means, enjoy your Monster power, but buy it at Costco by the case and pay yourself the difference.

My clients tell me it feels so liberating once they have begun. The long-term peace of mind beats out the instant gratification any day.

DIVIDEND PAYING WHOLE-LIFE INSURANCE ON STEROIDS AND THE POWER OF NONDIRECT RECOGNITION

My Introduction to Bank On Yourself

A friend suggested I read Jordan Adler's book, *Beach Money*. When the bookseller didn't have it he suggested I read *Bank On Yourself* by Pamela Yellen. I bought it, thinking it was an "If it is to be, it is up to me" book. I had no idea at the time it was my real ticket to financial freedom. As I read, the light bulb went on.

Fund a Bank On Yourself policy and take the cash value accumulation to pay down credit card debt while the ever-increasing values of the policy fill my retirement bucket. Awesome!

It gets even better! I take the cash value accumulation to pay down credit card debt and I keep earning interest and dividends as if I never took it out. What? This seems hard to wrap your brain around. It seems too good to be true. "Nondirect Recognition" is the feature that makes it true.

This is one of the ways the wealthy get wealthier, and this is how you are going to build your wealth, too.

It is really very simple. Cash value, when borrowed, is not viewed as coming from an individual policy but rather a company pool available for lending.

Since it is not recognized as coming out of your policy (nondirect recognition), you get to spend your money and earn interest and dividends on it at the same time. Think of the lost opportunities you can recover because your money is growing simultaneously inside and outside of your policy. The leverage of growing your retirement bucket while paying off debt is huge. It gets really exciting when your own bank starts funding all your recurring expenses instead of charging it and agonizing later.

Found Opportunity

One question prospective clients have is, "Do I have to borrow my own money and pay interest to use it?" Seasoned policy owners know they get back every penny with their growth and equity and are glad to do it. You get the exact dividend whether your money sits or is in motion. You want the same funds working for you simultaneously in multiple ways.

Let's do it. Here is our process:

1. Pay ourselves first, as we have already determined.

2. Capitalize the "Bank of _____(your name goes here)."

3. Borrow cash accumulation to pay off other banking institutions.

4. Replenish. Redirect payments previously going to other institutions back to Bank On Yourself.

Capitalizing your policy may bring on a slight setback to paying off your debt, especially if you cut back on credit card payment amounts to start your bank. Initially, you may not be able to fill as much of the debt hole as you would have. The first year may only be 50 to 60 percent of it. The next year will increase 60 to 70 percent, then 80 percent and so on. Remember, you are not just filling a hole anymore. You are building your wealth simultaneously.

Nick and Amy's Story

Quicksand. Somehow Nick and Amy had stepped into it. Had that many unexpected financial obligations come up? They awoke one day to the reality of having $50,000 in credit card debt. Encompassed with that sick feeling of realizing they hadn't done something right financially, Nick and Amy knew they needed rescuing and something had to change.

Nick and Amy were able to refinance their home and lower their payment. Among other things, they found $500 over their minimum payments to start moving their debt mountain.

Bank On Yourself Advisor to the Rescue

When I met Nick and Amy, they were filled with determination and I honored their enthusiasm. But imagine paying $500 extra on their debt mountain per month for 9 years 3 months and ending up with a zero balance.

I introduced them to the idea of becoming their own financing source while filling the hole. The simple strategy: Put $500 a month into a Bank On Yourself policy, borrow the cash values to pay off debt, then pay the policy back.

It would take 13 years instead of 9.3 years, but they also achieved 9 years 3 months time value of money, which makes a difference.

What exactly is the difference?

No Bank: Pay off the debt in 9 years 3 months, then continue to save to year 13, resulting in $18,000 in savings.

Bank: Put $500 to work in their Bank On Yourself policy and their cash value in year 13 is $90,694. That's $18,000 vs. $90,694.

Let's not forget the insurance coverage of $259,334. Nick and Amy transferred the risk of their human life value to the insurance company.

All the while, their policy serves as their liquid emergency fund, vacation fund, vehicle purchase, etc. Instead of spending their money and saying goodbye to it forever, Nick and Amy are moving it in and out of their policy, using it, using it and using it again to their good.

The Time is Now

1. Pay yourself first and build the "Bank of _____(your name goes here)."

2. Use cash value accumulation to eliminate debt while building your wealth.

3. Replenish and leverage multiple uses for the same funds.

> *"I dwell in a sea of abundance. I see clearly my inexhaustible*
> *supply. I see clearly just what to do."*
> ~ Florence Scovel Shinn

Seize Your Future

When something enhances your life, you want to share it. The gracious bookseller who introduced me to *Bank On Yourself* wanted to give what he was given. I could have nodded, smiled and done nothing, but something in his passion drove me to action. For something to change in your life, something has to change in your life. Next year and in years to come, you could still be climbing the same debt mountain or sharing the view from the top.

About Bekki

Bekki Harper is a principal planner and producer with Strategic Advisors Group LLC. Her passion for financial services ignited more than nine years ago and her constant hunger for excellence keeps her in the forefront of her profession.

As a dedicated Bank On Yourself advisor, she is an advocate and educator in financial freedom. She is a certified cash flow coach, a member of Tucson Marketing Professionals and a supporter of various other professional organizations.

Being an investor herself, Bekki is enthusiastic about deepening the pockets of investors and regularly sponsors and coordinates investor workshops. She is known for caring as much about her clients' money as they care about it themselves.

Bekki cofounded what is now known as the Strategic Advisers Group's College Positioning Division. College positioning is essential for families desiring the best college experience for their student. She is known for getting good students free money for college. Tens of thousands of dollars are available to students who draw the attention of college recruiters and follow the steps provided to them. Families are able to navigate the process of college acceptance and enrollment with confidence and ease. Bekki is instrumental in lowering cost burdens and safeguarding family assets via Bank On Yourself strategies and more.

In addition, Bekki works with school officials to coordinate scholastic essay contests at the middle and high school level. Every year, the winning students and their families are awarded ongoing personal college coaching that continues throughout their college career.

Bekki lives in Tucson, Arizona, with her husband of more than 22 years and their daughter. She is very active in charitable causes and regularly participates in efforts to give back to her community.

"Introducing my clients to companies that have stood the test of time for decades, companies that have prospered faithfully for more than 100 years, is rewarding," she says. "Discovering solid financial tools resonated in me that all the people I know and care about need to know about this.

"I love going to sleep at night, knowing no one is ever going to get hurt, and their lives are only going to be better because I was in it."

To learn more about Bekki, visit www.StrategicAdvisorsGroup.com or call (520) 577-5506.

CHAPTER 17

INTEREST RATES: Do We Really Understand Them?

BY DENNIS BAIRD

"It isn't what we don't know that gives us trouble;
it's what we know that ain't so."
~ Will Rogers

Interest rates! Everywhere we turn in our financial world we are confronted with interest rates. We pay a rate of interest to the mortgage company, and we hopefully earn a rate of interest on our savings. We pay interest rates on credit cards. Everyone wants a higher rate of return on their 401(k) or IRA. We are programmed by banks and financial institutions to think about and measure our financial decisions on interest rates. But could the banks and the financial institutions have an ulterior motive, or could they even be misleading us? A very good friend and mentor of mine asks the question, "If what you thought to be true turned out not to be true, when would you want to know?"

A CAUTIONARY TALE

I believe we have been conditioned to think about interest rates in a way that might not be true. Consider the following story from Ted CeDe, told in his own words.

A few years after graduating from college and getting married, my wife and I found ourselves with two children. We were planning to have more children and knew eventually we would need a bigger car. We had learned that the closer the children were to each other, the higher the probability for trouble. There was poking and grabbing, and one child always wanted what the other child had. We thought one way to avoid this confusion was to have more room between them and a larger car would serve this purpose.

We had saved some money and we considered the possibilities to make the money grow. We thought about investing the money in a mutual fund or individual stocks, but we were also aware of volatility, and ups and downs in the stock market, and we knew we could possibility lose part or all of our money if we invested it. We considered leaving the money in the mattress because we did not want to lose any of the principal. We had worked hard for the money and we knew we would need a better car in the future.

We settled on a certificate of deposit (CD) at a local bank. We had been banking there for a while and felt comfortable with our decision. We purchased a CD in the amount of $10,000 for five years, earning 4 percent.

TED TRIES TO CLAIM HIS CASH

Days after the CD matured, Ted went to the bank and showed Jeannie, at the counter, the paperwork. Jeannie had been the bank employee who helped him when he had purchased the CD. He told Jeannie he was ready to cash in his CD. She politely told him she did not have authority to give Ted his money and the branch manager would have to do that. During his five- plus years doing business at the bank, Ted had never met the branch manager.

Jeannie went to the branch manager's office and he returned with her. The branch manager shook Ted's hand and called him Mr. CeDe. After only waving to Ted now and again, Ted was suddenly Mr. CeDe. The branch manager invited Ted into his office where he quizzed Ted about his money. After chatting a bit the branch manager made Ted a proposal. He suggested that Ted leave his money in the bank by extending the CD for another five years. Ted's $10,000 had grown to a little over $12,000 since his original purchase. He would continue to pay Ted 4 percent on the new balance of $12,000. He then wanted to loan Ted $12,000 for five years but he said he would have to charge Ted 6 percent for the use of the bank's money. Ted was initially very offended until the banker said he could prove to Ted that Ted would have more money in five years if he followed the branch manager's advice.

I have shared this story with many of my clients over the years. I pause at this point in the story and ask them what they would do under these circumstances. The overwhelming answer is, "I'd take my money and run." Ted told me his gut reaction was the very same. But the bait from the branch manager was that the banker would prove that Ted would have more money in five years.

THE BANKER'S PROJECTIONS

Of course. Ted asked the branch manager to prove what he said because Ted thought he understood interest rates and this did not sound like a winning proposition to him. The banker took out his HP 12C calculator along with a yellow notepad and proceeded with the calculations. The branch manager did a projection showing Ted how his money would grow and what it would be worth in five years. Figure I shows a future value projection from a similar financial calculator ($12,000 earning 4 percent over five years.) Yes, Ted's money would grow and his new balance would be $14,600 in five years.

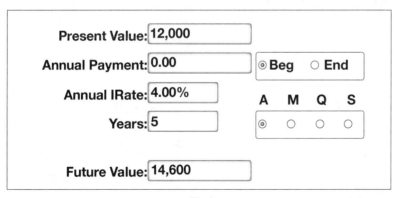

Fig .I

The banker then ran a projection showing the payment to the bank for the use of the bank's money over the five year period. The sum of $12,000 paid back to the bank at 6 percent over five years would produce an annual payment of $2,687.51 to the bank.

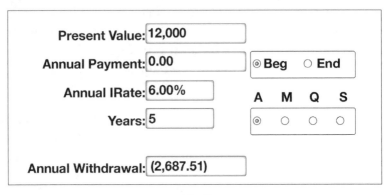

Fig .II

Let's review the facts in this case. The banker is proposing Ted pay a difference of 2 percent more for the use of the bank's money because the bank is paying Ted 4 percent for the use of Ted's money while Ted is paying the bank 6 percent for the use of the bank's money. Yes! Arbitrage (the difference between interest rates) is a factor in this example and is part of the equation. The principal sums are the same at the beginning of the calculations and the period of time is the same throughout both contracts.

ADDITIONAL CALCULATIONS

Now, the branch manager said there were two more calculations to arrive at the answer. Would Ted be money ahead by exercising the banker's proposal? The first calculation was to figure the total amount paid to the bank by Ted. All the banker did was multiply the annual payment of $2,687.51 by five years. The second calculation was to subtract the total payment to the bank from the amount Ted's CD would produce. Figures III and IV show these calculations.

Fig .III   *Fig .IV*

Now we have the answer. The banker was correct. If Ted followed the banker's advice, Ted would, in fact, have $1,162.45 more money at the end of the five year contract.

So, did interest rates tell the whole story in Ted's case? No! Not at all! In fact, they only confused our thinking in this scenario. The interest rates were misleading to our thinking. How can that be?

THE IMPACT OF PRINCIPAL BALANCES

The answer to the puzzle is in the principal balances. The principal balance in both cases was $12,000. But the balance in the amount borrowed from the bank was decreasing. So Ted was paying interest on a smaller balance each year. The interest paid on the CD was compounding and increasing. So Ted was earning interest on a larger balance each year.

I have shared this example with most of my clients on the trail of their financial journey at some point in time. I use this principle to teach a variety of concepts in financial matters. One of those principles is the power of the uninterrupted compounding of money. But that subject is big enough for another chapter. Most of my clients study the numbers for a while before the really understand the principles and concepts. Most people are confused about the apparent difference in interest rates.

THOSE MYSTIFYING INTEREST RATES

I few years back I logged onto a colleague's website. As I reviewed some of the links and posts, I was drawn to a question posed on the front page. It said, "Test Yourself!" I love these kinds of things because I want to know if I can calculate the correct answer, and if I do not calculate the right answer, I will probably learn something. I took the test. This was the question: "You invest $1,000 at a 20 percent rate of return for two years. How much would you have?" The question was multiple choice and there were four answers to choose from.

Before reading further or looking ahead, you might want to have a go at this exercise.

The choices were:

a. $1,440

b. $1,280

c. $800

d. $0

I got my pen and paper and started the exercise. I worked my calculations twice just to make sure my answer was correct. I entered my choice and clicked the submit button. I was stunned when I saw the response on the next page. It said, "Actually, any of these answers could be correct" and then showed the reasoning:

a. **$1,440** (First year: 20 percent increase; second year: 20 percent increase)

b. **$1,280** (First year: 60 percent increase; second year: 20 percent decrease)

c. **$800** (First year: 100 percent increase: second year: 60 percent decrease)

d. **$0** (First year: 140 percent increase; second year: 100 percent decrease)

How did you do on this exercise? I will ask again…interest rates! Do we really understand them?

Since I worked this problem the first time I have learned there is a big difference between average rate of return and actual rate of return.

Let's try another example. You are on an airplane and the woman next to you is an investment advisor and she says she will guarantee a 25 percent average rate of return over the next four years if you invest $12,000 with her. We'll use the $12,000 figure because that's what Ted CeDe left in the bank to earn 4 percent interest on. Yes, at the end of four years she will guarantee an average 25 percent rate of return. Are you investing your money with her?

I use this example with many of my clients and most of them are ready to pull out their checkbooks. Let's see how this could work:

• The first year your $12,000 doubles. You now have $24,000, an increase of 100 percent.

- The second year your $24,000 hits tough times and you lose 50 percent. Your balance is now $12,000.

- The third year your $12,000 doubles; again, an increase of 100 percent. You have a balance of $24,000.

- The fourth year your $24,000 drops to $12,000, a loss of 50 percent.

The four years are up. How much is the advisor giving you at the end of the four-year time period? Answer: $12,000. The guarantee was a 25 percent average rate of return. Did she keep her part of the agreement? Let's review.

- Year 1 = +100%

- Year 2 = -50%

- Year 3 = +100%

- Year 4 = -50%

Add up the rates of return for each year and divide by the number of years. The answer is a 25 percent average rate of return over four years. The advisor did, in fact, keep her promise. But you were probably expecting something more than just the return of your original $12,000, right? You not only get back just the original principle, $12,000, but you lost the opportunity to save and compound your money—no risk and guaranteed growth of your money over the 4-year period. This is called opportunity cost.

AND THE WINNER IS...

Now, I'll ask an important question. Who had the most profit (actual money) in their account at the end of the two contracts we have talked about? Ted CeDe, who earned 2 percent less on the arbitrage of his CD at the bank, or the investor who realized a 25 percent average rate of return with the financial advisor? Yes! Ted is the winner. He has $1,065 more profit in his pocket even after paying the bank 6 percent for the use of the bank's money.

Remember my friend and mentor's question: "If what you thought to be true turned out not to be true, when would you want to know?" In our airplane advisor example, you had to wait four years before you realized an average rate of return that could produce zero profit. How much fun is that? Right! Zero! Financial institutions and banks report average rates of return in their literature. It is easy to see why people get confused about where to put their money and realize results other than what they expected.

NOW DO WE UNDERSTAND INTEREST RATES?

In conclusion, let me make some recommendations. Not all of these recommendations were discussed in this chapter, but they will improve your ability to create and hold onto wealth.

1. We walk around with an illusion of knowledge. We already know everything. Don't be quick to dismiss a new or different idea. We cannot learn less. We must adjust your thinking.

2. We must recognize where money is flowing and who is in control of that money.

3. We can only achieve financial success when we understand how the product and design of the product will impact our financial success.

4. Since the subject of this chapter is interest rates, we would commit a fatal error in thinking if we consider financial matters only as a function of interest rates. That just ain't so. Wealth is much more than just interest rates.

5. We improve our situation any time we can eliminate the payment of interest to others and direct the same market rate of interest to an entity that we own and control.

6. We should diligently look for products that solve the problems of taxes (not just postpone them), risk, volatility, inflation, penalties and value of the dollar.

7. You must find an advisor who does not spout the same rhetoric as everyone else. Creativity and innovation have a place in our financial planning.

About Dennis

Dennis Baird was born in Payson, Utah, where he grew up working on the family farm. He graduated from Orem High School.

In 1969, he joined the Utah Army National Guard. He also served in the Pennsylvania and California National Guard, assigned to military intelligence in all three states.

Dennis graduated from Brigham Young University in Provo, Utah, with a bachelor of science degree, where he also served as president of Samuel Hall Society, a highly acclaimed service organization at the university.

Dennis has worked for Xerox Corp., National Inventory Control Systems and Medtronic, a medical devices company. He is involved in politics and ran for state Senate in the state of Utah. He does business and personal consulting and has served on the board of directors for Washington School of Graduate Studies and Washington School of Law.

Dennis owned an Allstate Insurance agency for six years. He owns commercial property and other businesses. He is the principal at Strategic Wealth and Insurance Services LLC. He works with businesses of all sizes and individuals as a wealth strategist. He is also proficient in college expense planning and college admission strategies. He is available fee for service if that serves the client best.

Dennis holds series 6 and 63 licenses and has active insurance licenses in 16 states. He speaks and presents financial seminars across the country. He is available for speaking and training to corporate and private groups of any size. Subjects include college planning, the myth of 401(k)'s and qualified plans, the real causes of wealth decline in America, and misinformation propagated by banks and financial institutions. The information he teaches will empower you financially.

Dennis may be contacted at drbaird@reagan.com or by phone at (801) 369-4081.

CHAPTER 18

PROTECTING YOUR BUSINESS UNTIL SALES, RETIREMENT OR DEATH DO YOU PART

BY GRANT THOMPSON

What about you, the business or practice owners? The backbone of our country. You are the ones willing to work 18 hours a day for yourselves; busting your tails, taking all the risk, maybe going into debt to reach your goals and dreams. Then we hear about government elites. These are the ones who never had real jobs and have the nerve to say, "You didn't build that."

I beg to differ. To make it today in business, you must think and plan right. I had the great fortune to grow up in my family's business. I watched my dad and mom put in everything they had to create a retail shoe and sporting goods business. Just like you, they gave their blood, sweat and tears. Witnessing the rights and wrongs were great lessons for me.

I'm very blessed to be in my profession and want to take those lessons and experiences and share with you how to incorporate the Bank On Yourself strategy into your planning. Giving you the safety, the liquidity is needed to grow and protect your business, ultimately, leaving your hard work to your family in a lasting legacy.

Why did you choose your profession or business? I know you want to help folks and hopefully you are accomplishing that goal. However, that's a result of doing what's right. However, be honest: You did it because you want to afford for you and your family the dream lifestyle. Don't be ashamed to say it because I'm glad you feel that way. You're busting your tail and you deserve it. You're building your dream business and hopefully you have now graduated from president of the toilet brush in your practice, to a thriving and growing business professional.

WAYS TO BULLETPROOF YOUR BUSINESS

Buy/sell or buy/sell stock redemption agreements, key man, succession planning and executive bonuses and how all this can fit together in your business or practice.

First, let's protect your baby. Let's focus first on buy/sell agreements. There are many items to put into this agreement and you will need the right pros on your team. What is a buy/sell agreement? Here's the short answer. It's a will for your business or practice. It's what you want to happen with your business/practice in the event you are selling, retiring or dying. Without it you are totally exposed.

Recently my business partner Chris Thurman and I met with a business comprised of three partners. All they had was a handwritten agreement with only the percentage of each partner's interest and a guess at each other's ownership value. Furthermore, they told us they had only verbally agreed to how they would handle each other's retirement or exit and what they would pay surviving partner heirs at death. It was basically to be determined as the events occurred. Nothing in writing will turn out to be a disaster in most situations. Having a written plan is a MUST! So what do we do about it? Read on.

BUY-SELL AGREEMENTS

A buy-sell agreement is a contract that assures the continuation of the business by obligating the company or co-owners to buy, and obligating you or your estate to sell, the business interest at the occurrence of specified events such as death, disability, withdrawal or retirement. Drafted properly, a buy-sell agreement will help set the value of the business for federal estate tax purposes, and may reduce the chance of valuation disputes with the IRS.

A buy-sell agreement:

- Guarantees a buyer

- Establishes a fair price

- Sets the terms of the purchase and identifies the events that trigger a buyout

- Assures a smooth transfer of the business

- Provides cash to you in the event of a disability, withdrawal or retirement and liquidity to your estate

- Avoids conflicts

- Assures the continuation of the business

A Family Scenario

I work with a family business that dad and mom started 40-plus years ago. They have three kids. Two joined the business profession and have contributed to its growth for more than 30 years. Their third kid decided not to go into the family business. Nothing at this point had been done to ensure that the two sons would be able to continue the family business when dad and mom retired or died.

The two adult kids were concerned and arranged for me to visit with dad to lay it all out. When we all met, dad abruptly jumped up and said, "Hey, we are family and we trust each other. We don't need some dumb agreement. All of this will be taken care of in my will." Tense situation but I'm used to it.

I looked at the will. What a mess…Imagine the tension in the room when his two kids found out the will said, "All my kids split evenly"! Yikes! Ever heard the quote, "Crap hitting the fan"? Problem is the third kid, who wasn't involved in the business, would receive a one-third ownership of the business, not having contributed anything to the business. Easily fixed with a professionally written and funded agreement in place. We can make everyone happy, happy, happy.

This problem isn't much different in nonfamily businesses. Many times friends form partnerships and have terrible splits because they lack a proper plan. Furthermore, a written agreement is just as important for exit planning. You may be s considering selling your practice and need to bring in an associate. That buy/sell will help things go much smoother.

A Partnership Example

Many years ago I helped two partners set up their life insurance plans for a buy/sell but they never implemented a written agreement. "We are just too busy," they said. Guess what? One partner was killed. I delivered the claim but the surviving partner ended up keeping most of the life insurance that was intended to buy out the surviving spouse's interest, with two small children. We supplied the cash but they never implemented a written buy/sell agreement. It was a travesty, to say the least. I saw the surviving partner take advantage of her and she didn't really have much recourse. It all ended up in court. That little piece of paper would have made that go smoothly and fairly. No hassles. Instead, lawyers got most of it.

Just get your darn agreements set up and fund them properly with life insurance. Then everyone knows what is going to happen when that day comes, and those days will come.

Once you have determined value, determine where the funds will come from to complete the buy-out of the partner's interest. On the living side, you will need enough cash to buy out your partner(s). That could take a lot of cash. If you take it from the business cash assets, that could be big drain and stress the business. You could go to the banker. Ah, the banker … Welcome to slavery. You're a new boss. Isn't that swell? That's assuming they will loan it to you. And who wants to go into more debt? Not me.

I do hear this quite often. "My banker will do anything I want." Really? Can you go to your "banker buddy" and get money whenever you want? Maybe, but what if your banker buddy dies or decides not to be your buddy anymore because the bank's stockholders decide you're no longer a good risk. Have you been watching the news? Money is drying up.

You could take on a new partner by selling your exiting partner's interest. This could be an option if you find the right fit. But how long will it take and do you really want that to be a forced option? By the way, without a buy/sell, your partner could sell to someone else without your permission.

You could do a payment stream to the existing partner. It's a viable option as long as the business continues to be profitable. However, for the exiting partner this could be a big risk. What if the remaining business owners later file bankruptcy or get sued. Oh, I know, you say it won't happen but it happens all the time.

Bank On Yourself policies will take care of all those issues and give the cash you need to buy out existing partners as well as surviving heirs. Two for one. Takes care of the living side for buy-out of the exiting partner and the dying side for the buy-out of the heirs so your business can continue.

OWNER KEY MAN POLICY

What about the economic loss you will experience with the loss of that partner? Why did you decide to take on a partner in the first place? You need to plan for that economic loss when the partner leaves or dies. Death can be abrupt and this will give you the capital to continue the business.

This also works when you have a planned purchase for your business or practice. It self- completes the plan of living and dying.

CREATING CAPITAL

Now we have the business or practice set up. Let's talk about creating capital for starting or growing your business. Ever finance or lease anything for your personal or business use? Of course. If you have the capital in your policy, you now can start Banking On Yourself. When you create these plans and use them for financing, you can keep the compounding going on those funds while you're leasing or buying your own stuff.

Most business and practice owners borrow money for most things. How about financing yourself? That's how you create real wealth. When you owe money to a bank or leasing company you now have become a slave to the lender. Here is a great quote: "Those who understand interest collect it. Those who don't pay it." Are you the collector or the payor?

Ever heard of the T.I.N.S.T.A.A.F.L. theory, which is the acronym for There Is No Such Thing as a Free Lunch. My 12-year-old son, Blair, can even quote it to you. Banks don't lend for free, do they? I'll give you an example.

One day I was headed across the street to grab to lunch in a bank building when I ran into three bankers I know. I joked and said, "Hey, you got a billion dollars I could borrow?" They all laughed and one said, "You bet, Grant, but I would need you to stop by and sign this little piece of paper first." We laughed, then I said, "At 0 percent, of course?" Laughing again, he said, "Sure, Grant. But then, of course, we own you! I guess everyone has to be owned by someone." They walked off laughing. Kind of ticked me off, if you want to know the truth.

Unfortunately, that's the banker's mentality. Go read the book, *The Creature of Jekyll Island*. Sadly, our society has been brainwashed into believing banks are the only way we can obtain capital. Hogwash! The reason we can't save is because we are giving all our money to the banks. So my question is, who owns you? Go start a Bank On Yourself plan and end the slavery. That's how you create lasting wealth. It takes a little time but it will happen.

Two years ago, Chris came in the office screaming about what he witnessed on TV the night before. The news interviewed a farmer about the great wheat harvest. During the interview the farmer said, "Yep, it was great harvest. Now we can pay back the banks." They are just living off the banks. Starting a Bank On Yourself policy will create the wealth you need and reverse profits to the bank back to you. No begging your banker any more or them telling you how to run your business.

My favorite part of doing these plans is that you can get money whenever you want and for whatever purpose you choose. You don't have to tell the banker what you're doing or beg for the money to do it. Furthermore, you don't have to put a business plan together for the bank and jump through their hoops anymore. Freedom to do, not just hope to do, is power.

BUSINESS SUCCESSION PLANNING

What is your written succession plan? Seriously, more than 90 percent of the owners we speak with don't have a written exit plan for their practice or business. Many are relying too heavy on their business as their retirement plan. That might work out to some degree, but what are you doing to be ready? What if Wally World (aka Wal-mart) decides to be in the same business as you and moves next door? Most business can't compete with them. Furthermore, what if the government passes legislation that hurts or even forces you to close? Your business may not bring what you think. You better get a plan. Just wishing isn't a plan.

Succession planning for the business can give you a precise road map for exiting your business and making it much more desirable for the buyer and more profitable for you. Think about how great it would feel to know who is taking over. Your clients, partners, staff and family will feel much more secure if you have that plan laid out in writing. Securing the buyer at a predetermined price is the exit strategy that makes the most sense.

Having a Bank On Yourself plan even gives you a great option of becoming the financing source for the business. I've had fathers or mothers finance the business for their kids. That could make the transfer even easier and create a great income stream for you. Plus it may give you a say if trouble arises in the business.

EXECUTIVE BONUS

This is a great employee benefit to attract and keep talent. You want to keep your "A" staff. There are multiple arrangements but keep it simple. The nice thing about setting up a plan is you can pick and choose who you set it up for and you don't have all the administration nightmares or expenses like with 401(k)'s, profit sharing and the like. Furthermore, you could still get a tax deduction for the business. This plan is much easier to administrate without all the government hoops. Government plans are a hassle and really not always a great choice. Plus your employees will love how they will be able to use their money now and still create their retirement. This teaches employees how to stay away from debt as well as protecting their families in case something happens before retirement. It's self-completing.

This was a short course and many options are available. Just make sure you have a qualified professional help you in these decisions. Implementation is the key. "There has been more lost from inaction than from any action ever taken." One last thing: Never apologize for being successful. Just be thankful and humble.

To your success!

About Grant

Grant Thompson has been working with business and practice owners for more than two decades.

With his business partner, Chris Thurman, their firm implements financial solutions for business/practice owners as well as for families. With all the "noise" or misconceptions in the financial world today, it can be difficult to get to the truth. They bring that truth. Their clients appreciate the education and share how much they appreciate having trusted partners on their team.

Growing up in the Texas Panhandle is where they received their values. Their experience and knowledge has helped their clients nationwide reach their financial dreams without worry and fear.

To schedule a consultation, call (806) 352-3480 or (800) 352-3480, or visit www. ThompsonThurman.com.

CHAPTER 19

SURVIVING SPOUSE

BY JEFF HOCHWALT, CLU, ChFC

Author's note: While this is a true story, it is important to note that identifying details have been changed to protect client privacy.

I truly believe that we are on this earth to learn from others and give of ourselves to make a better world. Yes, there are stories about how some people take advantage of others for their own gain, but in reality, they are the ones who lose so much in the end. Challenge yourself to help your fellow man to the best of your abilities, doing the thing that you were set on this earth to do. What you find is that rather than simply making a living, you make the ideal life for yourself and for those who you are able to help. One kind gesture starts another and another, until you have a movement for positive change.

"A human being is a part of the whole, called by us 'Universe,' a part limited in time and space. He experiences himself, his thoughts and feelings as something separated from the rest—a kind of optical delusion of his consciousness. This delusion is a kind of prison for us, restricting us to our personal desires and to affection for a few persons nearest to us. Our task must be to free ourselves from this prison by widening our circle of compassion to embrace all living creatures and the whole of nature in its beauty. Nobody is able to achieve this completely, but the striving for such achievement is in itself a part of the liberation and a foundation for inner security."

~ Albert Einstein in a letter published in *The New York Times*

The story you are about to read is one of a beautiful lady and her two children, and how I endeavored to help them to the best of my abilities during the most difficult of times. I learned so much throughout the process. At the same time, I hoped to play a significant role in helping this wonderful family become all they could be so that they too could serve their fellow man to the best of their abilities. It is all one can ask.

It was 5:30 p.m. on a Tuesday in February 2011, when I made a return phone call I would never forget. The caller had left a couple of disjointed messages earlier in the day, and when we finally connected, I learned that she was the spouse of my business client. I remember her voice sounding elegant and composed, yet in a certain level of shock. She informed me that her dear husband had suffered a horrible stroke and was not expected to last through the weekend.

"Oh my, how terrible," I told her. "What can I do to help?" I listened carefully as she quietly explained how she thought her husband might have switched his checking account some time back, but may not have succeeded. She also felt it was quite possible that, in the process of doing so, his life insurance with us may no longer be active. She asked if I would be so kind as to inquire with the insurer and then let her know. I honestly wanted to tell her everything was going to be OK, but at the time, I really did not know if it would. I consoled her and told her that I would find out first thing in the morning, and let her know as soon as I could.

The next morning, much more prepared, I again reached out to my client's wife to inquire about her husband's condition. Unfortunately, he had deteriorated to grave condition and would not likely survive the day. He was only 53 years old, and his death would be tragic and untimely. After telling her how sorry I was to hear this news, I explained that her husband had, in fact, prepared for the unthinkable and that his insurance was very much active and in place. I whispered that the face amount of coverage was $1 million. Even with everything happening, I could hear the relief come from her heart. She had two young, beautiful teens to take care of. Now there was hope.

Next is her story of recovery, the role that her husband's proper life insurance planning played, and how we applied Bank On Yourself (BOY) tools to help her maintain stability and balance so she could go on living without fear of running out of money.

MY COMMITMENT TO SERVICE

Being called upon to step up and help has truly been one of the greatest privileges of my career. It makes me proud to be the life underwriter and trusted advisor for this surviving family of three. I wanted to share this story in the hope that it might help others either prepare a little more or learn how to build a rock-solid, "infinite bank" of their own that can last as long as they do to provide a lifetime of income without all those ups and downs of the market.

A CLIENT'S STORY: 2011 FACTS

A mother of two young teenagers, whose first panic was to ask, "Are we going to lose our house?" I was so proud to assure her that, because of her husband's prior insurance planning, she would be able to preserve her home, educate her children and know that when she was ready to retire, her family's needs would be well taken care of without financial worry.

a) Her husband was a corporate officer with significant holdings both at home and abroad. Unfortunately, he had never created a will. I immediately introduced her to an excellent probate attorney and sat by her side through as many meetings as it would take to help her arrange her estate.

b) In all honesty, as her financial advisor, I would have been sweating bullets if not for the life insurance that had been placed on her husband a decade earlier. As it turned out, he had an additional $100,000 in life insurance through his employment, giving them a total of $1.1 million in life insurance proceeds, income tax-free. In addition, his company generously agreed to continue to pay his salary of $10,000 per month to her for three years, plus Social Security would pay out enough to basically cover the taxes on the continued salary.

c) She had just finished recent schooling and was hoping to start a career in energy work.

THE FIRST-YEAR SOLUTION

I knew it was my charge never to let these precious monies become compromised or lost due to market volatility. I completely placed myself in this wife and mother's shoes. What would I do in her position? I recommended that she fund a personally-owned Bank On Yourself (BOY) dividend-paying, whole-life plan at a rate of $150,000 a year for four years. We would transfer these amounts from her life insurance proceeds held at the insurer. This BOY policy is staged and ready to fund back-to-back college tuition for both her children for eight years—beginning in year five—in the amount of $20,000 per year, tax-free, as well as some $45,000 per year for her retirement when she turns age 67.

We also took out a BOY policy loan right away to pay off her balances on auto loans and credit cards, with the idea of having her pay herself back over time. That way she does not lose out on the growth and interest she could have earned had she simply paid those balances with cash.

As for the balance of her life insurance proceeds, I researched and found a very unique equity indexed annuity (EIA), which at the time was guaranteed to double its benefit base for income purposes over 10 years.

Here is how the combo worked:

INSURED	PLAN NAME	INITIAL DEATH BENEFIT	ANNUAL PREMIUM	YEAR TO PAY	PROJECTED INCOME*	PROJECTED AGES
(1)VALUED CLIENT	BOY PLAN	$2,758,428	$150,000	4.00	$45,000	67-90
(2)VALUED CLIENT	EIA	$500,000	$500,000	1.00	$53,000	63-100
	TOTALS	$3,258,428	$1.1M**		$98,000/YR.	

* Contains guaranteed and nonguaranteed values available at the stated ages listed.
** Represents total funding contemplated over first four years.

For illustrative purposes only—not valid without complete NAIC compliant illustrations

THE SITUATION IN AUGUST 2012

In August 2012, it was time for the surviving wife's six-month review. Note that it has been 18 months since her husband passed away.

a) The moment we met for our review, it became apparent that our visit was very necessary. If nothing else, for a little hand-holding. She basically wanted to know that everything would be okay. This was completely understandable and reminded me of why our six-month reviews were so important. Earlier, she had met with her holistic physician who challenged her to step back and perhaps turn down the focus on her career and spend more time healing. In our meeting, she asked me if she should end her path of her chosen career and pursue a job that would simply support her family from a food-on-the-table point of view. I paused and asked her what *she* wanted. She wanted safety and assurance that everything would be okay. During our visit, she made a statement that her remaining $400,000 in life proceeds were so important from a peace of mind standpoint and it dawned on me that she was losing sight of the incredible liquidity of all the programs we had created. (Note that her income goal was to have $8,000 to 10,000 per month at all times.) So I stepped back and started to add up the opportunity capital and was delighted with the result:

Long-Term Income Resources If All Assets Were Repositioned to Produce Income Immediately

CAPITAL SOURCE	ACCOUNT VALUE	AFTER-TAX TRANSFER	POTENTIAL ANN. INCOME AT 6%
CASH HELD AT INSURER	$400,000	$400,000	$24,000
BOY POLICY (SEPTEMBER 2011)	$130,500	$44,000 (NET OF LOAN)	$2,640
EIA NONQUALIFIED (SEPTEMBER 2011)	$550,000	$550,000	$29,250 (AGE 55 GMIB^)
CONTINUED SALARY	$10,000/MO.	$7,000/MO.	$84,000 (TO MAY 2014)
SOCIAL SECURITY	$3,000/MO.	$3,000/MO.	$36,000 (ENDS IN 5 YEARS)
COLLEGE FUNDS SET ASIDE			
BANK ACCT. 529 PLAN	$115,565	$115,565	$6,933
TOTAL	**$1,196,065+**	**$1,109,565+**	**$182,823/YEAR**

Source: For illustration purposes only. All values include dividends, which are not guaranteed.
^GMIB refers to guaranteed monthly income benefit available through certain equity indexed annuities (EIAs)

I believe that the process of illustrating all her assets in a way that demonstrated the possible amount of immediate income helped. The bottom line, I told her, is that because of her husband's gift of prior planning, she was able to choose to continue to do what she loves for her career, if that is her true calling. He basically bought her time to decide with the life insurance he purchased.

THE 24-MONTH PLANNING SOLUTION—PROPOSAL

Having this new peace of mind, we are now proceeding to review the surviving wife's options on how to manage the newfound wealth that is about to transfer from abroad, some 24 months into our planning. It's a large sum of $750,000 in U.S. funds. (It is important to note that as of this writing, the majority of these funds are still held up in legal finagling with the foreign revenue service and will likely take more months to transfer. In that time, sadly, more than $100,000 has been lost to the foreign exchange rates.)

So, what to do with these new dollars? Her earlier BOY design is a four-pay premium, which could just as easily become a 10-pay premium, if we wish. Obviously, if we fund a full five more years of $150,000 premium, all the benefit projections will increase measurably. The question is, what to do with the cash we are about to receive until years five through ten? How about funding a single-pay BOY plan? This "high premium/low relative death benefit" design would be considered a modified endowment contract (MEC), which means that distributions would be taxed to the extent of gain and there would be a 10 percent tax penalty prior to age 59 1/2. As much as I love to show non-MEC's, the death benefit would be too large, so we are recommending the single-pay BOY version. The amazing part of this solution is that it maintains a huge amount of liquidity as well as provides a full long-term care (LTC) rider built in as backup protection for our mother of two, as well as more life insurance protection.

The liquidity enables us to have a resource that would effectively provide 5 to 6 percent income replacement off the cash surrender value now, if necessary. We would also have the freedom to consider using the money in her second BOY policy to continuing overfunding her first BOY program's $150,000 premium, should we be so inclined. If she were to do that, it would increase projected college funding to $35,000 for eight years and retirement to $107,000 for 24 years, tax-free. All of her other investments stack on top.

Income/Capital Sources Projected at Her Age of 67

CAPITAL SOURCE	SUM	AFTER-TAX TRANSFER	POTENTIAL ANNUAL INCOME AT 6%
~~CASH HELD AT THE INSURER~~	~~$400,000~~	~~$400,000~~	~~$24,000~~
BOY POLICY 1 (SEPTEMBER 2011)	$1,698,490	$1,698,490	$107,000
BOY POLICY 2 (PROPOSED)			SURPLUS
N.Q. EIA (SEP 2011)	$1,000,000	$1,000,000	$57,000 (AGE 67 GMIB)
(BENEFIT BASE NOW DOUBLED)			
~~CONTINUED SALARY~~	~~$10,000 MO.~~	~~$7,000 MO.~~	~~$84,000 (TO MAY 2014)~~
SOCIAL SECURITY ???	$2,000/MO.	$2,000/MO.	$24,000 ?
PLUS: $2.75 MILLION AND $2.1 MILLION INITIAL LIFE INSURANCE BENEFIT AND INITIAL LTC BENEFIT OF $8,700/MO.			
PLUS: TOTAL OF $280,000 AVAILABLE THROUGH THE YEARS FOR COLLEGE			
TOTAL			$188,000/YEAR

Source: For illustration purposes only. All values include projections and dividends, which are not guaranteed.

SUMMARY NOTES

As you can see, we have built the surviving wife's plan in two stages. In stage one, we were able to transfer her tax-free insurance proceeds into both BOY as well as the EIA. Based on current projections, she will potentially enjoy $20,000 over eight years for her kids' college funds, as well as $45,000 for 23 years in retirement for a total of $1,195,000, which could be taken tax-free under current tax laws. Plus, she now has $2.75 million in new personal life insurance protection. The $500,000 EIA adds in $57,000 annually for life at age 67. Over 30 years, that would amount to a grand total of $1,710,000. When added to the BOY solution, it produces more than $2.9 million, which is decent leverage off her initial $1.1 million.

Stage two will grow her college and retirement projected income by more than $1.5 million on top of stage one.

WHAT WE HAVE LEARNED

Never underestimate the power of life insurance to be there exactly when needed. Imagine the surviving wife and mother's world without it. Yes, she probably would have managed, given the benevolence of the former employer for the first three years, but would she be truly able to pursue the career of her dreams on a timetable that made sense for her and her family's recovery? Then imagine if she were advised to place those funds where they could have become forfeit to market turbulence. Not on my watch.

About Jeff

Jeff Hochwalt, CLC, ChFC, is managing member of Financial Resource Partners LLC. His goal has been to help his clients grow their wealth without the risk, worry or volatility of stocks, real estate and other investments, to achieve financial security and to reach their short- and long-term financial goals and dreams.

One of only 200 life insurance agents in the country who have successfully completed the rigorous training and continuing education required to become a Bank On Yourself authorized advisor, Jeff has earned the distinction of top five in this group. He is also a chartered financial consultant and chartered life underwriter.

Outstanding client service, ethics and professionalism have elevated Jeff to qualify for the exclusive "Top of the Table" of the Million Dollar Round Table (MDRT), the premier association of financial professionals. He is a 12-year MDRT life and qualifying member and a first time Top of the Table qualifier. "Attaining Top of the Table membership in MDRT is a distinguishing career milestone, reserved for a select few like Jeffrey who have proven that they are among the best of the best, "says MDRT President D. Scott Brennan. The Round Table's membership represents the top life insurance and financial service professionals worldwide.

Jeff is a current member of the Society of Financial Services Professionals—Rocky Mountain Chapter and a registered representative of Cambridge Investment Research Inc., Member FINRA/SIPC where he holds his Variable Products, Series 6, 63, 65 licenses and is a registered investment advisor (Corporate RIA). He has also been a member of National Association of Insurance and Financial Advisors since 1981.

When Jeff's not working, you may find him enjoying photography or skiing, although preferably not at the same time.

In order to provide his clients with the level of service he believes they expect and deserve, Jeff only takes on a small number of new clients each year who are committed to achieving lifetime financial security.

CHAPTER 20

BANKABLE LEVERAGE

BY MARC BESHEARS

An insurance agent said to me the other day, "None of us intended to be here selling insurance; it just happens that we are all here now." That comment struck me and reminded me of something I said once. During the '90s, I was managing beautiful resorts and working 80 hours a week, and I remember saying to the tired staff during a meeting, "What a great work environment and we are so fortunate," followed by " … it sure beats selling life insurance for a living." The irony is too comical to me. Now, I not only sell life insurance, I love it and I love what it does for my clients and the future of the families and the next generations to follow.

MY STORY

My introduction to dividend-paying whole-life insurance was while I was under enormous financial stress. I started a development company in 2001. I presold $50 million of a "to be built" waterfront condominium community in south Florida. I marched into a major bank and they lent my company $40 million to build 140 units. Don't be impressed; the bank had no business loaning me the money and I was shocked with my newly-found creditworthiness. I thought I had made my fortune. As we erected the 10 four-story buildings in 2003, several hurricanes repeatedly knock down my buildings, causing more than two years of painstaking delays. That's right, at that point, we were on the edge of the real estate collapse. So fearing the worst in 2007, I went to see my attorney with the simple question: What do I do to protect myself? He went through his checklist of items and his last question was, "Do you own whole-life insurance"? My question back was, "Why? Do you think the bank is going to take me out?" He laughed, then explained that cash value life insurance in most states can be considered creditor- proof. At that point, he had my attention and I went home and immediately started to study the features and benefits of whole-life insurance. By accident, but with miraculous timing, I answered an advertisement for Bank On Yourself, which I came to find out is a whole-life insurance product.

MY EPIPHANY

Once I heard all of the features and benefits I realized that my past methods of high risk and high reward was not the way. So now, armed with knowledge and enlightenment I declared to my amazing wife, Lori, that we had been doing our personal finances all wrong. In my excitement, I failed to prepare for the conversation. Lori has worked in the banking business her whole life and even her father was a bank president. She was an honor student in finance and held the position as the head of banking for all of Florida with a major International bank. She has all the financial licenses and is very book smart.

As I proclaimed to her that we were handling our short- and long-term investments all wrong, she stared at me as if I had gone mad. All of sudden, this conversation was going downhill fast and it became extremely more difficult than the $40 million construction loan I had been awarded. Both of us were career professionals and had accumulated the typical 401 (k)'s, IRAs, stock portfolios and 529 plans that were typically invested in the same old mutual funds that you watch ebb and flow with the emotion of the markets. On top of that, we made investments by leveraging our borrowing power and purchased plenty of speculative real estate. You can predict the result of those investments so let's move on.

Lori and I were married in 1997, and as a dual-income family with no kids we had nice cash flow. However, with my method I was taking on more risk than needed to get ahead for the future. I did what most do: Buy more qualified plans and then speculate on what was hot at the time. When you are in your 30s and making money you have this false sense of security and that if you lose some money, then you will make it back. I was so wrong. In the '90s we saw our portfolio rise on the dot-com era, only to see it crash. That was followed by a slow recovery and again the market correction in 2003, then the last straw in 2007 housing crash and the financial crisis of 2008.

What is awful to think about is that when the markets were up—on paper—I was very creditworthy and the banks were happy to loan me money. Then in a blink, the market corrects and you have less money on paper and more debt than you can afford. What is wrong with this picture?

A WHOLE NEW APPROACH WITH WHOLE-LIFE INSURANCE

I studied the whole-life product and fully investigated the features, benefits and 100-year track record. Once I knew Bank On Yourself chapter and versus, I scheduled a family financial meeting with Lori in her office at the bank. She knew I was serious and she was ready to listen. During the discussion she even pulled out a financial estate planning book from her bookshelf to verify some of the technical terms I was using instead of debating me. Funny enough, in her studies she had highlighted the very term (paid-up additions) that I was teaching her. During this meeting, we traced our financial steps for the prior 10 years. Had we followed the Bank On Yourself plan versus our speculation and the traditional qualified plan method, we would have been seven figures ahead and stress-free from all of the peaks and valleys for our retirement. Yes, hindsight is 20/20 but the problem was that no one provided us with this option in 1997.

After this meeting, we agreed that we would no longer rely on the markets or the like.

We determined that we would not repeat the same mistake for the next five decades and become free of the market volatility and the need for bank lending. This plan could not happen overnight, but in short we still could reposition our current assets and frontload two cash value policies—one on each of us. We nicknamed them "Bank Of Beshears."

Once the policies were in place we immediately leveraged the policies to reverse the direction of our debt payments. The simple definition of leverage is "to make more efficient." Once we were able to leverage our own capital, even while it is growing for the rest of our life no matter what, changed our lifestyle and our future. In my excitement, I declared that we had bankable leverage. Yes, a newly coined phrase. I always wanted one. Any person, family or business that has a cash balance of any kind along with a positive household cash flow has bankable leverage.

Bankable leverage is easiest explained as repositioning current assets into a whole-life policy which you can in turn leverage by taking a loan against your policy and buying the note that you may have with any third party lender.

HOW BANKABLE LEVERAGE WORKS

Let me explain. When a bank loans you money, that loan is an asset to the bank and a liability to you. So what happens when you take a loan from your policy and pay off the third party lenders is you are basically buying that asset off of the bank. My wife totally understood this concept since she had been lending money on behalf of the bank for more than 20 years.

Now, I did not say that you get out of paying for the debt. Once you own the note you are now in two positions: both the lender and the borrower. So as an example. Let's say you have an outstanding loan balance on your car and you have 36 more payments. As each month comes along, you continue to make the same car payment. However, every time you send a payment to your policy it becomes liquid again. So at the end of the remaining 36 payments on your car you made back to yourself (your policy), you have accomplished the following:

1. You have 36 monthly payments back in your possession, available to use again.

2. You have not lost any scheduled growth on the money you loaded into your policy. This is what I mean by bankable leverage. You load your money to grow no matter what, followed by removing third-party lenders from your life and reversing the flow of the money toward you instead of away from you. This process will always be in your favor.

I hear too many people misuse the words interest rate and rate of return. I listen to clients tell me that they have a zero percent loan on their car.

I ask, "If it is zero, then how much money will you have at the end of the 36 payments?" They answer, "Well, whatever the value of the car is what I have." Then I ask, "Can any of those payments earn any interest for you the rest of your life?" Of course not. I follow that with a third question: "Would you rather have the value of your car and the cash value of 36 payments and growth on your original capital?" Of course they say yes. So what we can agree on is that a zero percent interest loan really means that your loan amount is "gone money" and if there was a method to have growth on all of my money and to recapture the loan payments then that would be better than a zero percent loan.

Yes, that is better, but the next question commonly is, "How?" Once you lose control of your money and your debt payments you are going backwards. I want society to learn and be aware that they can make certain that their money never stops earning and at the same time they can self-finance many of life's needs through their cash-value life insurance policy.

Now think for yourself about how much you have spent using lenders, credit cards, student loans, large cash purchases, and so on. Even worse, what if the value of that account declined in the meantime and you still made all of your car payments to GMAC. Those dollars are gone forever, never to work or earn for you again.

ADVICE YOU CAN BANK ON

Here is the simplest financial advice I can give anyone. First, make sure every hard- earned dollar you make has a chance to compound for the rest of your life. Second, preserve and protect those dollars by not spending outside your means. Third, avoid giving up control of your money where you are at risk of market swings, rules and regulation, and potential tax treatment. Fourth, leverage the first three items.

You may ask how and where can you do those for items. It starts with a venue and that is dividend-paying whole-life insurance engineered just right. Once you have this product you can save your money and the dollars you load with continue to grow for your lifetime. Lastly, when you need to purchase your next big item, you use your policy as the financing arm.

Again, you are wearing two hats in the spending cycle. You are both the lender and borrower in the equation, and at the end of your purchase your wealth stays with you, and your original capital or savings never changed course for long-term gains, wealth, security and a legacy. All money must be stored somewhere, and I cannot find a venue that has all the features and benefits that are provided in a properly engineered dividend whole-life insurance plan.

MY CLIENT STORY

Now let me tell you a story about one of my first clients and how we built a plan that solved so many financial issues. Let's call my client Brutus, which is not his real name but that is all I can think of when dealing with him. He is in the commercial real estate and apartment building business. Brutus had several properties, some great and some underwater. His situation was very unique because due to the real estate crash and the financial crash he found himself in a dangerous spot. His bad assets were going back to the bank and his good assets were solid. However, his bank note on a 16-unit, cash flowing apartment building was coming due and the bank was not going to renew because of the credit crisis in the country. The property was worth $1.2 million. It was cash-flowing. He only owed $300,000 and the bank would not renew.

Now, Brutus had a balance sheet with some assets that you may be familiar with. It just so happened that he and his wife had accumulated $350,000 in a variety of financial products. His money was residing in venues with and without tax implications. Now, he was at a major crossroad. His choices included selling the wonderful, cash-flowing property to pay off the bank, fight the bank or take on private investor money. All the options were less than good. Due to his nonperforming properties, he lost his credit worthiness. And due to the financial crisis banks were not lending money. He was stuck—but not really.

I ran figures showing a scenario of repositioning his assets and purchasing a high cash value life insurance policy. This policy would allow him the ability to borrow against the policy, which would be used to pay off the uncooperative commercial bank. Upon doing so, going forward the same $5,700 mortgage payment he once made to the bank would be directed to his policy, paying off the policy loan.

So in summary here is what took place. Brutus loaded up a cash value policy to the point that he was able to do a policy loan of $300,000 to pay off the third party lender. He now owns the property free and clear of any commercial bank. However, he now is the note holder of his own property. That is right. He must be honest with himself and pay himself back. So as he sends the $5,700 toward his simple interest policy loan, he will have paid himself back in fewer than six years. At the end of six years, he will have all of the $300,000 back in his control and he will have received six full years of growth on the entire cash value policy.

But the best part is that his credited growth on the value of his policy for each and every one of those years is on the full value of his policy. To be clear: he was awarded growth on the $350,000 each and every year even though he took out a loan for that amount. So his balance sheet and wealth never skipped a beat and he removed a third party lender from his life forever. In regards to his future value of this policy it will be worth more than $1.4 million at age 61, not to mention other accomplishment he will achieve by leveraging his policy.

I know that this example is using serious amounts of money, but even if you remove a zero or two, you can ask yourself if you would like to replace your debt payments with wealth-saving payments. To do so, you first must reorganize your portfolio and fund your own bankable leverage policy. You now have been given just enough information to conduct your own research and I hope you take full advantage.

About Marc

Marc Beshears is the founder of Top Wealth Agenda and has helped his clients grow their wealth without the risk, worry or the volatility of stocks, real estate and other investments, as well as achieve financial security and reach their short-term and long-term personal and financial goals and dreams.

Marc has put his clients on track to building more than $40 million of additional wealth they would most likely not have had otherwise, through safe, proven financial strategies.

Marc was born and raised in Farmington Hills, Michigan, and obtained his marketing degree from Ferris State University. He also was an avid golfer and went on to join the PGA of America, where he started his first career as a PGA golf professional. His journey led him quickly from being a club professional to the general manager of luxury resorts. He was promoted again to the position of regional director of 11 high-end golf resorts for the largest golf corporation in the world owned by Goldman Sachs. His territory ranged from Hilton Head, South Carolina, to Naples, Florida. In this role, he managed a staff of 2,000 and was accountable for a $50 million budget. In this industry Marc was awarded national manager of the year and was consistently recognized as the manager with the highest client satisfaction rating.

In 2001, as an entrepreneur, Marc followed his desire to be in the real estate development industry when he was the managing partner and led a variety of residential and commercial projects with sales of more than $60 million.

At the end of the real estate bubble of 2007, Marc discovered Bank On Yourself and immediately decided that he would make this his next career advancement. He founded his independent practice promoting this stress-free wealth building method.

Marc lives in the Naples area with his wife, Lori, and their two children, Jay and Elly. When Marc is not working, you may find him coaching little league, playing golf or trying to catch fish in the Gulf of Mexico.

In order to provide his clients the level of service he believes they expect and deserve, Marc only takes on a small number of new clients each year who are committed to achieving lifetime financial security.

CHAPTER 21

WEALTH DOES NOT RESIDE IN CHAOS

BY MARILYN BLOSSER

How well I know from personal experience that wealth does not reside in chaos. As a young, divorced mother of two very small children, I was in the same position that many Americans are in today. Living paycheck to paycheck, my finances were in chaos (filling my chaotic life with even more stress) due to credit card debt, car payments and day care expenses. One day a friend suggested I look into becoming an insurance advisor. I thought, "I can't do that" I need a steady paycheck, but she explained to me all the advantages of becoming an advisor. First, I would get professional training that would teach me how to get my personal finances under control so I could help others, while at the same time have unlimited earning potential.

As a female, up until then I had been limited by the corporate 'glass ceiling'. My original decision to change professions was based on what it would do for me with no idea of how my passion for this business would change. Within 18 months, I was for the first time in my life in complete control of my finances, but more importantly, I was in a position to help others gain control.

Two years into the business I delivered a check for $100,000 (a lot of money in the mid-'70s) to a young mother of three whose husband had died in auto accident. They were among my first clients. I was the advisor who had pointed out to the young mother's husband, when he was alive, the need for life insurance to protect his wife and family. The proceeds enabled his widow and three children to remain in their home and continue the lifestyle she and her children were accustomed to. I will never forget delivering that check and at that moment my passion for this business shifted from me and my head to my heart, where it remains today some 37 years later.

MY PRACTICE: A SNAPSHOT

Seventy-five percent of my practice is almost equally divided between three diverse groups:

1. Affluent families, millionaires and multi-millionaires

2. Small business owners

3. Middle to lower income people who are deep in consumer debt, credit cards, car loans, student loans and personal loans

Each group has its own diverse financial chaos (and stress) and I'd like to point out that for about the past 25 years, for some insane reason schools quit offering any kind of financial training. Not even simple bookkeeping! So children graduate high school and either go out into the workforce or on to college. Neither group received any formal education on finances (except for those actually studying finances) so unless they got it from their parents they didn't get it at all but they could get credit cards!

Schwab did a survey some years back and found that 70 percent of Americans teach their kids how to do the laundry, but only 34 percent teach them how to balance a checkbook, and even fewer (29 percent) explain how credit card interest and fees work.

Those in the first group are for the most part financially savvy by knowing how to create and read financial statements; cash flow and P&L statements, etc. and are keenly aware of their net worth. Their finances are organized and orderly but they have been so busy building and/or maintaining their wealth that they have not taken the time to plan for the transfer of their wealth to their heirs. Many do not have a trust or a will.

I was referred to a client who wanted to buy $3 million life insurance policy. During our first meeting, I asked him if he had set up a trust, and his answer was "no." I asked, "How about a will?" "No." I asked, "Do you know that if something were to happen to you tomorrow, the State of Florida is going distribute your $4,000,000.00 estate and you don't get to vote?"

Due to the chaos in his estate planning (like there wasn't any), we were not able to submit an application for the life insurance he wanted as I didn't know how the plan should be properly structured. Who should be owner and beneficiary of his policy(s); would the trust attorney recommend setting up an irrevocable life insurance trust (ILIT) for estate tax purposes; would he recommend the client's wife be the owner of the policy; should his corporation be the owner? These were questions that needed to be addressed prior to submitting an application. I knew what I would suggest, but not being an attorney or a CPA, this client needed additional professional advice.

THE NEED FOR A BUSINESS EXIT STRATEGY

This client is not alone. It has been my experience that many financially-affluent clients have no exit strategy, have not thought about who is going to get what and when. They have not considered who would be entrusted to physically take care of their minor children. Meaning who would be responsible for taking their children into their home to care for them emotionally and financially. I explain that is not only a big moral responsibility but also a huge financial responsibility: food, clothing, medical expenses, educational expenses, to name a few. It is a decision that takes time for parents to decide. This chaotic issue could be handled within a properly designed family trust.

Then, of course, there are the estate taxes that will have to be paid on the estate. Do they want their heirs to pay 100 percent of those taxes from the proceeds of the estate? Would the heirs have to liquidate assets in order to come up with the taxes that are due within nine months from the date of death? The 2013 estate tax rate is 40 percent! Setting up a Bank On Yourself plan specially designed to fund an irrevocable life insurance trust to cover the estate tax liability would be a far better solution to paying those taxes out of the estate proceeds. Two months later that's exactly what we did and now there is no chaos in his financial affairs.

SMALL BUSINESS CHAOS

The small business owner usually has some of the same chaotic issues as the affluent, millionaires and multi-millionaires that is created by their business, and if there are business partners these issues are multiplied. The majority of small business owners who begin with a partner or partners never get beyond setting up their entity, LLC, S Corporation or C Corporation status and get right to work. No thought (much less a formal agreement) has been given to what happens to the business in the event of a death of one of the partners.

What happens to the spouses and/or children of the deceased partner(s)? Do they get any remuneration for their spouse's share of the business? I recently asked a business owner client if he was he incorporated and who the shareholders of the corporation were. He proudly stated, "Oh, yes, we are incorporated. I have one partner who owns 40 percent of the business."

I proceeded to ask him if he had a formal buy-sell agreement, and he hesitantly said they did not. So I asked, "If something happened to your partner, what you would do?" He responded like most business owners who do not have an agreement respond: "Well, I'd sell the business and move on or maybe I'd keep the business."

Move on how? What about your partner's wife—what would she get for your partner's share of the business? "Well, I guess since he's a 40 percent partner I'd give her 40 percent of whatever I got." So regardless of the amount you receive, you'd give her 40 percent and if she tells you, "But I know the business was worth a lot more and I don't think 40 percent is fair." Now the chaos really begins, especially if attorneys are called in to settle the differences of opinion. And we haven't even gotten into the potential tax liabilities that could be due. Bottom line is: Neither partner had a clue as to what would *really* happen in the event of a death to either of them and I didn't get into what might happen in the event of a disability of one of them. That came later once the business was evaluated, life insurance was in place and a formal buy-sell agreement was executed.

It's of utmost importance that the life insurance is in place before the agreement is signed. For example, let's say Bill and John, both married and in their 40s, are 50 percent partners in a plumbing business with an outside appraised value of $1 million. They set up as an S Corporation, went to their attorney and designed a formal buy-sell agreement that stated if one of them dies, the surviving partner has to pay the deceased partner's wife $500,000. If they sign the agreement and Bill is killed in an auto accident, John is now going to have to come up with $500,000 cash to pay John's wife. I have seen this happen and more chaos begins. Using a Bank On Yourself plan for all the partners to fund the buy-sell agreement will eliminate all the chaos.

I am not an attorney but from my experiences, when death or liquidation of a partnership occurs, the IRS comes in to determine the fair market value of the business to determine if there is a capital gain or loss. Historically, they generally place a value higher than what the business is actually worth, creating more tax revenue.

CONSUMER DEBT AND CHAOS

The last group, one that I was once a part of, has financial chaos of huge proportions. Their biggest problem is consumer debt. They have become slaves to credit cards and their solution is to play credit card roulette, as opposed to freezing their cards and quit spending. They think that transferring the balance from one credit card to a new zero interest rate card is the answer. But nothing could be farther from the truth. The cycle is equivalent to being a drug addict in denial. They do not consider debt service and while they try to continue to play that game, they are still charging on other cards they cannot pay off each month so credit card interest is still piling up.

The clients I have in this group had never filled out a cash flow or credit card spreadsheet. That is the first exercise I have them complete and it's mandatory because they need to see these two documents in black and white. Without this, they are never going to be in control of their finances. And I need to see them if I'm going to coach them and show them how to become financially sound. Once they have looked at these documents, 90 percent have the same reaction and say to me, "Marilyn this is a real eye opener!" And these are the people I can help.

Once the client has completed both spreadsheets, we go over the credit card spreadsheet first and I show them which cards to pay and how much to pay each card based on the cash flow sheet. I have always been able to find more money by adjusting their spending habits.

Worst case I've ever seen was a couple in their early 40s with 17 open credit cards with a total balance of more than $48,000. They were not making any payments on the 10 cards that had zero interest, paying a total of $750 monthly on the interest bearing cards, BUT worst of all they were still charging! The cash flow sheet had several frivolous spending items: helping a family member with $250 a month; paying $300 per month for car insurance for one child, who was working, by the way, while they were going deeper in debt. By reallocating $250 to the $750 they were previously paying they could begin making $1,000 credit card payments and be out from under that debt in four years. But only if they did not create any more debt and limited discretionary spending to the $300 they had been spending on the son's auto insurance.

On top of all this, we were able to find an additional $500 per month by cutting down on other needless spending to begin a Bank On Yourself plan for the husband, the major income earner. The death benefit would provide enough to pay off the credit cards and their house, leaving his wife financially secure. The projected cash value of the policy would be sufficient to pay off the remaining $24,000 of credit card balances. They now have a plan and a goal. They purchased a temporary term insurance policy on the wife with plans to convert it to a Bank On Yourself plan in two years. Both plans will be used for passive income at retirement, which under current IRS regulations would be income tax-free. After getting control of their finances, the client emailed me and said, "Yahoo!! I'm excited!" Reading that was exciting for me, as well, knowing that I had been instrumental in helping this family eliminate the financial chaos in their lives.

It's my ability to be able to employ and design sound strategies for not only each of these financially diverse groups but all my clients that fuels my passion for what I do. I feel very good about helping clients and prospects reach their financial goals with certainty by unique and proper case design and conducting six month reviews along with financial coaching and training, thereby eliminating the financial chaos in their lives.

THE BANK ON YOURSELF ADVANTAGE

In case you want to know about the other 25 percent of my clients—well, they all have had their Bank On Yourself plans for a number of years and have used them to their full potential. Many have borrowed from themselves to purchase cars and fund their family vacations. I even had one client borrow money to loan a family relative enough money to purchase a car. The relative is repaying the policy owner's loan, so it's a win-win for both parties.

Many clients use their policies to pay off high interest credit card debt, while a few paid off their student loans. Two other clients used the funds in their policies to open up new business ventures, another funded her daughter's wedding and several are building up their cash value to fund upcoming college expenses. And probably the most unusual of all: I had one client borrow money to pay for his hair transplant.

The bottom line for all of these clients is they have no financial chaos in their lives. How would it make you feel to know your financial house was in order, that your financial future was secure, and that there was financial security for your loved ones in the event of your untimely death? Would you sleep better at night? All of my clients do.

About Marilyn

Marilyn is a Miami native with more than 35 years of experience in the insurance and financial services industry. During that time, she has taught hundreds of individuals and business owners how to build their financial nest-egg using the Bank On Yourself® concept, which provides income tax-free, guaranteed growth under IRS regulations that have been in place since 1913.

Because no one has the same financial goals or is in the same financial position, Marilyn designs each client's plan to meet his or her individual financial goals, improve his or her financial position and eliminate financial chaos. She meets with her clients on a regular basis—no less than annually and more often depending on each client's circumstances. As a result of her individualized coaching, she has helped many clients become completely debt-free and on their way to financial security.

Marilyn received her associate of arts degree from the University of Florida and Miami Dade College. She has served as president on both the local and national board of directors of Women in Insurance & Financial Services with a combined service on these boards of more than 15 years. She has been a member of the Miami Association of Insurance and Financial Advisors for more than 17 years and is active in several community service organizations, including the American Legion.

Marilyn M. Blosser
Blosser Financial Services Inc.
www.blosserfinancial.com

13305 SW 109 Court
Miami, FL 33176-6009

Office: (305) 251-5208
Toll-Free: (888) 251-5436

CHAPTER 22

THE RETIREMENT PLAN EVERYONE WANTS BUT NEVER HEARS ABOUT

BY PAUL J. NICK

What type of retirement plan do you want? Do you want a plan that only allows you to spend 3 to 4 percent of your retirement savings each year or one that allows you to spend down your savings? I often jokingly tell people, if you don't spend your retirement money, your children will be happy to after the government gets its share. While there is an element of humor to that statement, it is also packed with truth. Often people don't want to spend their money because they are afraid of running out of money and leaving their surviving spouse with nothing.

So how long does your money need to last? Until you and your spouse die, right? I think most people would agree that this is a true statement. Today, if you and your spouse make it past age 65, one of you has a 50 percent chance of living past age 90. It's typically the female–sorry, guys. So, if you don't know when you are going to die, then you have to make your money last a long time. Unfortunately, this fact alone will put most people in financial handcuffs throughout their retirement.

Let me ask you a few other questions. If you knew without a doubt that all your assets would be replaced 100 percent after you died, wouldn't that free you up to spend down your savings throughout your retirement years? If your spouse and family were taken care of, wouldn't you have the freedom to spend your money and enjoy your retirement? Isn't that what retirement should be about?

In this chapter, I will be sharing with you a simple way to get the retirement plan that allows you to spend your money, and you can do it without any additional out-of-pocket costs.

CONVENTIONAL FINANCIAL PLANNING HAS FAILED AMERICANS

I don't know you personally, but I can probably tell you what your retirement plan looks like. You have a 401(k) or some other qualified plan that you have been funding for years because that is what everyone else is doing. You may have an IRA or Roth on your spouse, you have been putting some money in 529 plans for your children's education and you have life insurance through your employer just in case you don't make it to retirement. All of your investment money is typically in mutual funds. You have also been told that the market will average 8 to 10 percent per year over the long term and you should be able to live off the interest of your savings when you retire. So how is that working for everyone? Folks, this is not a retirement plan; this is called a "hope and pray plan." Yet this is what 90 percent of working Americans are told they should be doing to plan for their financial future. Why are the majority of Americans' savings funneled to mutual funds with massive risk, fees and tax implications? Why are there no guarantees for Americans' retirement? And who benefits the most from this type of plan? Is it you or the people who run these plans?

If you could think of the perfect business model, what would it look like? You would probably get the government to create tax incentives for using your product. You would entice participants with the potential for higher rates of return with your particular investments (i.e., mutual funds). You would use arbitration clauses so the customers could never sue you if you made a mistake or lost their money (Google "New York Times When Winning Feels a Lot Like Losing"). You would have the government create rules and penalties for early access to the money. Then you would charge a nice fee for many, many years regardless if the account performs well or not. Does that plan sound familiar? The only guarantees in a qualified plan are that the government will get its taxes, the mutual funds will get their fees and you, my friend, will put up all the money and take 100 percent of the risk. This sounds more like a retirement plan for the financial representatives than for you.

A LOOK AT THE 401(K) IN ACTION

If tax rates continue to go up, which is likely, why would anyone push a large amount of income to the future where it will be taxed at a higher rate? That just doesn't make sense. When would you rather pay taxes, while you're working or in retirement? Let me clarify for you. You are not saving taxes, you are deferring taxes to a later date and the IRS will tell you at that time what rate you are going to pay. If you are in a high tax bracket today and knew taxes were going down in the future, then it might make sense. But you are likely in a lower tax bracket today than you will be in the future because the government is not slowing its spending. See Figure 1 and 2.

Figure 1: You deferred $75,000 so you could pay the IRS $174,000. Huh?

Annual Contribution	$12,000
Current Tax Bracket	25%
Withdrawal Tax Bracket	25%
Years Until Withdrawal	25 years
Investment Return	6%
Account Balance	$697,877
Your Share	$523,407
Amount Due IRS	**$174,469**
Apparent Taxes Deferred	**$75,000**

Figure 2: After-tax contributions that come out tax-free are exactly the same as before tax contributions that come out taxable, given the same tax bracket and interest rate.

		Tax Def. Cont Taxable WD	After Tax Cont Tax-Free WD
Annual Contribution	$12,000		
Current Tax Bracket	25%		
Withdrawal Tax Bracket	25%		
Years Until Withdrawal	25 years		
Investment Return	6%		
Equivalent Contribution		$12,000	$9,000
Gross Withdrawal		$697,877	$523,407
Amount Due IRS		**$174,469**	**$0**
Actual Net Withdrawal		**$523,407**	**$523,407**

So, if we are not saving the taxes we thought we were, and we will end up with the same spendable amount, does it still make sense to tie up all of our savings in a tax-qualified plan?

Today, when a corporation hires a new CEO, some compensation guarantees have to be put in place; otherwise, it will be difficult to find someone. Many of these guarantees come in the form of retirement packages from the life Insurance industry using pension annuities and permanent life insurance. The banking industry purchases huge amounts of permanent life insurance on the top 25 percent employees. For example, Bank of America has more than $16 billion in cash values. I guess Bank of America doesn't think cash value life insurance is a bad deal. If it did, it certainly wouldn't have $16 billion of the bank's money in it. This can be verified on the FDIC website by pulling up its financials. Even our representatives in Congress and the Senate get a lifetime pension after serving only one term. Why are the wealthy and government officials setting themselves up with guaranteed income accounts for retirement, and we get to wing it with a 401(k)? Annuities and properly structured permanent life insurance contracts provide lifetime financial security, period.

Only four financial products offer growth that can be tax-free: municipal bonds; Roth IRA; Roth 401(k); and permanent life insurance. That's it!

Naturally, people tend to be skeptical at the first mention of life insurance or annuities. The media tells everyone that life insurance is a bad deal and annuities have high fees and surrender charges, blah, blah, blah. Yet people will continue to send hard-earned dollars to Wall Street even after they see blatant fraud and thievery of clients' money (e.g., Madoff and Stanford). The reality is that people are not getting the whole story.

Let's forget about life insurance for a minute and just talk about benefits. In any vehicle one would use to accumulate money over time, a major desire would be to maximize benefits in addition to achieving a decent rate of return. If you could get any benefits you wanted, what would you ask for? Most people can only come up with three or four items, max. Here is a list of what everyone would want if they could get it:

- Tax deferred growth

- Access to your principal and gains tax free, under current tax law

- A competitive rate of return

- Interest guaranteed

- Invest in anything you choose

- Protection from creditors and judgments

- High contribution limits

- Access to the money

- Use as collateral

- A way to bypass estate tax

- High liquidity options

- Disability waiver (if you couldn't work due to disability, the financial institution would fund your plan to age 65)

- Tax deductibility

So, how many of these benefits do you get with your current plan? If you're like most people with a 401(k), you have three of these items in your current plan: tax deferred growth, protection from creditors and tax deductibility.

A properly structured permanent life insurance contract with the right company can provide all the benefits mentioned above, except contributions to a life insurance contract outside of a qualified plan are not tax deductible.

There are two types of life insurance companies, stock and mutual. Stock companies are owned by stockholders and the stockholders get the dividends. Mutual companies, on the other hand, are owned by the policy holders. There are no stockholders, so policy holders receive the dividends from the company.

My family has a long history of policy ownership. Our family holds close to 50 policies among my parents, the adult children and the grandchildren. In 1969, my Dad purchased a whole-life insurance policy from a mutual insurance company a few months before I was born. This particular policy had an annual premium of $1,054.33. However, he only paid the premium for 19 years. He had contributed $20,032.27 of his own money to this policy over that 19-year period and hasn't paid a premium since 1988. In 1988, he changed the dividend on the policy to pay the premium and also to go toward increasing the cash value. The dividend paid on this policy in 2012 was $5,598.02. That's 5½ times the original annual premium. Additionally, the cash value in that policy as of last year's statement was at $153,058.26 and it has a death benefit of $237,271 (the original death benefit was $100,000). The cash value increase on this policy last year alone was $7,598.32. That is equivalent to about a 5 percent net rate of return. If my father would have cashed in this policy in 2012, the company would have sent him a check for $153,058.26. What was the cost of Insurance over that 43-year period? Nothing. He made money, right?

All of the policies my father owns today are in addition to all his other investments, so this is not an either/or situation. It should be looked at as a way to enhance your current retirement plan.

So what about "Buy Term and Invest The Difference?" This has to be one of the best marketing slogans anyone has ever imagined. When I ask clients what the "difference" was, they can never tell me because they just bought the term insurance and don't know how much more they would have paid for permanent insurance. One problem with term insurance is that only 1 percent of all term policies ever pay a death claim. The insurance companies know this and that is why it is so cheap initially. However, it's not so cheap in your 60s and 70s when you're closer to life expectancy. So if your financial plan includes buy term and invest the difference, it means that at some point in the future you will be self-insuring, right? If you don't have life insurance, and you take on that risk yourself, you are self-insuring. There is nothing wrong with self-insuring, but there is a cost to this, which is much higher than permanent life insurance. Here's why: If you don't have life insurance, you can't spend down your assets because we have to leave something for the surviving spouse to live on. So without life insurance you can only take 3 to 4 percent per year. However, with life insurance, you could take 5, 6, or 7 percent. At least you have the option to take a higher income.

By the way, the 4 percent rule is now being challenged (Google "Wall Street Journal Say Goodbye to the 4% Rule for Retirement")

Figure 3: Self-insuring is also paying an insurance premium.

WITHOUT LIFE INSURANCE		
Account Value		$1 million
Withdrawal Rate	4%	$40,000 per year
WITH LIFE INSURANCE		
Withdrawal Rate	7%	$70,000 per year
Difference		**$30,000 (Self-Insured Premium)**

What do you call it when you give up $30,000 in income to provide a benefit to your spouse after you die? That is called "life insurance" and you will pay a premium either way. You either give up income in retirement or you send income to an insurance company. What if you could do it for $15,000 with the insurance company? You could take $55,000 of income and still have access to the cash in the policy. That is a 37 percent increase in your income.

Long-term care (LTC) is another area where I see people self-insuring when they don't have to. You don't have to be old and living in a home to use long-term care insurance. You could bump your head, fall down, have a stroke, etc. However, something major could wipe you out. Many planners are failing to educate their clients on alternatives to paying LTC premiums. In the past, our only option was to pay a premium for life, and then if we didn't use the coverage we lost all that money. There is new and improved long-term care that allows you to place a specific amount of assets with the insurance company or pay a premium for just 10 years. Here is how it works. Recently I helped a friend of my father who had a traditional LTC policy for which he was paying around $7,000 a year. The problem is that his premiums were not guaranteed and could go up substantially in the future. The other problem was that his benefit was only for three years. Here is how we saved him $140,000 and increased his cash flow by $7,000 per year:

Old LTC Policy	$7,000 per year for 20 years = $140,000 in premiums
	If he doesn't need the coverage he loses $140,000
New LTC Policy	One deposit $130,000
	Maintains access to funds
	Initial monthly benefit grows to $11,000 per month at age 83
	Money back any time
Savings @83	**$140,000**
Cash Flow Increase	**$7,000 per year**

This brings me back to my original question. What kind of retirement plan do you want? One that is restrictive or one that lets you spend your money? If you knew that your spouse would be taken care of and that the assets you spent in retirement would be replaced 100 percent, would that free you up to spend your money the way you always wanted to?

What will your retirement picture look like?

So now you know the retirement plan that everyone wants is one that lets you spend your money. Consider the above recommendations to enhance your plan.

Happy retirement!

About Paul

Paul J. Nick, owner of South Texas Financial Group, has practiced as a financial strategist and retirement specialist since 1993. Paul has successfully designed progressive strategies that have continuously increased his clients' wealth (even when the markets tanked) and provided certainty for their income during retirement.

His experience and customized approach empowers his clients to embrace revolutionary planning concepts that instill wealth-building habits, provide peace of mind and ultimately lead to an abundant lifestyle.

Paul is unique in that he grew up in the financial services industry. Paul's father built one of the largest financial services companies in Texas that specialized in a conservative approach to retirement planning.

Paul has been a student of nutrition for more than 30 years. His health and wealth strategy helps clients understand the importance of eating quality, nutritious foods and staying away from the foods known to cause health issues. Paul states, "If we can help our clients stay out of the doctor's office, not only will they feel better, they will have more money to spend on themselves and their family."

Paul is also the founder of Houston Energy Corridor Connections, a 5000+ member networking group on LinkedIn, which hosts four live networking events for the Houston energy industry each year. The focus of the group is to bring people together from the energy industry and help them build their personal networks and improve their businesses and careers.

A former Marine and avid pilot, Paul has logged more than 600 hours in high performance aircraft. When Paul is not working with clients, he enjoys flying, spending time with his family, coaching his daughters in soccer and volunteering at their school.

Paul lives in Houston with his wife, Kim, and daughters, Kennedy and Avery.

CHAPTER 23

THE REST OF YOUR LIFE IS GOING TO HAPPEN NO MATTER WHAT YOU DO!

BY SCOTT ADAMSON

The question is: Will you be one of the ones who did…or one of the ones that wish they did?

When it comes to money, there are very few sure things out there. For awhile it seemed like the stock market was a sure thing. After it went south in 2000, it seemed like real estate was the ticket for a few years. The collapse of the real estate market in 2008 proved that wasn't the solution.

Looking back through history, there are many other examples of things that were sure winners, like tulip bulbs, ostriches, gold, silver, stocks, real estate, tech companies and others. The truth is they have all been winners at various times and complete losers at other times.

When the dust settles the story is always the same…the people who got in before everyone else and got out before everyone else were the ones who made all the money. It's also true that the people who had the cash to take advantage of the opportunity when it arose are the ones that profited the most.

Five years ago (in 2008), the real estate market in this country came crashing down upon us with houses in my area dropping 40 to 50 percent in value. A lot of banks were teetering on the brink of collapse and the banks left standing wouldn't loan money on a house that was on sale for half of what it sold for the year before.

The amazing thing is that when the price was twice as high, the banks were tripping over themselves to loan money and when the price went down they wouldn't or couldn't loan money to people to buy a house at a greatly discounted price.

A friend of mine in the banking business explained it to me in a simple enough way for me to understand. He said, "Banks will lend you all kinds of money if you don't need it."

If you had access to cash after the real estate market crashed there were and still are many opportunities to take advantage of some great deals.

I grew up in the agriculture world, farming, ranching and feeding cattle. I always say my father never met a steer he didn't think he could make money on. The cattle feeding business for those who don't know makes the stock market look pretty tame in comparison. When my father started in the business he was very successful and even though the cattle business can be very volatile he made more money than he lost and continued to reinvest the profits back into the business by owning more cattle.

His twin brother was his partner and they put in place a buy-sell agreement that was funded with whole-life policies taken out on each other. That way, if either of them died, the other would have the money to buy the other's share, providing money for his family.

Over the years, the business borrowed lots of money to operate with and also to purchase the necessary equipment like trucks, tractors, pickups, land, buildings and so on. The operating line was structured as a line of credit and most of the equipment was acquired with installment loans.

Over the years, there were several business disasters like markets crashing and bad winters that caused big losses. The worst was when we shipped several truckloads of cattle to the packing plant one day and after they took them in, the plant declared bankruptcy at noon and locked the gate with our cattle inside. We were left with no money for our cattle and a note at the bank.

Luckily, it had been a few years since the life insurance policies were purchased so we could get money from them to keep the bank happy. Over the years that happened at least two more times and the last time we had to cash the policies in to keep the business going.

At that time, I didn't know anything about the power of dividend paying whole-life and how to use it for financing. So I went along with the idea of cashing out the policies to give the bank the money. I had no idea that the bank could have just done a lien on the life insurance policies and, if they were smart, loan us the money for premiums if we needed it.

When I left the business at age 38 and moved to sunny Arizona, I started my career in the financial services business. Over the years, I was educated on the various investment options and was licensed to sell all kinds of life insurance and annuities, as well as stocks and bonds.

In 2003, I came across the Bank On Yourself concept in its earliest form and immediately the light went on. I knew instantly that my family had the basics for this concept to work but didn't know how to do it. I sat at my computer and calculated how different things could have been if we'd used the policies to finance the equipment and land purchases. When I was done the first thing I did was stick my head between my knees and try to not be sick to my stomach.

The difference was staggering…several million dollars difference for my family if we had used our own capital to finance the business instead of the banks. Worse yet, we let the bank force us to rob our own bank to satisfy them.

When my dad asked me what I was doing one day, I told him I'd just started working with the Bank On Yourself concept. He, of course, asked what that was so I told him that the simplest way to explain it was to think about using the money from the old life insurance policies as a banking system, and that we could have all the money we paid out in interest in our pockets instead of the bank having it. His face lost all its color and for a second I thought he was going to pass out.

The biggest mistake we made was not understanding that the life insurance policies were much more valuable than the business was and the longer we had them the more valuable they would become.

We made serious money on cattle when times were good. For example, in the good times we could put down $150 and borrow the rest to buy a steer and the required feed. The profit potential was $200 in 120 days. So under perfect conditions that $150 investment could make $600 in one year. The problem was the same then as it was in the real estate market. When we were making so much money it was no problem to keep expanding and stay leveraged to the hilt. But eventually, the market tanked and we experienced big losses and the banks were reluctant to lend us enough to get back in. The people who had cash could buy back in at a huge discount and make even more money.

One thing I know for sure now that I didn't know then is that everyone needs his or her own financing source. The bigger the source is, the more prosperous you will be and nothing can change that. Opportunities are going to come along in your lifetime for you to take advantage of some type of investment that is selling at a great discount. It could be houses, gold, cattle, stocks, land or something else, or you may just finance the things in your life that most people use banks for. Stuff like cars, houses, college educations, vacations, furniture or maybe even a new set of golf clubs. By understanding your own financing capital and using it properly you will build your net worth and it won't matter what else is happening in the world.

When you look at a Bank On Yourself plan it's easy to see what you will have at any date in the future. Try doing that with your 401(k)! One of my favorite questions to ask is what will your 401(k) be worth in 10 years. No one knows what it will be worth next week, let alone in 10 years or at retirement.

Funny how things changed as I get a little older. I'm only 53 but it feels like 80 is coming at me so much faster than 50 did when I was 23. The older I get, the faster it goes and so on and so on. I heard that so many times when I was younger, and even though I believed it, I don't think I could really appreciate it, and I'm sure as time goes by it will only get worse.

The good news is that I now know a few things that I didn't know a few years ago. I think one of the most important things I know for sure is: The rest of my time here is going to happen no matter what I do or say about it. I've finally figured out the only thing you can count on for sure is time. The clock is ticking and will continue to tick until I graduate, kick the bucket, croak or do one of the many other ways there are to say it.

The only question is if I'll have my financial house in order when that day comes. the only way to do that with 100 percent certainty is to use dividend paying whole-life insurance. The best part of using whole-life is that it accomplishes so much at that same time. It's a source of financing, emergency cash, retirement income, vacation money and money to take advantage of investment opportunities and tax-advantaged growth, as well as money to make sure my family is OK financially when I'm gone, no matter if that's sooner or hopefully later. It doesn't depend on the stock market or any other market to grow and the longer I have it the better it gets.

Let's talk about what I call the four lies about life insurance:

1. **Term is the cheapest insurance.** Term has been around for long enough to be accepted as conventional wisdom now so that's should make you nervous. The truth is somewhere around 1 percent or less of all term policies sold pay a death claim. Using simple math I can determine that means 99 percent of the premium dollars paid into term are a waste of money. It gets more expensive the longer you have it and it's designed to fail.

2. **You don't need insurance when you're older.** I don't happen to think you ever need life insurance. I think you should buy it because you want it. What I mean is that you want to ensure what you want to happen will happen even if you die before you accomplish it. Life insurance does that for you and if you do it correctly it also gives you advantages you can use while you are still here. I will say that if there is a time when you need it, it's when you die and statistically that's when you're older.

When I worked at a bank here in Phoenix, I had the opportunity to sit with several widows who'd just lost their husbands. We would go through their assets and figure out the best way to manage their money going forward. Not one time when I asked how much life insurance they had did I hear them say: "We had way too much and now I don't know what I'm going to do with all this money."

225

It didn't matter how old they were, it seemed like their lifestyle was going to take a hit because when their spouse died they lost income. So whoever came up with the idea that you don't need insurance when you're older has never sat across from a widow who didn't have any and figure out what her income was going to be going forward.

3. **Buy term and invest the difference.** As long as you can guarantee the investment is going to outpace the death benefit of the whole-life policy this could work. The problem is you can't and it won't. On the other hand, buying dividend paying whole-life and borrowing from it for your investments and paying the loan back with interest when you make money from the investment can work very nicely.

4. **Whole-life insurance is the most expensive.** I would argue the only way this is true is if you cancel the policy in the first few years. Since the way a Bank On Yourself Policy is structured so it builds cash value in the early years, it doesn't take long for the cash value to equal what you paid in. Once you get to that point it will always be worth more than you paid for it. On the other hand unless you die while the policy is in force term insurance premiums are 100 percent expense.

When I was working at the bank I used to have older people who would come in and ask what they should do with their money. I would give them some options and it was common for them to say, "I won't be around that much longer so I don't want to tie my money up."

I would always say, "That makes it so much easier...just let me know what day you're going to be checking out and we'll figure out how much you can spend every day until then." Of course, they would say they didn't know and what if they lived longer?

I would say, "Then how about we plan for the worst and hope for the best?" What I meant was, let's put a plan in place that works no matter how long they live and no matter what happens in the markets or the rest of the world. They always seemed to like that idea and forgot all about how long they were tying up their money or how much longer they would be here.

The point is we all get hung up on the wrong things when it comes to money. The important question is: "Will you be one of the ones who have a plan that works no matter what happens? Will you have a plan that, if all your investment plans pan out, is simply that much better because you also have a whole-life insurance policy? Or will you be one of the ones who wished after the stock market or real estate market crashed and cut their retirement plan way back that they had at least something that worked, no matter what?

You decide…there's still time.

About Scott

Scott Adamson was born in a small town in Northeast Colorado. After graduating from Colorado State University with a bachelors of education degree, he had a one-year internship in Chicago working at the Chicago Board of Trade and the Chicago Mercantile Exchange.

He then joined the family business in Northeast Colorado, which included commercial cattle feeding operation, a small farm and ranch, trucking and a composting business.

He was very involved in the state and national cattle organizations, and the state and national politics. During those years, he was elected as the youngest president of the Colorado Cattle Feeders Association (it's now the Colorado Livestock Association), was a member of the Central Yuma Groundwater Management District, and was a nine-year member of the local volunteer fire department.

In 1998, he decided to leave agriculture and venture to Phoenix, where he worked as a senior investment representative for BankOne, which is now Chase.

In 2003, he came across the book *The Infinite Banking System* by Nelson Nash. He immediately knew that was what he wanted to do as a career—and the rest is history.

Through Nelson, he met Pamela Yellen, the creator of Bank On Yourself, and has been an Authorized Bank On Yourself Advisor since then.

When I came across this concept, I understood it completely and immediately knew it was the way to help anyone and everyone become more financially secure.

I've been very fortunate over the last 10 years to be able to help a lot of people who started out as clients and are now friends.

CHAPTER 24

MIDDLE-CLASS INVESTMENT SECRETS

BY SHAWN KIELEY

"We are responsible for the fortunes of our family. Tremendous amounts of money will flow through our hands during our lifetime and by controlling the flow we ensure our prosperity."
~ Shawn Kieley

THE FIRST SECRET: PAY YOURSELF FIRST

It's really a simple decision and when I made it, little did I know that "simple decision" would also be the seed of revelation that would change the course of my life. It changed the way I looked at money and lead me to the solution I share with all my clients.

If you have read my biography, you would know I am a man of passion when it comes to my faith, my family and ensuring that I have and leave enough financial wealth to enjoy life, as it was intended.

Along the way I have suffered like many people my age; through financial mistakes, I followed what I believed to be the best advice: Buy term, invest the difference, pay cash for everything possible, have three to six months of expenses in an emergency fund, invest heavily in stocks when you're young and add more bonds as you get closer to retirement–only to have to live from paycheck to paycheck.

During this journey I realized I was putting everyone and everything else first in my life when it came to our money. Taxes, charities, car payments, credit cards, living expenses ... and where were we on the list? Dead last.

I remember feeling hopelessly stuck while sitting in my office poring over a stack of bills. Do you know the feeling? If so, perhaps you have heard it too; that tiny little voice, the one that comes from deep inside of you, and stops every thought with a quiet flash of inspiration. That morning I heard it loud and clear. It simply said, pay yourself first.

As those words sunk in, my mind froze and I felt a sense of calm and it was like a veil had been lifted and I thought; we could do that! Why not–what we were doing up to that point was getting us nowhere fast. I shared this with my wife and we decided from that point forward, a part of everything we earned would be saved for our family first, no matter what.

The next step was to decide what type of financial vehicle should be used as a storehouse. Maybe a tin can, a savings account, a money market, CDs or something else. Leaning on my years of experience in finance, I have learned there are 10 wealth destroyers that every plan must take into consideration to be successful. Taxes and inflation, two of the wealth destroyers, play a major role, eroding the purchasing power of safe money accounts.

To illustrate, imagine you are the owner of a small plantation that grows bananas. Each week for the next four weeks, you go into the field and harvest 10 ripe bananas, which are placed into your storehouse. The math would tell you that at the end of the month you would have 40 bananas, right? When we account for taxes and inflation, we end up with far fewer bananas than the math would indicate. As a successful plantation owner, you will qualify to be in the top tax bracket of 35 percent. When you complete your tax return, you learn you have to send in 14 bananas to pay your taxes on the harvest. After taxes, you now have 26 bananas.

If you have ever bought bananas and stored them for any length of time, you know many of them turn bad and decay. This is similar to inflation. An average inflation rate of 3 percent means we will lose another two bananas, leaving only 24 in your storehouse. As long as the bananas are kept in a storehouse that does not keep up with inflation, your harvest will continue to decay, leaving you with less and less purchasing power.

Perhaps you are living on your savings and you have experienced this very thing. Interest rates are very low and the little interest paid out is taxed as earned, leaving you with even less money to live on. It's not your fault. We have all heard that when you get close to retirement, you should shift your money out of risky investments like stocks and into safe investments like bonds and CDs to protect your principal and live off the interest.

So where does this leave my wife and me? It left us to start where we were. We decided to use a savings account now due to the convenience of transferring money from our checking accounts. We then started putting money regularly into it before we wrote out a check to anyone else. The first thing we noticed immediately is how liberating it felt. What a sense of accomplishment!

At the same time we didn't want to go broke safely so I immediately began to perform an extensive search to learn if there was a better place to use as a storehouse for our safe money.

THE SECOND SECRET: WHERE YOU STORE AND GROW YOUR WEALTH IS MORE IMPORTANT THAN THE TACTICS AND STRATEGIES USED

The search for a better place to store and grow our savings lasted almost two years. The reason it took so long is because it was hidden in plain sight like the picture hidden within a stereogram.

In fact, it's not something new—it's been around from more than 200 years and you probably have heard about it. I certainly did, but I dismissed it because everyone knows it's a terrible investment vehicle and they're right because it's not an investment vehicle—it's investment grade insurance.

So what makes "Investment grade insurance" a perfect place to store and grow your savings?

Investment grade insurance, when properly designed, eliminates or severely reduces the effects of the 10 wealth destroyers and stands alone against all other accounts that we would typically use to store safe money.

Table 1 is a summary checklist that highlights which financial vehicle is strongest in each categories of the 10 wealth destroyers

Table 1: Investment Grade Insurance Plan
Vs. Traditional Safe Money Accounts

		INVESTMENT GRADE INSURANCE	VS	TIN CANS, MONEY MARKETS AND SAVINGS ACCOUNTS
1	INFLATION	WINNER		–
2	TAXES	WINNER		–
3	OPPORTUNITY COSTS	WINNER		–
4	NEW TECHNOLOGY	WINNER		–
5	PLANNED OBSOLESCENCE	WINNER		–
6	LOAN AND CREDIT INTEREST	WINNER		–
7	FINANCIAL COSTS	–*		WINNER
8	INTEREST RATE DECLINES	WINNER		–
9	STOCK MARKET CRASHES	WINNER		–
10	LAWSUITS	WINNER		–

*Initial cost certainly goes in the direction of the other vehicles. However, there are other advantages in a policy that offset the costs as outlined in the details below.

If you want to dig into the details, read on. If not, skip down to the bottom of this section.

1. Inflation: The policy increases by a contractually guaranteed amount each year. The other account types do not have guarantees and lose purchasing power every year.

2. Taxes: The cash values are tax-advantaged, meaning money inside the policy grows tax-free, the death benefit can be received income tax-free, and under current tax law it is possible to use the equity in your policy with few or no tax consequences. Dividends you leave in your policy are not taxable. Dividends you take out are not taxed until they exceed the amount of your cost basis, at which point you could switch to borrowing your "cash value" tax-free, as long as the policy remains in force (IRS Tax Code, Section 72). The other account types are taxed as earned.

3. Opportunity Costs: If you pay for major purchases by borrowing your equity from your plan to pay cash for these items, and then pay your plan back with interest, you could ultimately recapture most or all of the interest you would have paid to a third party lender and your plan will continue to grow the same as if you never touched it. We will talk more about that later.

In the other accounts, when money is taken out it is no longer working for you and you lose the interest those dollars were earning forever.

4. New Technology: This includes cell phones, pay-for-TV and other monthly expenses our grandparents did not have. When you pay for things as described above, you could also recapture those dollars in your plan, so you can use them again.

Other Accounts: When money is taken out to pay for new technology, it is no longer working for you and you lose the interest those dollars were earning forever.

5. Planned Obsolescence: This is when you replace things that wear out (for example, a car). When you pay for things as described above, you could also recapture those dollars in your plan, so you can use them again.

Other Accounts: When money is taken out to pay for the replacement items, it is no longer working for you and you lose the interest those dollars were earning forever.

6. Loan and Credit Interest: When you pay for things using Investment Grade Life Insurance, you are redirecting the interest you would have paid back into your account for the benefit of your family. This feature is powerful and supercharges the cash growth within the plan.

Other Accounts: When money is borrowed from third-party lenders, the interest paid is lost forever because it is sent to their accounts.

7. **Financial Costs:** The policy expenses are fixed and become more efficient every year.

   Other Plans: Have lower initial costs but are missing tax-free growth, uninterrupted growth of money placed in the plan, a contractually guaranteed increase, and a guaranteed maturity value, which can go to your family tax-free. My calculator says these benefits far outweigh the costs.

8. **Interest Rate Declines:** These will not affect the guaranteed annual increase. Interest rate changes may affect the dividends. The other plans have no guaranteed increase and the amount of interest credited would decline with decreases.

9. **Stock Market Crashes:** Once credited to your account, both your guaranteed annual increase and any dividends you may have received are locked in, unaffected by stock or real estate market swings. Other accounts are not affected by stock market crashes.

10. **Lawsuits:** The money in your plan may be protected from creditors and lawsuits. Other accounts are not likely protected (consult with legal counsel to determine what's applicable in your state).

Now we knew the answer to the question "what is the best financial vehicle to store and grow our safe money"; we set up our investment grade insurance policy and began to fund it by rolling in our existing savings and tax refunds; restructuring debt; reducing unnecessary spending, and only funding our company 401(k) to the full match. We went all in.

THIRD SECRET: CONTROLLING YOUR CASH FLOW BY SELF-FINANCING WILL MAKE YOU VERY WEALTHY

The advantages of an investment grade insurance policy means it can be used for much more than a glorified savings account. One of the not-so-obvious uses is your ability to self-finance.

When we learned how this worked we set two goals: Take back all the interest we were losing when we made payments to third party lenders, and self-finance all of our major purchases.

How was this possible? When you use the cash values of our policy to self-finance major purchases, you pay yourself back just like you would if you were using someone else's money. So you'd win in three ways:

- First, the cash value continues to grow and you receive the same guaranteed annual increase.

- Second, dividends that may be paid are credited to your account.

- Third, when you pay yourself back, just like you would any lender, you also get the interest you would have paid to a third-party source.

Why is this better than what you're currently doing? It's better because when you recapture the opportunity costs and redirect the interest you are currently losing for your financing needs, you become wealthy.

Take a look at Table 2, which represents an average American family. John and his wife, Sandy, have some credit cards, a house payment, a couple of cars and some student loan debt. Each month, John and Sandy are making monthly payments to third-party lenders. Direct your attention to Table 2:

Table2: John and Sandy's Payments and Interest Breakdown

DEBT	MONTHLY PAYMENT	MONTHLY INTEREST	YEARLY INTEREST LOST FOREVER
CREDIT CARDS	$ 647.00	$ 97.05	$ 1,164.60
HOME	$ 1,795.00	$ 1,346.25	$ 16,155.00
CAR 1	$ 524.00	$ 104.80	$ 1,257.60
STUDENT LOAN	$ 274.63	$ 87.88	$ 1,054.58
CAR 2	$ 259.00	$ 51.80	$ 621.60
TOTAL	$ 3,499.63	$ 1,687.78	$ 20,253.38

Every month John and Sandy are making $3,499.63 in payments and $1,687.78 is going to the interest. What this means is that 48 percent of every dollar is being lost to finance charges.

When annualized, the interest John and Sandy will have paid in a single year is more than $20,000, and I don't have to tell you that's a lot of money flying out the window. The good news is, with an investment grade life insurance plan and the proper strategy, we can change the flow of money and bring those dollars back.

How is this done? We do that by setting up our plan and then pay ourselves first to capitalize to the policy. Working with clients we can often find the money to do this without making any major changes to the family budget.

As soon as possible we will start buying down the family debt, taking a loan from the policy and paying off the first debt on the payoff schedule.

The plan will continue to grow as though it was never touched, and as you send the money that was servicing the debt into the plan, your family will get all the interest that would have been lost forever... back! We will continue paying off the other debts on the schedule in this manner until all debt is paid off.

It doesn't stop there. Once all the debts are paid off, we will continue to send those payments into our storehouse, which will cause our balances to grow and grow and grow. This works much better than the way most debt elimination plans work, which will get you out of debt but leave you with very little savings.

When you are diligent with this strategy and your cash flows through the plan as described above, you will become very wealthy and you will have more than enough income to live on and support your family, as well as enough to pass along to your children and your grandchildren and support the causes most dear to your heart.

Today, our balances are growing larger every month and our biggest regret is that we did not know about this sooner. Our plan has guarantees and there is no guessing and hoping that the money will be there when we need it. No special skills or training is required to run the plan and we are both confident if something happened to one of us, either of us could manage our plan without a hiccup and we sleep much better at night.

Experience has taught me that people don't plan to fail; they simply don't plan. I don't want that to be you and if you do have a plan but you're not using this financial vehicle, you owe it to your family to take a long, hard look. Dear reader, I ask you this: Think about your financial position. You know it better than I can say and if you find you would

like to discuss your situation and learn if this is the right solution for your family, then don't hesitate to send an email to:
LetsTalk@coppergrove.com

About Shawn

Shawn Kieley is a Veteran and a well-known financial educator in the Seattle area who has been recognized as a leading expert in middle income family investment strategies. For the past 10 years, he has been working with families to help them save, spend, invest, insure and plan wisely for the future.

Shawn has uncovered the areas in which many families are exposed to the 10 wealth destroyers and shows families how to avoid common financial mistakes found in following conventional wisdom.

Having a great desire to learn and to continuously improve, Shawn has completed the rigorous training required to be a Bank on Yourself authorized advisor and has become one of only about 200 such advisors in the United States and Canada. Using this knowledge, he has developed an expertise using whole-life insurance in a specialized way that most individuals and even insurance agents could never have imagined to live a prosperous life.

Shawn lives with his wife, Heather, who is a stay-at-home mom, and their children in the Seattle area. His hobbies when he is not helping clients are reading, enjoying family time and taking long drives all over scenic Washington state.

CHAPTER 25

HOW TO LOSE YOUR DEBTS *WHILE* KEEPING YOUR ASSETS

BY STEVEN H. STEP

One truth that I have learned in 28 years of helping my clients achieve their financial goals is that it is those who have the discipline to save who are the most likely win the financial game. "Regular savers" flock to Bank On Yourself-designed whole-life policies because of the safety, guarantees and tax advantages of these instruments. However, many people feel that even if they are (or can become) good savers, they cannot really take advantage of all of the benefits of a Bank On Yourself policy because of the high amounts of debt they are carrying.

A MIDDLE-AGED COUPLE'S DILEMMA

Jason and Roberta are a warm, fun loving couple in their forties with two kids and a dog. They fell into that category when they first met with me. Over the previous few years, they had accumulated a lot of debt. They painfully explained to me that while they understood and liked the whole Bank On Yourself concept, they had amassed $16,000 of credit card debt along with student loans and a loan for a time share. They owed almost $50,000 in addition to their mortgage.

Jason explained that while they both had good jobs with good incomes, it would be very hard for them to create any new savings to go into a Bank On Yourself plan while paying their regular living expenses and $2,000 a month just to service their nonmortgage debts. Roberta lamented, "We keep working harder and harder and yet we are not getting ahead...and at this rate, we never will."

Jason realized that they should try to cut back on current expenses and apply any new savings to simply paying off portions of their existing debt. I explained that those with high debts are really making high monthly payments of both the Interest and the principal to other people's banks. This creates a situation in which their financial health spirals down—lower and lower—with high payments that seem to go on forever. Sometimes even more debt gets added on. All of this money gets paid out...never to be seen again. You have less in savings that is earning money and greater amounts of hard-earned money being spent on debt. Making matters even worse, some people end up making just the minimum payments required and at 10 percent or more, compounded interest will take decades to pay it off.

Jason also said that he understood the importance of saving and that before their total debts had gotten as high as they were he and Roberta had actually been pretty good at saving. They had put some money into a stock account and with some appreciation, it was worth about $20,000. They also had a CD and checking accounts worth $33,000. They were earning less than 3 percent on their savings of $53,000 with one group of banks and they were paying interest payments equal to 20 percent on almost the same amount of money to another group of banks. Specifically, they had put $50,000 plus interest into the banking pool and had borrowed almost the same amount from the same traditional banking system. They were paying almost $9,000 to banks and financial institutions every year to be able to borrow the same amount of money that they had put into the banking system.

At this point in the meeting I asked them, "Who's money are you borrowing?" After a few moments, Jason looked down and then got angry before he said, "We have been borrowing our own money!"

The couple realized that they could simply pay off all of their current nonsecured debt with all of the money in these stock or savings accounts, but that would mean that they would have absolutely no savings to fall back on if something were to happen to either one of them or their incomes. Besides, they felt that if they did lose income or suffer some type of emergency, they could suspend or stop most of the debt payments and still have their savings liquid and available.

I understood their dilemma and I could see and feel the frustration the debt was having on them and their relationship as each blamed the other for portions of the total debt. I explained to Jason and Roberta that by using the principles behind the Bank On Yourself concept and repositioning the money that they had already saved up, they could pay off all of their debts off in just over two years time. Even more exciting, they could actually recapture the interest they would otherwise have to pay for years to come to other banks. Best of all, their money would continue to accumulate as their long-term "safe" savings and would be available to take out as retirement income down the road. Roberta laughed and said, "If you can show us how to pay off all our debt without using up all of our savings, then you will be our new marriage counselor, too!"

BANK ON YOURSELF TO THE RESCUE

When we met a week later, I showed Jason and Roberta how they could roll $26,000 of their savings into Bank On Yourself policies, insuring each of their lives in each of the next two years. Then in each of the first two years, they would borrow $24,000 and pay off all their debts. Then they would then simply make the same payments that they were currently making to their creditors back to themselves and their own policies. They also saw that once they had paid all of the loans back, they would have the same amount of accumulated savings they would have had had they not taken the policy loans out to begin with. In a few short years they will have eliminated all of their nonsecured debt and still have all of their savings.

Once the policy loans have been paid off, Jason and Roberta will be able to put all of the money that used to go into debt payments into more savings. Those savings will grow without taxes being taken out each year and can be used to finance cars or trips to their timeshares, and recapture interest they would otherwise pay to banks. Their plan will also create a significant retirement income from those savings that is tax-free under current law. Lastly, the permanent life insurance protection on each of them would help to guarantee that most of their financial goals and dreams would be realized even if either one of them were to pass away before they had saved up enough to achieve those goals.

Jason and Roberta became very relieved and very happy as they realized that their whole financial future would be dramatically improved by following these Bank On Yourself plans and my advice. They could see that they would be able to reverse the financial winds that were spiraling down with debt for a long time into winds that spiraled upward with more savings and opportunities. They were also glad to learn that we would be reviewing their plan every six months to make sure that both the plan and they were on track.

A RETIRED COUPLE'S SITUATION

One might believe that older Americans (those over 65) would have less debt and are mostly living off their retirement plans and savings. The truth is, however, that many older Americans are coping with significant debt, as well. We do not hear of their plight as much because they are the "silent generation" that does not talk about financial problems or ask for help. The situation for seniors is often even more precarious in that often they are living on fixed incomes while facing higher costs for medical insurance and health care.

This was especially true for Ron and Darlene—a sweet retired couple who were quietly living off his pension plan and their social security payments until the day Ron suffered a heart attack and had triple bypass heart surgery. Thankfully, the surgeon, hospital and staff all did a great job and a few weeks later Ron was feeling better than before.

Even though Ron and Darlene had Medicare, they were left with unpaid medical bills of more than $19,000. Since they could not come up with that money all at once, they paid the bills with a credit card, which came with a 14 percent interest rate. They were trying to figure out how to pay off the balance and avoid having to pay $400 a month to the credit card company for the rest of their retirement years when they learned about Bank On Yourself.

Until his medical emergency, Ron and Darlene had no other debt besides the mortgage and had managed to save just over $30,000 in a bank certificate of deposit that was going to come due in a few weeks. The new rate was going to be less than 2 percent (a lot lower than the rate they had been earning for the previous five years).

During our first meeting, I told Ron and Darlene that I would put together a plan for them using Bank On Yourself that would enable them to pay off their high interest rate credit cards, and begin paying the loans back to their policy, where the interest paid ultimately benefits them. They would also be building an emergency fund to help cover future unexpected expenses.

A SOLUTION FOR RETIREES

They were very skeptical but agreed to keep an open mind and meet with me again in a week. The following week, Ron and Darlene came in, still doubting that I could help them. I showed them that even though Darlene was 68 they could purchase a single premium whole-life plan with Darlene as the insured person and fund their plan with the money that was about to mature from their CD. There would never be any future premiums to pay. The policy is projected to earn interest and dividends that are higher than the CD over the long term. While the gains that they earn will be taxable (just like the CD), they could almost immediately borrow out the money from the cash value and pay off the entire credit card debt. The couple was even more astonished to learn that when they pulled out the $19,000 policy loan, none of it was taxable since they had not yet earned any interest.

Ron and Darlene then simply started to pay themselves back with the same money that they would have had to pay to the credit card company anyway. This way, though, all of those payments will go back into their new Bank On Yourself plan. Once they have paid back the loan from the policy, if either of them were to suffer the same type of financial emergency again, they would be able to handle it the same way while never taking away from their savings. Try doing that with a CD from the bank.

Darlene's demeanor changed completely as she gushed "this plan not only solves our current predicament but will provide us with piece of mind moving ahead—especially since our savings would be earning more than the CD." I reminded them that unlike with the CD, they would decide when to take out money and it would grow without taxes being taken out each year until then.

THE BANK ON YOURSELF CUSTOMIZED PLAN

An authorized Bank On Yourself advisor is qualified to help you analyze your particular situation, and then design a customized plan that will help you reach your financial goals. He or she will:

1. Review and take stock of your current financial picture.

2. Determine where are you currently saving or investing. He or she also will ask, what are your goals and do you have a plan for achieving them? What percent of your income are you able to save and what are you earning on those savings? How much debt do you have and what interest rates and fees are you paying on that debt? If you do not know where you are or where you are going, then any road will take you there.

3. Examine what percent of your income you are currently saving.

YOUR NEXT STEPS

If you saving little or are earning almost nothing on your savings while carrying high debt and paying high amounts of interest, you are losing the banking battle, and it will be difficult to achieve your financial goals. Put together a family budget and see if there are ways that you can save more. Good savers are able to put away at least 10 percent of their income and often find ways to save 20 percent or more.

I have clients who earn more than $250,000 a year and still find it difficult to save much. I have other clients who make less than $75,000 and manage to save a third of it.

Make sure that the money that you are saving is guaranteed to grow. Good savers really love their Bank On Yourself policies because it allows them to grow their nest egg without being taxed every year whether they have taken out money or not. In addition, Bank On Yourself policy holders are able to use their savings to self-finance cars, trips, college educations and even other investments with the money in their plans without ever taking away from their long-term savings.

Many people have been misled into believing that the money they have placed into stocks, bonds, mutual funds and other markets are savings. But since these investments can go down in value these are not really savings. What is the point of saving if you end up losing some of the money?

Analyze your current debts and calculate how much interest is being paid out to your creditors each month, never to be seen again. Many American families have accumulated a high amount of both mortgage and other personal debt and are often shocked to see how much of their hard-earned income is going to service their debt. Not having to pay 10 percent on credit card debt is better that earning the same 10 percent on your investments. Even if you did make more on other investments than what you were paying in interest, that income would likely be taxable (and may even push you into a higher tax bracket), while the money you pay out as interest payments is generally not deductible.

A Bank On Yourself authorized advisor is uniquely qualified to help you analyze each of these three areas. We can help you clarify your goals and review your current financial situation. We charge no fees to put together a customized solution that enables you to save in a better way while paying off your debts. Then we show you how to turn those savings into income tax-free retirement income and permanent life insurance.

About Steven

Steven H. Step is president of A Step Ahead Insurance & Financial Services. He has helped more than 285 clients grow their wealth without risk or worry, reduce their taxes and achieve their dreams of financial security.

Steve has put his clients on track to building more than $86 million of additional wealth they would not have had otherwise, through safe, proven financial strategies. That's why his clients think of him as their "secret weapon," helping them build and safeguard their wealth.

One of only 250 financial advisors in the country who have successfully completed the rigorous training program and continuing education required to become a Bank On Yourself™ authorized advisor, Steve has consistently ranked as one of the top 25 Bank On Yourself authorized agents over the past eight years and has been in the financial services business for 28 years. He holds a master's of business administration degree in marketing from the University of Southern California and a bachelor of arts degree in economics from Denison University. Steve's articles on financial planning have appeared in many publications, including *The Daily News* and *Senior Life.*

Steve lives in the San Fernando Valley area of Los Angeles with his wife, Zena, and their daughter, Samantha. When Steve's not working or at family activities, you may find him traveling, playing golf or just watching a ball game. Steve is also active in the community, including his synagogue and the American Cancer Society, of which he is a past recipient of the Outstanding Achievement in Legacies and Planned Giving Award for his work in helping substantial donors save taxes and earn income by doing good.

In order to provide his clients the level of service he believes they expect and deserve, Steve only takes on a small number of new clients each year who are committed to achieving lifetime financial security.

CHAPTER 26

SIMPLE SOLUTIONS FOR REDUCING FINANCIAL STRESS AND MAKING COLLEGE AFFORDABLE

BY STUART GROSSMAN

"Help me, Stuart. Our oldest child is heading off to college soon and we don't know how to pay for it. What should we do?"

Among the 15 to 20 families I meet with on a weekly basis, this same question gets asked to me more than any other…by a large margin. It's no secret: Paying for college is one of the biggest financial investments a family will ever make. And unfortunately, most parents are woefully unprepared.

Many families search for the best way to help pay for their student's college costs. Many vehicles that are often used do not provide them with peace of mind in their savings plans. This is where the Bank On Yourself system comes in. It offers a safe, low-risk, predictable savings opportunity with unique tax benefits, which makes it an ideal method for saving money for important major purchases, including college.

In fact, the Bank On Yourself system offers one aspect that is not available in almost any other college savings plan: The money you save in these specially designed, whole-life insurance plans is not counted against you in the U.S. Department of Education's financial aid formulas when calculating your expected family contribution (EFC). This could help you avoid overpaying for college by tens of thousands of dollars per year.

Of course, one of the most enticing aspects of the Bank On Yourself plan is that the money remains in your control and is always available for your use, without paying interest to financial organizations or penalties for withdrawal. So you can use the money you save for college and still have it available for your retirement. You don't need to make that heart-wrenching choice that many parents face: sending your child to college or retiring in the manner and timeframe you had planned.

THE PROBLEMS PARENTS ENCOUNTER

In conducting hundreds of workshops for parents of high school students all over the western states, I have found that parents have two major problems when it comes to sending their kids to college:

Problem #1: The cost of college is higher than ever and almost unaffordable for many families.

Problem #2: Parents are finding it difficult to afford the high cost of college and still have a comfortable retirement without going heavily into debt.

Indeed, the cost of college has risen dramatically over the years. The average cost to attend in-state university is approaching $25,000 a year for in-state tuition. A private university averages $45,000 to $60,000. How is a family supposed to pay that?

Without good planning, they cannot. As a result, student and college loans now exceed the total debt from credit cards in this country.

In addition, many families have problems saving enough money for retirement. That may be because of decreased pensions or because their pensions were changed to 401(k) plans dependent upon mutual fund or stock market values, which have not been good over the past 13 years. Or, because of the recent recession, many breadwinners either lost their jobs or had to cut back their retirement funding.

So what can families do to solve the college problem? They want their kids to get a college education in a field they will enjoy, which also will assure them a good income and solid career prospects. They know a college education is the key to success. Yet families don't want to go heavily into debt and they need to have adequate money for retirement.

A VIABLE SOLUTION

The Bank On Yourself concept is a revolutionary solution that, among other things, helps families solve the "college problem." In fact, I have used this concept for hundreds of clients, including my own family. Bank On Yourself solved my family's college problem and it can do the same for you.

Many families have saved some but not enough money for their kids' college through 529 plans or other plans. Some hope to pay for part of it through their income cash flow. Others are expecting to borrow money for college. Some shift the responsibility onto the kids to take out student loans. Many settle for a community college education. But most find that they do not have enough money saved to pay the full amount of the rising cost of college.

SO HOW WILL THE BANK ON YOURSELF SYSTEM HELP SOLVE THE COLLEGE PROBLEM?

The Bank On Yourself system is a way to have money available from your own source of funding. You can then tap into the cash value of your Bank On Yourself policy and use it to pay for college (in addition to other purchases such as cars, house repairs, vacations, etc.) and have additional money to fund retirement. The key is to treat your Bank On Yourself cash value like you would a loan from a normal financial institution and pay yourself back with interest so the money will be replenished and available for you to use again.

So let's talk about Bank On Yourself's five major benefits:

Benefit #1: The money in the Bank On Yourself plan is in a special type of whole-life insurance policy, which is not counted in the U.S. Department of Education's financial aid formulas when figuring out a family's expected family contribution (EFC). These repositioned assets could make families eligible for more financial aid and decrease the family's portion of college cost.

Benefit #2: The money is very safe in a low-risk environment where it is guaranteed to grow every year. This eliminates worry about fluctuations in the stock market or real estate investments. It's a very predictable program that can be counted on to grow your money in a steady manner. Rates of return will vary based on how the program is set up, but rates of return are generally significantly higher than current interest rates in savings accounts, CDs and money markets.

It's important to have money in a program where you don't have to worry about the variability or unpredictability of its growth, because when you need money for college, you can't wait for several years for it to regain its value after a big drop like the market experiences in 2001 and 2008. It's crucial to have the money available when you need it.

Benefit #3: The money is liquid—you are able to get to your money when you need it, easily and without hassle, and without penalties. The Bank On Yourself whole-life policy is easily accessible through withdrawals and policy loans, which you can normally receive within a week or less.

Benefit #4: There are some great tax benefits in a properly set up Bank On Yourself plan. According to current tax law, which has existed over the past hundred years, it's possible to access the gains in your plan with no taxes due.

Benefit #5: There are life insurance benefits involved. If something happens to one of the family breadwinners, the death benefit can help pay for college, retirement or raising the children. This can be very important and comforting to the family, and truly is a self-completing plan.

HOW WILL THIS WORK IF YOUR STUDENTS ARE CLOSE TO GOING TO COLLEGE?

If your high school students are close to going to college, you don't have much time to build up your plan. But we have developed a system using student loans as a bridge to pay for college costs while we are building up cash value in a Bank On Yourself plan. When your students graduate, and payments on the student loans start, you will have enough cash value built up at that point to pay off the loans. After that, instead of making payments to financial institutions, you will pay back your Bank

On Yourself plan—and the interest that would have gone elsewhere now goes to help improve your own wealth.

This can translate to a huge difference in your overall financial success. This method works very well, even for families where the kids are juniors or seniors in high school.

FINDING MONEY TO FUND A BANK ON YOURSELF PLAN

There are many sources of money we have found to make this work. Sometimes families have monies saved already in various investments and savings accounts that can be put into their Bank On Yourself plan. Along with assets in retirement and qualified plans, this repositioned money will not affect a family's EFC under the Department of Education's formula.

Money in a Bank On Yourself-type policy also grows safely and predictably and is insulated from the dramatic stock market losses suffered by many 529 and other market-based plans. Sometimes the money can be found in 529 plans, Roth IRAs, savings accounts, CDs, money markets, even mutual funds. Those are all good sources for money if the family has designated them for college and retirement planning.

Another source is restructuring people's debts. Often, refinancing a house can reduce mortgage payments and pay off other debts in the process. This will improve a family's cash flow with very low mortgage rates, plus tax deductible interest.

Another idea is decreasing nonmatched contributions to company 401(k) plans, as well as money put into IRAs. This money can better serve a family by putting it into a Bank On Yourself, where it will further diversify what they are doing with their assets. It will be there for college and retirement.

It's important to go through a family's expenses and budget and see where they're spending their money, so they can see where they can trim their spending habits and improve cash flow.

CRUNCHING THE NUMBERS...MEET THE DAVIS FAMILY

The Davis family came to me for help with college funding. Their son, Jason, is a high school senior and daughter, Caitlyn, is a junior, and mom and dad were hoping they could send both to private colleges believing they would get a better education with smaller class sizes and more individualized attention.

They had saved some money for college but not nearly enough and their cash flow was tight, even though they had a combined income of $130,000. Both students had good grades and would have no problem getting accepted to the private schools they chose.

Each student had $30,000 in UGMA accounts to be used for college funding, which would count against them in the financial aid formula. The parents had $150,000 in savings and mutual funds and $40,000 in 529 plans they had set up for their kids' college educations. They also had approximately $300,000 in retirement accounts.

They were putting $300 a month into these 529s and were putting about 15 percent of their income into their retirement account annually, Four percent of that was matched by their employer. Their debts included a mortgage and $10,000 on a car (on which they paid $450 a month) and credit cards that they were trying to pay down quickly at $400 a month.

When we originally estimated their Department of Education financial aid formula, need-based financial aid didn't look promising. The family would be responsible for paying about $44,000 each year for each child. Yikes!

However, by repositioning money that was above the parents' asset protection allowance into a Bank On Yourself-type whole life plan— including the savings, mutual funds and 529s which otherwise would have counted against them—we were able to reduce their responsibility from $44,000 to $30,000 per year. That's a hefty savings of $14,000. Plus, when both students were in college, this amount more than doubled, giving them $30,000 in financial aid—a dramatic improvement in their situation.

They were very happy with the improvement in financial aid, but they were still concerned about their out-of-pocket costs for attending a private school. We estimated these expenses at $90,000 per student for four years of private college, totaling $180,000 for the two kids—a huge amount!

So we had to come up with a plan for this cost. First, we restructured their debt by changing their 15-year mortgage to 30 years. This improved their interest rate and payment, and incorporated their credit card and car loan debt into their new mortgage, increasing their monthly cash flow by a whopping $1,300 a month—money they desperately needed for college and to fund their Bank On Yourself plan!

We also modified their 401(k) contributions. We put their contributions above the 4 percent match by their employer into their new plan, along with the $300 a month they contributed to the 529. Now they were able to put $2,000 a month into a Bank On Yourself plan. They also used the kids' UGMA 529 assets to help fund a Bank On Yourself plan in a separate policy.

WITH THEIR NEW BANK ON YOURSELF PLAN, THE DAVIS FAMILY:

1. Didn't have to be concerned about potential drops of their mutual funds and 529s in the stock market

2. Could have access to this money to pay for college, buy vehicles, do some home improvements and have additional funds available for retirement

3. Received very good tax benefits by having all their gains in the Bank On Yourself plan, which in essence was a pot of money they would build up, with potentially no taxes due on it

4. Could recapture into their Bank On Yourself plan the interest they would have paid had they used conventional student loans and paid them off over a 15 to 20 year period plus. All future interest they would have had to pay on car loans, credit cards and any other money they borrowed for big ticket items

After we put this plan together for the Davis family, they were extremely happy with the results. They were able to fulfill their dreams of sending their kids to private colleges, reduce the overall cost of college, and pay for all college expenses in a comfortable manner. They also added the benefit of having more money for retirement that they could count on without the risk of being in the stock market.

WHY CHOOSE COLLEGE FUNDING SYSTEMS?

Ten years ago, one of my clients asked me about how to fill out financial aid forms to get more financial aid. Also at that point, my own kids were getting ready for college. So I did some research and realized there's a huge need for legitimate information on how to fund a college education. I joined the National Association of College Funding Advisors, which taught me what it takes to help families fund college and get the best prices for college. Through their training and 10 years of experience working with hundreds of families one-on-one and conducting seminars, I have learned many things that can help students and parents.

It's very rewarding to talk to clients who have been with us for several years, to find out how happy they are to have used our many years of experience to help them minimize college costs as much as they can. Their biggest benefit is the Bank On Yourself plan.

We have hundreds of incredibly happy clients. Not only do we help people get started with their plans, we are there for them when they have questions—and when they need policy loans, they can work through our office to properly set those up. We have reviews every year to make sure their plan is going as they expected it to, or to possibly change it when that is necessary. This is another important service we are proud to offer.

About Stuart

Stuart Grossman is president of College Funding Systems and Grossman & Associates Financial Services Inc. He has helped hundreds of clients with a wide array of financial services for the last 25+ years.

He grew up in Spokane, graduated from Ferris High School, and earned a degree in accounting and finance from the University of Washington. Returning home to Spokane after college, he worked in the family business for a number of years before establishing his own financial services practice.

Working in arenas such as college and retirement planning, insurance, and residential lending, Stuart believes that the only sensible financial plan is one that looks at the big picture, crafting a plan in which all the components of your financial life work together to help achieve your goals in a way that is consistent with your values.

After a lot of research, Stuart began helping clients with college financial aid issues 11 years ago. This service was valuable enough to his clients that he decided seven years ago to expand the reach of his services by conducting workshops. So far, he has conducted more than 200 workshops throughout the western United States with more than 5,000 people in attendance.

Stuart's college consulting services adhere to the same holistic philosophy that he brings to all of his clients. In addition to helping you maximize your financial aid, he can help you craft a strategic plan that can help you pay for college without massive debt and without sacrificing retirement savings. In fact, his goal is to increase your assets at retirement while paying for the best education your children can get.

Stuart makes his home in the Spokane, Washington, where he lives with his wife, Mary Kay (a noted dietician and author), and their children, Brent and Elyssa. Stuart also has two adult sons.

Stuart is the author of *How to Give Your Child a 4-Year College Education Without Going Broke* and is a highly sought-after speaker and media favorite with his insider's secrets on how to legally beat the high cost of college.

For information about upcoming college funding workshops, contact Stuart at (509) 924-9123, or stugrossman@msn.com, or go to www.grossmancollegefunding.com.

CHAPTER 27

PLAYING THE LONG GAME: PAYING LESS TAXES OVER YOUR LIFETIME

BY TREVOR LASTOKA

Naturally you'll want to know how the strategies in this chapter will be able to help you. But first let's get to know each other.

My name is Trevor Lastoka and I have been a CPA since 1991 and involved in the financial services industry ever since. Very early on I specialized in income tax planning and investment analysis. After a number of years I realized that I was tired of sitting in front of a computer for 70 hours a week during tax season. It was time for a change. I had always helped my clients out with investments and insurance and decided to dedicate all of my time to helping people reach their financial goals.

I enjoyed many years of success helping my clients eliminate taxes and save for retirement until the market crash in 2008, when almost everything went down. The fear and panic from this one event made it clear to me that many of my clients were not as comfortable with risk as they said they were.

This led me to take a firm stance on my view of how much risk I feel is acceptable for myself and my clients. I believe you should only have money in the market that you are comfortable losing. So even if you did lose everything you invested in the market, you did not put your retirement at jeopardy. As for everything else that you cannot afford to lose, that money should be in savings vehicles that are guaranteed not to lose money and will provide a secure retirement. By focusing on safety I am helping my clients reach their goals without worrying about the ups and downs of stock and real estate markets.

Obviously, you will recognize as you read on that you will require help in applying the strategies throughout this book. I look forward to meeting you so I can understand your specific situation and what you would like to accomplish. After I have that understanding I can guide you on the path to accomplish your goals. That may be by using strategies that you find in this book or one of the many other strategies that I employ.

REDUCING TAXES AT THE OPTIMAL TIME

One of the best tips I can give you is to change how you look at paying taxes. Most people are focused on paying the least amount of taxes this year and I can understand that. The problem is that approach may actually cause you to pay higher taxes in the future. My mission is to help you focus on paying the least amount of taxes over your lifetime instead of just focusing on this year.

My fellow CPAs are partially to blame for this short-sighted focus on paying taxes. They want to be helpful to you so when you pick up your tax return, they give you free advice to put money into IRAs and 401(k)'s because it reduces your current year taxes. By focusing on the short term, your CPA might feel good because you are happy paying less in taxes this year, but this is only a short-term focus. They are not planning for the long game, which is to pay the least amount of taxes over your lifetime.

Now the mass media also tells you to defer as much income as possible into IRAs and 401(k)'s because you will be in a lower tax bracket when you retire. However, in real life, many people are in the same tax bracket when they retire as when they were working. Many people who are already in low tax brackets follow this generic advice and put the maximum allowable into their IRA or 401(k), which does not make sense! Why would someone choose to avoid paying a low tax now to put their money into a government retirement plan, where they will pay taxes on a potentially larger amount of money in the future at a tax rate that could potentially be much higher.

I am curious. When you and your financial advisor sat down and reviewed how much you will pay in taxes when you withdraw your money from these retirement plans, and how long it will last you, what did you come up with? Hmmm ... you haven't looked at that yet ... I wonder why they haven't talked to you about that. That is something you should know before you stuff money into your IRA or 401(k) plan for another 10 to 20 years.

For the last 10 years we have had the lowest federal tax rates since 1931 and I can't see them going lower during my lifetime. With our national debt in excess of $17 trillion to pay for consistent involvement in foreign wars and entitlement programs with more than $100 trillion in unfunded liabilities, most people would agree that taxes are more likely to be higher in the future. Would you rather pay taxes now, knowing what the rates are, or gamble that rates will be this low in the future?

I've had many clients come to me after contributing for years to a 401(k) or IRA and they want me to help them get their money out without paying taxes. The taxes on their IRA withdrawals were going to crush their retirement income and cause most of their Social Security income to be taxed. In many cases, their 401(k) or IRA is their only savings vehicle. At that point they have painted themselves into a corner and will have to pay the taxes. It never fails; they tell me they figured that taxes would be less in retirement because that is what they were told.

CONTRIBUTING TO 401(K) PLANS AND IRAS

I also see many clients who have faithfully contributed to their 401(k) plans to get the company match while they are paying double digit interest to credit card companies. They have to average more than 25 percent return every year in their 401(k) to equal the after-tax interest they are paying on the credit card debt. If this is your situation, please stop contributing to your 401(k) until you have paid off your credit card debt.

Also keep in mind that the free match you are getting from your company is zero if the markets go down. To ensure you are actually keeping that match it needs to be in the lowest risk option available.

So when should you be contributing to IRAs and 401(k)'s? Here are some things to consider:

1. If you are in the top two highest tax brackets now, are you sure you will be in a lower tax bracket in retirement and have no high interest rate debt?

2. If you are in the lower tax brackets, are you sure you will be in a lower tax bracket in retirement, have no high interest rate debt, can afford to lose that money and have sufficient savings so you will never wish you could get at it before retirement?

Wait a minute, what do I do if I can't say "yes" to those requirements? You need to play the long game and think tax-free growth.

HOW TO GET TAX-FREE RETIREMENT INCOME

There are primarily two ways to get tax-free growth and tax-free retirement income:

Option 1: Roth IRA (the first option is well-known and my least favorite of the two). If you qualify, you can contribute a limited amount each year to a Roth IRA which grows tax free but it has a number of drawbacks, as well:

- You have as much chance of losing money as growing it if you have your Roth invested in the stock market;

- The growth has to stay in the Roth for five years from starting your first Roth or until age 59 ½, whichever is longer;

- You cannot put back any principal that you take out;

- The 2013 income restrictions eliminate this as an option for singles folks earning more than $127,000 and married couples earning more than $188,000; and

- The Roth can only be a partial solution for most people because of its 2013 annual contribution limits of $5,500 for people under age 50 and $6,500 for those age 50 and over.

Option 2: The specially designed, dividend-paying whole-life insurance policy

This is my favorite option, made popular by the national bestselling book Bank On Yourself by Pamela Yellen—but it is not for everyone.

Not everyone can qualify or has the discipline to save consistently and pay back their loans. A small sample of the benefits for those who do qualify is the ability to:

- Set your own maximum annual contribution limit based on your personal financial situation;

- Have contractually guaranteed growth every year that is locked in and backed by the claims-paying ability of insurance companies that are rated A or better;

- Have access to your money through policy loans without impacting the growth of your policy; and

- Make this a complete solution for most to get tax-free growth, as there are no income restrictions to participate.

As a business owner, I have many of the same savings and cash flow issues and concerns that everyone faces. If I leave my savings in the bank, I earn almost nothing and I am not keeping up with inflation. If I invest in the market I run the risk that the market is down and I lose money just when I need to use it to grow my business. I don't know about you but I don't like to lose any of the money I worked for. I know many of my clients feel the same way, which is what led me to find a solution.

In 2006, I was introduced to the Bank On Yourself concept and Pamela Yellen. I was skeptical at first because some claims sounded too good to be true. I spent a good part of a year learning the concept as I took the training to become an authorized Bank On Yourself advisor. During this training, all of my questions were answered. It was like any education …you don't know what you don't know until you learn it. I have been using Bank On Yourself-type whole-life insurance as my primary savings vehicle ever since. I have also used this concept to help hundreds of my clients safely grow their wealth, and eliminate banks and Mr. Market from their lives.

Some of my favorite client stories use this concept hand-in-hand with college planning for their families. But since I know my good friend Stuart Grossman is dedicating his chapter in this book to college planning, I will not duplicate his efforts. Instead, I would like to share a story about a business owner I work with and his wife.

A CASE STUDY

I met Bryan and Stacy in 2004. Bryan was at a place in his life where he was paying off school loans, having kids, and figuring out how he could buy his own medical practice. At that time, I helped him with an affordable term life insurance policy to protect his expanding family.

Over the next few years Bryan was able to get financing to purchase his own practice and in 2007, he started his first Bank On Yourself policy on his wife, Stacy. At the time, he did not have any insurance on Stacy but the main purpose of the policy was to create a safe place to grow his savings and still have it liquid. He wanted to be able to borrow from the policy for business purposes, if needed, and down the road use it to finance college for his kids.

The first three years Bryan had his first Bank On Yourself-type policy, he did not put the maximum possible into it. In fact, he just paid the minimum premium and a little extra into the paid up additions rider. This is a little unusual because most of my clients put in the maximum amount possible each year so their policy is growing at the maximum possible rate. But Bryan was planning for the future and knew he would be able to put the money in later. So each year, I would remind him that he should try to put more into his policy to get it growing at its maximum possible rate.

Starting in the fourth year, Bryan was able to start putting the maximum annual premium into his policy. Two years later, he was able to put in a large lump sum to catch up the first three years that he did not put in the maximum. In another year he told me that he wished he would have started his policy 20 years ago, which led him to thinking about his kids and their futures. He asked me if it made sense to get policies started for them now. Bryan did not plan to use those policies for himself but to get these in place so his children will never have to go to a bank for a loan.

We went over how his kids can really take advantage of the power of compounding by starting policies for them as early as possible. I told Bryan that he could be the owner of the policies until he decided to transfer ownership to his kids. That could be at age 18 or later depending on when he felt they were financially ready and responsible.

Bryan started policies on each of his kids and put the maximum premium into each of those, as well. But a year later he needed to reduce the premiums down to just above the minimums on all his policies because he was having business problems. He was sure glad he had that flexibility with his policies.

In 2012, Bryan had resolved his business problems and entered into a new business partnership. Now it was time to get something in place to fund Bryan's retirement and also get buy-sell agreements in place for the partnership. After several conversations, it was clear that the next step was to apply for a policy to fund Bryan's retirement and also have money available to fund his business financing needs. Together, Bryan and I are looking at business continuation planning in 2013. While he has come a long way since 2004, we have many more things to do together to accomplish all of his goals.

This is just one example of my client stories, but I have hundreds more and everybody's story is very different.

I sincerely hope I've led you in the direction of understanding the long game, and there's more understanding still that I'm sure that you might like. Because the strategies that we have shared in this book represent only a small sample of the strategies I use. So as I finish, now would be a great time to find a time that we could talk, get any additional questions answered and help you on your path to accomplishing what you really need and want.

About Trevor

Trevor Lastoka is a bestselling author and is regularly sought out by the media for his opinions on tax reduction strategies and college planning. He has helped more than 530 clients grow their wealth, reduce their taxes and achieve their dreams of financial security. He has put his clients on track to building more than $210 million of additional wealth they would most likely not had otherwise using safe, proven financial strategies.

One of only 200 life insurance agents in the country who have successfully completed the rigorous training program and continuing education required to become a Bank On Yourself authorized advisor, Trevor is a certified public accountant and personal financial specialist. He also is a registered representative and offers securities and investment advisory services through Berthel Fisher & Company Financial Services Inc. (member FINRA/SIPC).

Trevor lives in the Minneapolis/St. Paul area with his wife, Jennifer, and their children, Grace and Tyler. When he not working, you may find him playing with his kids, golfing, fly fishing and pheasant hunting.

Trevor is also active in the community, including attending New Hope Church and supporting Faith Search International. He can be reached at (877) 207-6350.

CHAPTER 28

TAPPED OUT AND DISCOURAGED? TRY SOMETHING DIFFERENT

BY TERESA KUHN JD RFC CSA

"Money frees you from doing things you dislike.
Since I dislike doing nearly everything, money is handy."
~ Groucho Marx

A study published in 2013 by the Employee Benefit Research Institute indicated that a record 28 percent of respondents had little to no confidence in ever being able to retire.

Job insecurity, inflation, tax increases and continued high levels of debt are just a few of the legitimate concerns that keep Americans from saving for the second half of their lives.

Another contributing factor is that the same money strategies that might have worked in the past, albeit often in a hit-and-miss fashion, simply aren't viable in this new age of economic flux. The evidence of this failure is hard to ignore—it's literally all around us.

I'd like to suggest that it's time to move on from conventional financial advice that has not served you well in the last few years and acquire a more contrarian approach to protecting and growing your wealth. If you're like most people, you've been content to let your CPA, financial advisor, banker or broker handle the details of your financial future, relying on your monthly statements or an occasional phone call from the advisor. And maybe you've augmented that with some iffy advice from one of the financial entertainment television shows or a newspaper column or two.

I am going to be so bold as to suggest that you need to change your money habits now, or risk being unprepared for what lies ahead. In the future, I believe that you'll find that more and more of life's big decisions—decisions about everything from how to protect your cash to how to handle your health care—will land squarely in your lap. You need to be prepared to take a more informed and proactive role in those decisions.

Is what you've always done working out as you expected? Are you where you want to be in life right now? Are you satisfied that you have done all you can do to ensure that you and your family have the best possible futures?

If the answer is "no" to any of those questions, then you must consider what I am about to tell you very carefully. It might run contrary to everything you think you know about money, but it might also be just what you need to hear in order to avoid making mistakes with your money from which you can never recover.

MYTH CONNECTIONS: HOW WHAT YOU THOUGHT YOU KNEW ABOUT MONEY IS ALL WRONG

In an attempt to wring one last breath of truth out of a very tired cliché, I would like to propose that you think about building your house on a solid foundation. I know, I know. You've heard it before—at church, from a relative, maybe even in school or at work.

However, truth is truth and there is no way to deny the power of a solid foundation for your financial future.

I work with a diverse client base with people in many different phases of building their own personal economies. Yet, even if I am dealing with my richest, most money-savvy clients, I always have them begin with a stable, secure mechanism for managing cash flow. For me, using specially designed, "turbo-charged" life insurance policies is the ultimate way to achieve steady growth while staving off the erosive forces that destroy wealth.

Having such as means of securing cash in place ensures that, should clients decide they want to take advantage of real investment opportunities, they can do so with greater peace of mind.

I'm often asked why, if my methodology is so effective and so much safer than exposing one's nest egg to banks and Wall Street, more people aren't taking advantage of it. The biggest barrier, I think, is the lack of financial education in our country. Most Americans aren't told the truth about money, especially when they are young. We aren't made aware that money is organic, that it is susceptible to erosion from forces over which we exercise little to no control. They don't call it a "nest rock," but rather a "nest egg."

Imagine you had a big box of rocks. You take those rocks to a secret location, bury them, and then return years later to collect them. What would you find when you opened that box? Rocks—still in the same condition as when you left them.

If, on the other hand, you buried a box of eggs and then, 10 years later, you went to retrieve them, what would you have? Reeking globs of organic matter that barely resembles the original eggs!

The reason for that transformation, of course, is that outside forces, such as heat, rain and the chemical makeup of the eggs themselves, have combined to transform them into something else; something we'll never be able to use. There's a reason eggs have expiration dates stamped on the carton.

Money, too, has its own version of an expiration date. While you don't actually see it printed on currency or advertised in the news, the idea that money expires becomes apparent when we don't make good money choices; when opportunities are lost or the high price of financial ignorance, or what I call the "dumb tax," must be paid.

Money only stays fresh so long. You have a limited window of opportunity after it is earned to put into place sound strategies that will help it grow safely, without exposure to risk, unnecessary taxes and other erosive elements. That's why getting a good financial education is one of the best things you can do to protect your future.

In the United States (and probably elsewhere as well), people certainly aren't given much direction as to what to do with money—how to grow it in a safe, steady and sane manner.

The results of this lack of education become apparent later in life when we are earning our own money and making our own financial decisions. This is the time when we fall prey to what I call "whizzdumb"—information doled out by our friends, family and the financial entertainment industry that isn't very wise at all.

We also watch television programs and read books that tell us things like "no pain no gains." Or "You have to put all your money on Wall Street to get ahead." We learn that permanent life insurance is bad and that we should always buy term and invest the difference. Slick marketing campaigns have many convinced that they must always court risk to make gains, and turn to our friends, the bankers, when we need a loan or a safe place to put our cash.

There are dozens and dozens of money myths that I could debunk. Due to space limitations, however, I want to focus on just a couple of the most persistent and pernicious of those myths.

1. ALL YOU NEED TO DO TO RETIRE IS TO FULLY FUND YOUR 401(K).

When the current economic crisis hit, millions of ordinary Americans saw their so-called safe and secure 401(k) accounts losing hundreds, sometimes thousands of dollars.

Unfortunately, a lot of those people were at or near retirement and had little time to recoup that lost money. Those same people also discovered another dirty secret: Many 401(k) plans contain hidden, but very costly fees that some financial advisors fail to take into account when designing plans for their clients.

If you are one of the rare people who actually read your monthly statement, the fees may not seem significant enough to cause worry. However, just 1 percent in excessive fees can hurt you ... big time! To further compound the problem, there are many plans where the fee is charged based on a percentage of your balance. This means that becoming a diligent saver actually hurts you.

What if there was something you could do to help you avoid paying unnecessary fees and help you get back some of the thousands of dollars you've been giving away simply because you don't know the alternatives? Would knowing this information help you reach your goal of having a safe, prosperous retirement?

I believe it would.

That's why I sponsor webinars and workshops to educate ordinary people on how they can become their own sources of financing for major purchases, business expansion, college tuition, etc. Using a simple but effective system, you can accumulate wealth more quickly and safely than you ever thought possible, and accelerate the process of getting out of debt.

Bad advice and myths share something in common: When either of them is repeated often enough and by the right people, they become so ingrained in a culture that anyone challenging them is seen as a virtual heretic. In the world of personal finance, as in other areas of life, myths can do a lot of damage, causing people to make decisions that, given the right information, they would never ordinarily choose to make.

Another one of the most common, and in my opinion, worst pieces of financial advice I have heard over the years is the venerable and oft-repeated mantra:

2. BUY TERM LIFE INSURANCE AND INVEST THE DIFFERENCE.

You've heard it on TV from those talking head financial gurus. Or maybe it was your mom or dad, looking stern and waggling a finger in your direction as they repeated it to you. Your significant other swears that "Warren Buffett does it this way." Your hair stylist, auto mechanic, the guy down at the grocery store, are all true believers in the idea that buying term and investing on Wall Street is the way to achieve financial security.

Buy term insurance and invest the difference sounds logical, doesn't it? However, when you dig a little deeper, you'll find issues that buy term and invest the difference doesn't address. For example:

• Most of the term policies advocated by financial "experts" do not increase the death benefit level during the policy term. This means there is no remedy for inflation. (And I believe that inflation is bound to be much higher in the future!)

Pamela Yellen, best-selling author of *Bank On Yourself*, did the math and she figured it out: A $250,000 20-year term policy, adjusted for 4 percent inflation, will have lost 56 percent of its value! Even policies that include an increasing benefits rider may not increase at a rate that will overcome the erosive effects of inflation.

• What if you lose your health during your insurance term? Some term policies are written such that if your health deteriorates during the policy term, your renewal rates increase. If you don't renew and try to seek coverage elsewhere, you might discover that you are uninsurable—at any price.

• You can invest the difference easily enough, but you can't time the market or accurately predict how much money will be in your account when it comes time to retire.

No one can possibly know the future, which, according to Barry Dyke, best-selling author of *Pirates of Manhattan,* is one reason that Wall Street investing is so risky and usually ends up losing you money.

With the types of accounts I design for my clients, they always know exactly how much they have at any given time, which is absolutely crucial to planning one's financial future accurately.

My clients don't have to worry about timing the ups and downs of the stock market and they have access to their money, when they need it.

• Buy term and invest the difference advocates usually know nothing about the specially-designed whole-life policies I use to structure my financial plans.

The reason for this is that these policies are only written by a few select companies and have special provisions which are unlike those of traditional whole life insurance policies. Any advisor who assists his or her clients with this type of specialized policy must have thorough training and must also be willing to forego the usual high commissions on whole-life in order to make the plan work for his or her clients.

Thus, policies used for becoming your own personal financing source are far beyond regular whole-life policies in both complexity and purpose.

- Most financial gurus fail to factor in the tremendous amount of money saved on interest and fees that result from implementing this type of plan.

By financing your large purchases (for example, your car) yourself, the interest you pay ultimately benefits you, as a policy owner. And there are no added-on fees—all fees are already taken into account in the premium you pay. (My clients love this!)

Now, just for the record...I believe that everyone who can afford to do so should have as much life insurance as possible. Term is a great way to get more coverage for less money and if you can get term, you should have it. However, the primary reason for getting one of the specially-designed whole-life policies has little to do with the death benefit. Instead, the idea behind these policies is to provide you with a savings and cash management vehicle that gives you growth, stability and safety, in sharp contrast to the ups and downs of the stock market.

Also, when you use the money in your policy to make major purchases, it can continue to grow as though you hadn't touched a dime of it. Only certain companies offer this feature, and I put my clients' policies with those companies. The permanent insurance you also get is just icing on the cake.

You can find out more about how to avoid paying too much money to banks and finance companies. There are lots more financial myths that threaten your savings. Do your own research and take action.

About Teresa

If you want to achieve steady, safe growth with your money but aren't sure how to do so, then you need to start a conversation with Teresa Kuhn.

A respected financial educator, radio show host, and strategist, Teresa is the president and CEO of Austin, Texas-based Living Wealthy Financial Group. Her passion is telling people the real truth about how money works and showing them how they can avoid exposing their wealth to eroding factors such as taxes, inflation, and Wall Street losses.

Using a powerful, proven blueprint, Teresa and her team have counseled hundreds of ordinary Americans across the nation, helping them preserve and protect their life's savings. Clients find her holistic approach to finances refreshing, positive and effective.

Business owner Larry Smith says: "Since working with Teresa and discovering Bank On Yourself, I now have control over my own money and don't have to stress about getting approved by banks when I want or need a loan. Bank On Yourself works and Teresa Kuhn ensures that it will continue to do so for me and my family in the years to come."

Austin photographer Kate Caudillo, a long-time Living Wealthy Financial client, appreciates having Teresa provide guidance for her personal and business financial choices. "Her vigilance and thoroughness, combined with her genuine concern for her clients, gives me the confidence I need to make the right decisions with my money," Kate says. "I know I only have one shot at getting my financial future on track. Knowing this, I am glad that I have someone like Teresa on my side, providing the guidance I need to make the right financial choices."

After graduating with degrees in finance and law, Teresa became a registered financial consultant and certified senior advisor. She is a member of the National Association of Insurance and Financial Advisors and the Financial Planning Association. She is also the past president of the Jackson Township Rotary Club (first female and youngest person to hold that position) and a graduate of Leadership Stark County.

To maintain the high quality of the customer experience she provides at Living Wealthy Financial, Teresa devotes herself to keeping abreast of changes in the financial landscape and connecting with any clients who are committed to doing what it takes to achieve true financial peace.

Contact her office today at (800) 382-0830, or email her at tkuhn@ livingwealthyfinancial.com to discover how Teresa and her team of experts can help you meet and exceed your financial goals.

CHAPTER 29

SERVING TWO MASTERS:
Making Sense of Sane Living in a Crazy World and Gaining Real Wealth Along the Way

BY MARK WILLIS

"Don't think money does everything or you are going to end up doing everything for money."
~Voltaire

Your brain is an amazing thing. It does an incredibly complex physics calculation every time you apply the brakes at a stop sign. It knows the emotions of another person simply by looking at micro-expressions on his or her face. Your brain, the three-pound knot of neurons in your head, can contemplate the most complex financial statements or consider the infinite vastness of the universe…but it all depends on how you think.

In the following pages, I will reveal to you the true secret to lifetime financial security—and wrapping your brain around this secret will not only make you more productive, joyful and more generous; it will bring real wealth to you and your family.

MY STORY

As a child, I'd joyfully drop my small allowance of coins and dollar bills into a crumpled paper bag. When I reached $50, my parents rewarded me by opening a savings account. I've never liked banks nor did I like parting with my hard-earned cash. It didn't seem right. It seemed like the adults were in a scheme to pull a fast one over on me. Looking back, those early instincts weren't that far from the truth.

Creativity and entrepreneurialism were the name of the game growing up. My parents taught me in a Christian context, so my faith impacted my view of finance and business. At first glance, Wall Street and the "Streets of Gold" may seem worlds apart, but in fact, all world religions deal with the topic of finance. More on this in a bit…

Student debt dominated my late teens and twenties. I laugh when I remember signing my first promissory note in a dim, dirty hotel room near campus before my freshman year. It was just like that moment from childhood when I handed that bag of coins over to the banker, only this time it was to a woman named Sallie Mae.

Thankfully, Sallie Mae was not the only woman I met at college. I married my beautiful bride, Katrina, and we began our life together. What we wanted out of life was simple: to love each other; to live with integrity; to live in community with others; and perhaps most of all, to live sanely in an insane world. Sounds nice, but I was already wed to another woman that wanted nothing to do with those values—and now Sallie Mae wanted a place in our marriage. Our six figures worth of student debt felt more like a mortgage payment, and we began to severely delay other financial goals. Would we ever break free? We were at a point of despair, but we discovered several important financial strategies I'll soon reveal that changed everything…

THE INSANITY

The more I hear stories of clients, friends and family, the more I realize our case is not unique. The system is rigged. Like Neo in the movie "The Matrix," we've spent our entire lives in an artificial media lifestyle that begs us to focus on all the wrong things–all of the unimportant things. Buy a bigger house! Chase that rate of return! Keep up with the Jones! George Fooshee, in his book *You Can Beat the Money Squeeze*, says it best: "People buy things they don't need with money they don't have to impress people they don't even like."

The following infographic depicts spending patterns through life stages. Notice how spending tends to eclipse income. Many people *appear* to have a luxurious lifestyle, but when we look at the numbers, they are living on more than they make—they are choosing debt regardless of income. This is true for people who have an annual income of $30,000, and it also is true for people living on $300,000. Consider the emotional states listed below that accompany the "Artificial Media Lifestyle."

ARTIFICIAL MEDIA LIFESTYLE

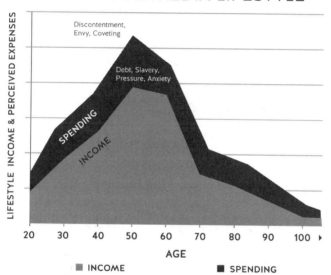

In addition to the temptations to live beyond our means, baby boomers specifically are now specifically being called the sandwich generation. Sandwiched between these two stressors:

1. college-bound children and

2. aging parents in need of major financial assistance

They're handling these responsibilities at the same time. Maybe that's why the *Los Angeles Times* recently reported that 25 percent of Americans are now raiding their 401(k)'s to pay bills, with those in their 40s being the biggest perpetrators. The future? Forty-five percent of baby boomers are expected not to have enough money to cover basic living expenses at retirement.

This insanity applies to people of all ages. Banks on average siphon 34.5 percent of your income without you even knowing it (see "If Time Is Money," below). They use this wonderful, terrible tool called "interest." As I teach my clients, those who understand interest will continually collect it, but those who don't understand interest will be doomed to pay it forever.

TIME AND THE BIG PICTURE

Banks understand interest, and for hundreds of years, they've maximized profits with interest. Imagine, for at least one third of your day, you're working for your creditors. Add Uncle Sam into the equation, and we may be looking at half of your hard-earned money disappearing before you can get a word in edgewise.

To see if the following infographic applies to you, answer the following:

- Do you use credit cards?
- Do you lease or finance a car(s)?
- Do you have other outstanding loans with compounding interest?

Who are you really working for? Yourself? No... Could cutting out these parasites on your finances be good for your budget? Your family? Your sanity? Yes!

IF "TIME IS MONEY"

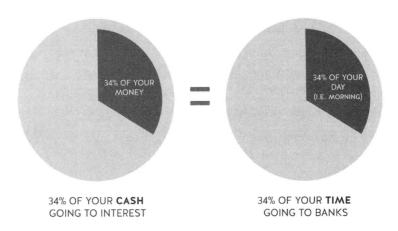

34% OF YOUR **CASH** GOING TO INTEREST

34% OF YOUR **TIME** GOING TO BANKS

HOW YOU MANAGE YOUR MONEY **DIRECTLY AFFECTS** HOW YOU SPEND YOUR TIME.

Wait a minute! What about paying cash directly rather than going into debt? Some people happily tell me that they are debt-free and pay cash for everything. While this is commendable, I have one more question most people overlook: Do you pay cash for big-ticket items, thereby losing interest you *could have earned* on your money had you invested it instead?

Let's zoom out for a moment. Imagine you're an alien dropping in on our planet, and you're observing our global financial system, where the elite banks and governments were collecting and hoarding the vast wealth of the many. Looks dramatic, right? Is this world mad? This system of financial insanity makes sense for those pulling the strings, but for the majority, we're just left with sense that the cards are stacked against us.

Is there any hope? Yes! What I am about to tell you is the closely-guarded secret to a lifetime of financial security, the key to unlocking the rigged system and breaking free from the insanity of our financial rat race.

THE SECRET TO FINANCIAL SECURITY

Money is first and foremost a spiritual force, only then is it a financial tool. No human can avoid that basic fact. Money doesn't care what religion you subscribe to—it wants the rights to your heart and mind. Spiritual gurus agree: we must let money serve us, not the other way around. It is written in the Talmud: "He who loves money will not be satisfied with money." Jesus is quoted as saying, "Wherever your treasure is, there the desires of your heart will also be." Even Lao Tzu says, "If you are content, you will always have enough." While I will soon be moving into some very practical financial strategies that earn real wealth, having the right financial product, a cushy income or the best financial advisor in the world is not the secret secret to lifetime financial security—it is thinking right about money as a spiritual force that makes all the difference.

When you're thinking right about money, your eyes are open to creative strategies, applications and approaches to finance. What you seek, you will find. If you take one thing from these pages, get this: Practice financial sanity—you will be more productive, more joyful and more generous. Live your values and you will increase your well-being.

FINANCIAL SANITY

The Jews have this wonderful practice called Sabbath. It is not about collapsing in a heap of exhaustion at the end of the week. Sabbath is about sane living, a rare commodity in our culture these days. Sabbath and financial sanity helps scale priorities in your life to their appropriate size. But for most of us, we're barely hanging on by our fingernails. Do not say to yourself, "I will out earn my spending habits," but rather, "In all things I will seek financial sanity." Let's review three exciting examples of how my clients are doing just that.

SANE AND GENEROUS HEALTH CARE

For 2012, annual premiums for employer-sponsored family health coverage reached $15,745, and since 2002, premiums have risen 92 percent. If you're not sick before you get health insurance, your bill alone is likely to put you in the emergency room. We have a broken health insurance system–there's no use in putting new wheels on a totaled vehicle. We need bold new solutions to traditional health insurance, with financial sanity in mind.

Solution #1: Health Care Sharing Programs: Rather than paying massive premiums to a for-profit company (whose best interests do they really hold?), let's cut out the profiteers and through a nonprofit, faith-based cooperative we can simply bear one another's (medical) burdens. Each month, my wife and I get a letter from the Health Co-Op letting us know that another member in the co-op has a medical need. This month, we paid our share to a family in Indiana who was paying for the father's gallbladder surgery. When we have a medical need, checks come pouring in from all over the United States to pay our bill. Additionally, the non-profit also offers an advocate to negotiate down the price of the hospital bill for us, so we can focus on getting well. Those who send us checks are encouraged to pray for us, which we joyfully welcome. This makes paying for health care more affordable and a spiritually meaningful act. Oh, and did I mention the monthly amount is 66 percent less expensive than comparable health insurance plans? So what would you do with all that saved money?

Solution #2: Bank On Yourself: What if you could become your own source of financing? At Lake Growth Financial Services, we specialize in working with people who want to create wealth like banks do, in a safe and predictable way. We wean folks off banks by recapturing all of the interest they throw away on student loans, mortgages, car finance companies and credit cards.

PRODUCTIVE, PEACE-OF-MIND BANKING

Being debt free is fine, but let me ask you: What do you get when you pay off debts directly? Just a pile of receipts! What if instead, you could pay off your debts and still have your money to earn interest for you? That's what the little-known financial strategy "Bank On Yourself" is all about. You don't have to be a billionaire to be your own banker. You just need the right chassis. We put it in a 160-year-old financial vehicle that has increased in value during every market crash, and every period of boom and bust–a custom-designed, dividend-paying whole-life insurance policy. Here's how it works:

- First, money grows at an incredible speed for life insurance, beating out ordinary whole- life insurance by a long shot, and over a reasonable period of time, outpacing most stock market portfolios.

- Second, the gains are guaranteed and protected from market fluctuations.

- Third, you can access money whenever without penalty or taxes due, and use the money without government restrictions at retirement.

- Finally and perhaps most amazing, you can use your money for whatever, and the money continues earning interest on the capital you borrow.

Only a handful of insurance companies offer this, and they are the only kind I trust for my practice. It is crucially important that these plans are built correctly and by a planner who knows what he or she is doing. At Lake Growth, we have passed the rigorous requirements Bank On Yourself advisors have to go through. In addition to building your ship to spec, we offer continual, free coaching to clients regarding the growth in their plan, and we teach how to use it to make purchases, so they can leave their old banker in the dust.

FINANCIALLY SANE EDUCATION

For my wife and I and many of my clients, as it is with hundreds of thousands around the country, we have become our own student loan company to ourselves, and now interest is flowing to us, rather than away from us.

FINANCIAL HOPES AND DREAMS

Clients come to me with new ideas and sane applications on their particular financial journey. I sit down with them in an advisory role and build a free, personalized plan just for them. Here are some of the ways these sane strategies are working for them. How might this look for you?

1. Building an emergency fund to cover any unexpected expense

2. Recouping the cost spent on the down payment for a house

3. Paying for your child's college and avoiding restrictions of the 529 and ESA, as well as keeping under the FAFSA's radar

4. Purchasing your cars and family vacations without guilt or loss of interest

5. Expanding your business and offering compelling and generous employee benefit plans

6. Planning for retirement

7. Generously leaving a legacy that will last for generations to come

When you recapture interest given to banks and write health insurance companies out of your expenses, you build incredible wealth—not just of dollars and cents, but sanity and time, too. All of a sudden, the 80-hour work week begins to look more like 40 or 30 or less. Maybe your spouse can quit his or her job, and both of you will have more time with the kids (or parents). Maybe you can allot more time to pursue your passions. When you've left the rat race and have taken control of your money (instead of letting it control you), you can truly give generously, out of your abundance.

Solution #3: Radical Generosity: Giving generously is a goal for many. This is a simple twist on the strategy mentioned above, which is offering many of my clients the satisfaction that they are leaving a legacy that will last. Microfinance is a relatively new term, but it offers great promise for good in the world when designed correctly. Increasingly, lenders give reasonable loans in small measures to an entrepreneur in another country. We see this with women and men in India, Asia, Africa and South America who are starting small businesses at unprecedented rates through the generosity of micro-financing. Sanely, you could "recycle" giving through your Bank On Yourself plan we've set up together to give generously, and your pool of reserves would never diminish; it would only grow through the guarantees in the contract. Micro-financing provides an opportunity to literally change the world– you're rescuing others from poverty and loan sharks, both domestic and international. We've seen people set free from the predatory bonds of checks cashed and payday loan establishments within the United States, too. Imagine all of the practical applications of radical generosity. The potential is endless.

FINANCIAL LENSES

Unfortunately, for most Americans, our finances are on autopilot. We've lost our capacity to dream big, hope big hopes and think critically about the system and how our money flows through it. We need a new perspective—new lenses to see the spiritual power of money in our lives, and then use that power for good. We don't need to be stressed out, insane, angry and confused. First, figure out what you value most, and then structure your financial strategy around those values. Remember: Like a telescope, money amplifies. If you are a jerk, boatloads of money will amplify the fact that you're a really big jerk! If you're an ethical person and you manage lots of money, you will accomplish great good in the world.

FINANCIAL WELL-BEING

Let's dream big and think critically about money. Today's economic climate demands more than ever from families, small business owners and investors. It is clear that many of yesterday's strategies are not sufficient for the future. We need fresh approaches to obstacles like retirement, college planning, starting a business and your dream. All it takes is faith and using that 3 pound knot of neurons in our heads. Practice financial sanity—you will be more productive, more joyful and more generous. Live your values and you will increase your well being.

About Mark

Mark Willis is a financial advisor and owner of Lake Growth Financial Services. As a leading expert in the field, Mark has helped hundreds of clients take back control of their financial future. Seen by those he works with as "the safe money guy," Mark helps protect his clients from the volatility of the markets, so they have the financial peace they deserve. Mark's interest in the intersection of spirituality and finance brings a unique perspective toward his financial planning practice.

Mark is married to the brilliant and beautiful Katrina Willis. He enjoys swimming, running and a friendly game of softball when he gets the chance. He plucks around on his mandolin, and you might even catch him cycling with friends around Chicagoland.

CHAPTER 30

DON'T BE A PRISONER OF HOPE

BY MARVIN WITTROCK

"I hope I have enough money when I get ready to retire."

"I hope my stocks will really start to do better."

"I hope this investment will turn out like it was predicted."

"I hope the real estate market will bounce back."

Webster's Dictionary defines hope as a "feeling that what is wanted will happen; desire accompanied by anticipation or expectation."

However, while growing up on a family farm in western Iowa as the oldest of nine kids, I learned at a very early age that hope was not the answer. If you wanted something to happen, you had to work to make it happen. Desiring or hoping for an outcome just didn't cut it. I had to have a plan, take action and see it through.

Chores like milking cows, feeding livestock, baling hay and driving a tractor at the age of nine shaped my foundation in life along with the love and support of my parents. This followed me through my school years, wrestling in high school, and six years in the U.S. Navy. After college I began working in agricultural sales. It did not take too many years to figure out that a change was needed. I started my insurance business.

No matter what part of my life I look back on, I have always held the philosophy that "What you see is what you get" when it comes to dealing with me. I just am myself and that's all I know how to be. I know that honesty is the best policy in all circumstances. I learned to listen to people and ask questions. I am not afraid to say I don't know an answer, but I will find the answer. I knew that if I helped enough people get what they want, I would get what I want. And I planned to have fun while I was doing that.

Ten years ago I began working with Pamela Yellen and started with Bank On Yourself. My personal philosophy fit in with them like a hand in a glove:

- Honesty

- Listening to what a client wants to accomplish

- Forming a plan of action

- Working as a team to reach their goals

As I have worked with clients looking at their financial futures, it becomes apparent that there are five common "hopes" people tell themselves:

1. Hoping that retirement will turn out OK

2. Hoping that the interest they are paying keeping their lifestyle going isn't sucking the life out of their income

3. Hoping their 401(k) is doing better than they think it is

4. Hoping their employer-matching dollars in their retirement plan is a good deal

5. Hoping that the stock market will bounce back by the time they retire

Now don't get me wrong. There is definitely a place for hope in our lives, but not when it comes to planning our financial futures.

With Bank On Yourself, we are able to look at the current financial picture of a person, talk about what they want to accomplish, and then put a personalized solution together to get where they want to be. This is a true, actual plan—not a wish or a hope that it will work out. We use companies that have been in business for more than 100 years and can document their successful growth. I can honestly say I own these same policies, my children own these policies, and my brothers and sisters own these policies. So when I sit down to discuss with my potential clients what their options are, I have every confidence to assure them this is what I do; I know it is best for them, also.

It is my job, my responsibility to give everyone I work with the best advice. I do not take this lightly. For the last 10 years I have taken advantage of any training provided to ensure that I represent Bank On Yourself to the best of my ability. The challenge to find out what a client wants to accomplish and then being able to recommend a plan to accomplish it is what keeps me loving what I do.

Let me share a story about Sam and Jean. When I got their information and saw that Sam was 82 years old, I wasn't sure how he would qualify with life insurance underwriting. But I have learned not to prejudge and reasoned that maybe I could help them in some way. I met them in their home and as we talked at the kitchen table, it was clear that 82-year-old Sam was indeed healthy. He also was looking for a better place to put his money than where it was sitting in CDs. He was getting very little return on his dollars and he knew better than to just hope that it would change.

While we visited I was able to go through a fact and feeling questionnaire with Sam and Jean. It is important to take the guesswork out of the equation. It also is important to listen to the clients to see what their goals are and what they want to accomplish. By completing this questionnaire, I learned that their house was paid for. So I brought the idea of a reverse mortgage to the table. This allowed them to use the equity in their home. They have a guarantee that they can live in their home. The mortgage company paid them a lump sum of money which we combined with the cashed-out CDs to purchase a Bank On Yourself for Seniors whole-life policy.

This accomplished several benefits. Sam knows his death benefit will provide for Jean. He has the cash value that he can take loans out of with no hassle. There is also growth in both the death benefit and the loan value. This became a win-win for everyone.

Most people don't even realize that they are becoming prisoners of hope. It usually comes on gradually. We get so busy with our day-to-day lives. We fall into the trap of living beyond our means. The banks and financial institutions are eager to loan money to us. Credit cards are readily available with great promotions of no- or low-interest for a time, or points to buy plane tickets, or cash back to buy tanks of gasoline. We think we'll get an income tax return that we can apply to our debt or a raise at work will be used to pay our debt. Radio advertisements tell us gold is the best place to put our money—even though gold prices rise and fall like the stock market with no guarantees. Somewhat famous financial people spout buy term life insurance and invest the difference. Even hiding your hard-earned dollars under your mattress stops any chance of growth on those dollars. Hoping you win the lottery or hit it big on the slot machines are just money games based on luck. But life happens and pretty soon we are looking at a mound of debt and statistics say that 34 percent of our income goes to interest. The retirement picture looks very scary.

The people that I work with want to stop this cycle of hoping their financial picture will turn out well. They want to find a way to purchase big ticket items like a house or a car or a college education for their kids and pocket every penny of interest they now pay to banks, credit cards, and finance companies. They want to be in charge of their own finances instead of being slaves to a bank or financial institution that holds their money and loans. They want to cut up their credit cards. They want control of their own destiny. They are really looking at retirement and being able to keep their present lifestyle as they reach their golden years. They are looking for a steady, predictable income for as long as they live. They know hope is not the answer.

As a Bank On Yourself advisor, I have had the privilege of being in homes all around Iowa. I find meeting face-to-face suits me. People like to know who they are working with. Like I said earlier, "What you see is what you get." That is exactly how I approached Dr. Tom and his wife, Cheryl. Both in their mid-50s, Tom and Cheryl each owned their own business. As many small business owners know, it often takes several years to get a business up and running and making a good profit. That is what Tom and Cheryl were facing as they really began thinking about retirement. While building a business, they had neglected to build a retirement fund. After all, there is only so much money and they chose to pour everything back into their businesses.

Then some good friends of theirs, who already were my clients, suggested Tom and Cheryl call me. As soon as I talked to them I sent them to the website www.findoutmorenow.com (passcode MW85). That showed some real interest on their part and gave them some basic information on the concept. Our first appointment was to gather information on the fact and feeling questionnaire. It is essential to find out what they want to accomplish. As an advisor, I had to find out what their problems were and then we could work to find solutions.

No two cases are the same. Unlike many insurance agents, I don't come to the client with policies I want to sell them. My approach is, "Let's see where you are at and where do you want to go." Then with Bank On Yourself specialized software, we customize an overfunded whole- life policy to meet clients' needs. The results are amazing.

Tom and Cheryl are relieved now to have a plan for retirement income that is very workable. They know the dollars going into their overfunded whole-life policies will have growth, both on the cash value and the death benefit. This is guaranteed. Think about that! There is a $100,000 Challenge at www.bankonyourself.com/challenge that anyone can take to compare their best investment or savings strategy with what we do. This showcases 18 advantages and guarantees of our Bank On Yourself solution to growing your wealth.

I don't hope, I know there are many stories I could recount from over the past 10 years since I've had the privilege of working with Bank On Yourself and partnering with Pamela Yellen. The satisfaction and enjoyment of working with people to give them solid, guaranteed solutions to their financial plans and giving them peace of mind is immeasurable. To be able to bring to the table safe ways for growing wealth and reaching dreams, makes for a calling that fits me to a tee. Knowing I can help people and still have fun doing it honestly and with confidence that it is the right way–well, it just doesn't get any better than that.

About Marvin

Marvin A. Wittrock, a Bank On Yourself authorized advisor, and owner of Wittrock Enterprises (www.wittrockenterprises.com), started in the insurance field in 1990. Then working with health/disability/life insurance, he always kept an open mind searching for new and intriguing options. In 2003, after reading a book by Nelson Nash and talking with Tim Austin of NACFA-BOY, Marv found his calling. He knew that Bank On Yourself was a way to help people get out of the money traps that they had fallen into and to get free of the grip that banks and finance companies had on them. Plus he saw a way to help people ensure that they had a safe retirement account.

Marv is one of only 200 insurance agents in the country who have successfully completed the rigorous training program and continuing education required to become Bank On Yourself-authorized. He is also a life underwriter training council fellow (LUTCF). He is a member of the invitation-only "Fast-Track to 7-Figures" Mastermind group, working closely with Pamela Yellen and Tim Austin.

Born the oldest of nine children to parents who operated a family farm in western Iowa, Marv graduated from high school and went to auto mechanics school. Following graduation, he enlisted in the U.S. Navy and was trained as an electronics technician. He served three years in Vietnam during his six years of enlistment. Coming home after his service, he worked before he entered Iowa State University (ISU) on the G.I. Bill. Upon graduation from ISU, Marv got started in agricultural sales and eventually moved into the insurance field.

Married for 39 years, Marv and his wife, Barb, have raised five children who are all now married and productive citizens. So far, nine grandchildren have blessed the family. Marv is active in the community, including in his church, where he serves as chairman of the trustee board, and the local VFW and American Legion chapters, and the Boone Sportsman's Club. His hobbies are hunting and wood-working projects.

For more information on Bank on Yourself, go to www.findoutmorenow.com and enter passcode MW85.

CHAPTER 31

THE FOURTH ALTERNATIVE

BY MICHAEL E. JASPAN

The purpose of this chapter is to try to help you become a better-educated, much more informed financial consumer. It has been my opinion that an educated consumer always makes an informed decision based on his or her overall financial goals, objectives and concerns. That's why there is never any risk or obligation to find out more about this life-changing financial strategy. In fact, the whole process takes only about an hour to determine how it can work for your personal situation. Most people are very pleasantly surprised when they learn how easily and effortlessly they can take back control of their financial lives. You don't have to be a rocket scientist or a brain surgeon to understand how this program works because it is fundamental and once you begin, your results are predictable and assured.

A SAFE ALTERNATIVE

Of the tens of thousands who have already started using this little-known financial system, not one single person has ever lost a dime. As a matter of fact, the two biggest regrets that most people have admitted regarding this revolutionary process are: First, they wished they had heard about it 20 years ago; and, second they wished they had started with a lot more money when they began. In most cases, it's actually a combination of the two.

Imagine yourself 20 years ago when you should have already been taught this valuable financial lesson but unfortunately were deliberately excluded by your banker. Then imagine yourself again, but this time filled with all the knowledge and experience that life has taught you over those last 20 years. Would you do everything exactly the same this time around? Do you remember when Albert Einstein defined insanity as doing the same thing over and over again and expecting different results?

The plain, simple truth is that most people do the exact same things over and over again expecting different results and sadly, never really come close to achieving any of their core financial goals or objectives. They always seem to be a day late or a dollar short when opportunity knocks and then they make unrealistic agreements with themselves that they will be better prepared the next time, only to watch with envy and contempt while others pass them by on the way to true financial independence.

What is it that separates the select few from the metropolitan of mediocrity? Why is it that most people seem to work harder and harder each and every year, and yet still seem to be going backwards financially while the fortunate few indulge in the many joys of life, taking month-long vacations and having time to spend with their families and loved ones? Is it a coincidence that only the wealthy are shown how to do this? Could there be a reason why this specialized knowledge has been withheld for so long? What do you think would happen if everybody in the world had equal access to all the advantages that were previously reserved only for the privileged few?

BACK TO BASICS

There is a basic principle when it comes to making money. It's not what you eat but what you digest that makes you strong, it's not what you learn but what you remember that makes you wise, and it's not what you earn but what you keep that makes you rich. There are a thousand different ways for you to earn a living and bring home a paycheck, but regardless of whatever it is that you do to pay the bills, there are only two legal ways for you to make money. One is where you trade your time for money by providing either a product or service to your customer in exchange for payment. However, since there are only 24 hours in a day and you must leave yourself time to eat, sleep, etc., there are obviously certain limits to how much time you have to trade for money. The other method is to work smarter, not harder, and let your money work as hard for you as you worked for your money.

What this really means is that while you are trading your time for money, you might want to consider directing some portion of that money to another financial vehicle that will bear interest and increase in value. When that vehicle has accumulated enough value over time so that it can now provide you with passive unearned income equal to or greater than the amount of money you previously were trading your time to earn, that is when you can begin to live your financial life on your own terms. In other words, this is how real wealth is created and you can achieve your own financial freedom. It does take some time and there is a process to follow but it is a one-time requirement that will provide you with a lifetime of benefits. Are you willing to put in the time it takes and to follow the process in order to be able to live your dreams?

The tragedy is that most people just don't have the discipline to do what is in their own best interests and they always end up putting everything else in front of their financial dreams. It's only human nature to want what others have and aspire to "keep up with the Joneses," but ironically, it's doing what other people are too busy to do, doing what's inconvenient for other people to do and doing what other people are too good to do that makes you financially successful. There will always be someone who has a bigger television, a nicer car, a larger house, a longer vacation and a whole list of other material items. They will always be there to tempt you to spend beyond your means, to keep you in financial bondage and to block your path to true financial independence as you struggle to keep up with them.

PURSUE YOUR DREAM

What price do you allow yourself to pay for all this financial decadence? What toll does this take on your physical and emotional wellbeing? How much quality time do you sacrifice with your family and loved ones? Where does it end? Is it really worth it? The only person who knows the answer to these questions and what you are willing to give up is you. Why not take some personal inventory of yourself and see how much you have lost already. The solution to your situation lies within you. In the words of Napoleon Hill, "You have to define your dream and get a burning desire for its achievement." If your dream is to be financially free, to be able to do whatever you want, whenever you want and wherever you want, then you must develop that burning desire for its achievement. You can do it!

If there was a way for you to recapture back all the interest and finance charges that you presently just give away to the banks, the credit card companies and all the other financial institutions in your life you would probably want to know—say "yes!" If you didn't say "yes," you probably didn't understand the question. For more than 160 years now, there has been a well-guarded, little-known financial secret that your banker hopes you will never find out because when you do, you won't ever need your banker again. Have you ever wondered where all the money really goes?

VANISHING DOLLARS

Let's take a look at a fixed rate $100,000, traditional 30-year mortgage and see what happens.

If you were to add up the total of all the payments that you would make over those 30 years–which by the way virtually nobody does anymore because either they refinance the mortgage, they move to another house or they just simply die—everybody knows that you would easily pay anywhere from $250,000 to $300,000 on that $100,000 mortgage. So the question that begs to be asked is, where does all that money go? Does it go into your house? Does it go in to your account or does it go somewhere else entirely?

You see, each month, when you make your mortgage payment to the mortgage company, which, by the way, is a bank, most of what you're paying actually goes toward the interest and only a very small portion goes toward the principal. Is it any wonder that it takes 30 years to pay off the whole mortgage? Wouldn't it be great if you could simply reverse that the other way and have most of what you're paying going toward the principal and only a very small portion going toward the interest? What if you could pay off the whole mortgage in half the time or less and recapture the entire principal plus all the interest? You would probably want to know how to do that—say "yes!"

A LITTLE-KNOWN SECRET

Well, you are at the right place at the right time. In the next few pages you will discover the little-known secret that your banker goes to great lengths to make sure you never find out because his very livelihood depends upon it. What that means is that your banker will do anything and everything he can to keep this information from you and guard this secret with the same resolve that a mother bear has when protecting her young cubs from predators. Remember this is your banker we are talking about and with this secret you can replace him on a permanent basis and never have to pay interest to an outside financial institution ever again.

Let's take a look at how you can finally and permanently rid yourself once and for all of any and all dependence on banks, credit card companies and all the other financial institutions you deal with. By implementing this one simple step, you can put all that money you were previously willing to give away back into your own account where you can recycle those dollars over and over again. This truly is the ultimate in leveraging your money to work as hard for you as you worked for your money.

WAYS TO LEVERAGE YOUR MONEY

Let's say you are in the market for a new car. Legally, there are only three options available to you when you are ready to get that new car. First, you could lease; second, you could finance the purchase; or third, you could pay cash for the car. Are there any other legal options available to you? When you lease, the leasing company puts up a lot of money and in return expects to make a handsome profit by charging you interest or finance charges. When you finance a purchase, the finance company puts up even more money and in return expects to make an even more handsome profit by charging you even more interest or finance charges. The question is how much money does either the leasing or finance company give you back at the end of the term? Say "nothing!"

That's why most sophisticated people don't like to lease or finance the purchase of their cars because they understand that they would end up paying out all those additional interest or finance charges on top of the actual purchase price of the cars and never realize a single dime. It becomes very apparent, then, that the clear choice would seem to be paying cash for their cars and avoiding this added expense, especially since everybody knows that cash is king, and accordingly, that is exactly what they set out to do.

They begin the long, arduous process of saving and saving and saving and saving…until after what seems like an eternity, finally that glorious day arrives when they have saved up enough money to be able to go out and buy their brand new car for cash. What an absolutely exhilarating feeling as they rush down to the bank to drain their account of all its contents on their way to the car dealership, where they pick out the car of their dreams appointed with all the options and just the perfect color— absolutely gorgeous! Then they complete a simple cash transaction without any monthly payments, without any interest or finance charges and drive away in their brand new fully paid-for car. There isn't a doubt in the world that at this very moment life is good!

Unfortunately, after about two or three weeks pass, they receive their statement in the mail from the bank and that's when it hits them like a ton of bricks. While they were saving, their account was always going up, up, up; it was increasing in value and it was worth more and more and more. However, as soon as they took out all the money from their account that suddenly stopped. This is what is called lost opportunity cost. Let me repeat that for you—lost opportunity cost. What it really means is that you finance everything you buy. You either pay interest or finance charges to someone else's financial institution or you lose out on the opportunity to continue having your money earning interest and making money for you.

To put it another way, when it's time for you to get your next big ticket item you have the three options discussed earlier. First, you can lease; second, you can finance the purchase; or third, you can pay cash. Just remember no matter which method you choose, you always finance everything you buy. You're either paying interest to someone else or you are losing interest on your own money.

THE FOURTH ALTERNATIVE

Fortunately, there is a fourth alternative for you to avoid financing everything you buy and it is safe, secured and guaranteed. It's called Bank On Yourself and it's where you literally become your own source of financing almost as if you have created your own personal banking system, minus all the brick and mortar, and in this method you not only buy the big ticket item for cash but you actually recapture back the entire purchase price plus all the interest or finance charges you were willing to give away in the first place. How would you like to make the same margins that the banks, credit card companies and all the other financial institutions that you deal with have been making off you throughout your whole life?

Sounds too good to be true, doesn't it? Well, this is only the beginning of the beginning of the beginning. What about earning interest on all the money you spend on all your big ticket purchases? How many cars will you buy over your lifetime? How many houses will you buy? How many vacations will you go on? How much money will you need for your golden years? When you implement the fourth alternative, the answer to these questions is whatever you want because you are in the driver's seat, you are in control and you get to call all the shots.

About Michael

Michael E. Jaspan lives in the Philadelphia suburbs and is the proud father of three children: Jared, Carly and Jordan. He is also very involved in community activities, including the F&A Masons, St. John's Lodge #115, the Scottish Rite, Northern Jurisdiction, Valley of Philadelphia, The Shield and Square, The Royal Arch and the Shriners. In the course of his business Michael enjoys traveling and public speaking engagements.

Michael advises clients how to grow their wealth, reduce their taxes and achieve their dreams of financial security. He has successfully put his clients on track to acquire more than $187 million of additional wealth. Michael promotes a very unique strategy to help his clients. He uses safe and proven money management principles to achieve this goal. His "Fourth Alternative" is a secret weapon in the industry.

Michael has been in financial services for 27 years. He is one of just 200 financial advisors in the United States to successfully complete the rigorous training program and continuous education to become a Bank On Yourself Authorized Advisor. Michael is also a seasoned Certified Senior Advisor.

To ensure the level of personal service you'd expect, Michael only accepts a limited number of clients each year who are committed to achieving lifetime financial security.

Michael E. Jaspan
P.O. Box 820
Richboro, PA 18954
jandcseniorfinancial@yahoo.com
www.michaeljaspan.com
(215) 860-3470

CHAPTER 32

THE GOVERNMENT MADE ME DO IT:
Wall Street Fallacies and What to Do About Them

BY RON CAMPBELL

I don't think there is a greater country on the planet than the United States of America. I love our country and I love the opportunities that exist for each person. We have seen great leaders emerge from within our ranks. However, I also believe that most of us have a tendency to be followers when it comes to areas of life that are riddled with uncertainty. One of those ambiguities for most people is the area in which I specialize, financial services. There are volumes of books written on the subject, the television and radio are filled with professionals espousing their opinions, and the government plays an ever-increasing role in creating laws that manipulate us toward certain investment vehicles. The good news is that, although most people appear to be followers, we don't have to get caught up in the crowd. We can be independent thinkers and make our own investment decisions even though they may not be considered mainstream. In fact, I want to ask you to step away from the traditional Wall Street mentality and consider options that may prove to be better for you and your family.

I have been extremely fortunate over my career 35-year career in financial services to have been affiliated with, and mentored and coached by some of the brightest minds in our industry today. It is my sincere desire to be able to pass on to others the great knowledge and outstanding strategies that have been instilled in me and have worked for hundreds of my clients.

YOU CAN'T GET THE RIGHT ANSWER STARTING WITH THE WRONG PREMISE

Traditional financial planning professionals typically tell their clients they will be able to live on less and will pay less in taxes when they retire. That is a very consistent message among them. In a recent workshop I conducted I asked the retirees in the room a couple of questions. How many of you are able to live on 70 percent or less of what you were making before you retired? No hands went up. How many are paying less taxes now than when you were working? Not only did no hands go up, but people began chuckling. The question that needs to be answered is, "How good can any retirement plan be if it is designed around a faulty premise that you would be able to retire on 70 percent of the income you received when you were working and you will be paying less tax?" Why do we buy into these false premises?

THE 401(K) EXTRAVAGANZA

If you ask a person 55 years of age or younger how long the 401(k) has been around, they will respond, "Forever." I suppose it has been around in their "forever," which began when they started working. But the truth of the matter is that the 401(k) legislation didn't take place until 1978. In 1980, the first official 401(k) was implemented. Before that you received your tax deduction from an IRA. In 1981, the government took away the tax deduction of the IRA and ushered us into the 401(k) world. Not long after that the corporations used that as an opportunity to walk away from defined benefit plans, which guaranteed that the company would pay its employees a pension during their retirement. The responsibility was then placed on the shoulders of the employee in the form of a defined contribution plan, which is a 401(k).

Where can you invest in a 401(k)? Is it done through insurance companies and banks or through Wall Street mutual funds? The answer, of course, is through Wall Street mutual funds. What a coincidence. When you really evaluate how Wall Street works in conjunction with government, you will realize that the tax code is basically the carrot on a stick.

Not only has our government steered us toward a 401(k) atmosphere by offering hard to resist tax benefits, but they have taken it even farther. From the first 401(k) in 1980 until 2006, employees had to take the initiative to enroll in their company's 401(k) program if they wanted to participate. However, in the Pension Protection Act of 2006, the legislature determined that when you work for a company who offers a 401(k), you will be automatically enrolled. Now, if you don't want to participate in the 401(k), you have to take the initiative to opt out. Why do you think that is? Do you feel that constant nudge by your government to follow the pack? There are reasons the government wants you to participate in your company's 401(k), and the reasons aren't necessarily in your best interests even though they would lead you to believe otherwise.

One of the reasons people enthusiastically flock to the 401(k) world is because they are sold a "rate of return." This doesn't happen in just qualified plans like a 401(k), but also in nonqualified mutual funds. The financial advisor is quick to boast about the great returns on a given fund that is hot right now. But, keep in mind that you can't spend a rate of return. You can only spend the actual dollars in your account. Allow me to illustrate what I mean. If you invested $100,000 and made 10 percent the first year, lost 10 percent the second year, made 10 percent the third year and lost 10 percent the fourth year, that would be a zero percent average rate of return (10%-10%+10%-10%=0%). But in actual dollars, your $100,000 is now worth $98,010. In this example, you had an average rate of return of zero, but you lost $1,990 in four years. When you factor in taxes, fees and expenses, your investment then experiences further erosion. You see, the average rate of return doesn't tell the whole story when it comes to investing.

COMPOUND TAX

Another factor that investors fail to consider is what I call "compound tax." Let me explain. Let's say you bring $50,000 to your investment broker and ask for his investment advice. He says, "I think you should invest your money in the stock market. After all, I can illustrate for you how you can get a historical 10 percent average rate of return in the stock market and in 20 years your $50,000 is going to grow to $336,000."

That sounds like a great deal, doesn't it? But, let me ask you this: How much will it cost you to get there? Most people would say, "$50,000, the cost of my initial investment." But what else did it cost? Well, there is something called taxes. Every year that you're growing that $50,000 in your left pocket, you have to put your hand in your right pocket to pay the IRS taxes on the 1099 they give you. In the first year you're going to lose about $1,700 in taxes. Using the rule of 72, in 7.2 years from now your $50,000 should be worth $100,000 and your 1099 is for $10,000 and you pay $3,500 that year in taxes on your investment earnings. Do you see what is happening? As your money is compounding, so is your tax obligation to the IRS. The bottom line is that over the next 20 years you will be growing your $50,000 investment in your left pocket, but you will be taking about $105,000 out of your right pocket in compounding tax.

LOST OPPORTUNITY COST

Now your investment has cost you $155,000 (your original investment of $50,000 plus your $105,000 in taxes) to get to $336,000. And where does the $105,000 come from during that 20 year period of time? It comes from your lifestyle. Are you familiar with the concept of "lost opportunity cost?" If you spend a dollar, not only do you lose that dollar, but you lose what that dollar could earn you. So now, that $105,000 that you paid in tax is also subject to lost opportunity cost. The lost opportunity cost of the $105,000 you had to pay in taxes over the past 20 years is about $148,000. That is, you could have invested the $105,000 over the course of the past 20 years and earned an additional $148,000. If you add up your $50,000 original investment, the $105,000 you paid in taxes and the $148,000 in lost opportunity cost, it has cost you $303,000 to earn $336,000. That's a net real return on investment of just $33,000.

THE EFFECT OF TRADITIONAL FINANCIAL PLANNING

Think about what traditional financial planning has done to the average American. It certainly hasn't reduced our stress. If financial planning was a science, there would be no losses in the market and everyone would be making money. We have been told by traditional financial planners that they have a solution to your problem. Then we discover there is a problem with the solution. There are too many variables for traditional financial planning to be effective. I read a book one time that had a chapter titled, "I Never Met a Man Who Made a Million Dollars in Mutual Funds." I have to tell you, that chapter changed my approach to my business and opened my eyes to many of the fallacies of traditional financial planning and mutual funds.

Here's a question to ponder. If you put money in a mutual fund and that mutual fund goes down in value, is it possible for you to still have to pay tax on your investment? You may be surprised to know that it is possible that you would receive a taxable 1099 from your investment even though the value of the investment has decreased. The mutual fund managers make constant decisions about buying and selling inside the mutual fund every year. If they happen to sell for a profit, for example, a particular stock that is part of the makeup of the mutual fund, you will receive a 1099 for your portion of ownership in that particular transaction even if the mutual fund lost money that year. Most people don't realize that and rarely are they told of that possibility by their broker. That type of taxable scenario is more common than one might think.

Unfortunately, we have been led to believe that the secret to our potential financial affluence is tied up in something that Wall Street has created and the government has endorsed. Do you think the government or the financial institutions are going to develop programs that enable you to keep a larger share of the money you earn? Unfortunately, history has taught us that the very opposite is true. Government and financial institution-based programs are always going to be tilted in the favor of those entities, not in favor of the consumer.

Friends, we have to make our own way. It has been said that we are left to the Yo-Yo method; that is, "You're On Your Own." I couldn't agree more! That's why it is imperative that you find the right advisor who is well-versed in the most current financial planning strategies and will be of the greatest benefit to you in your wealth accumulation efforts.

THE BANK ON YOURSELF SOLUTION

The Bank On Yourself concept is a way you can take care of yourself by literally becoming your own source of financing. You don't have to put all your money into a Bank On Yourself plan for it to be effective. The important thing is to simply start. You may want to begin with a simple strategy of using this plan to finance your next car purchase. Test it out and see how it works. But I will tell you that used properly, this concept can revolutionize your financial position and it can have a generational effect on your wealth. Here's what I mean by "generational effect." I'm sure you would agree that our country currently has some very serious fiscal problems. In fact, the country's financial crisis is now being referred to as a generational problem, which means it is a problem that will effect generations to come. Traditional planning is not going to solve that problem. We have to address a generational problem with a generational solution. If you can use the leverage of life insurance and pass a legacy down to your children, then your children will be in a position to set up a legacy plan to pass on to their children. Through proper financial planning, we can get our families back to the stable entity they once were instead of being splintered and struggling.

By using the Bank On Yourself strategy, you are able to maximize the utilization of your money. For example, in the dividend paying permanent insurance policies I use for my clients, they are able to borrow money from the cash value in their policy and still earn interest on that money as though they never withdrew a dime. There is absolutely no other place you can put your money that will give you that kind of benefit. Additionally, if they should pass away, their heirs will receive a death benefit that far exceeds the cash value of the policy. Under current law, they don't have to reach into their pocket to pay income taxes on that money as it's growing.

Consider this. Today we have 8 percent unemployment, 47 percent of today's population has zero tax liability and, according to the IRS website, the income tax revenue is projected to go up by 80 percent over the next five years. Where is the money going to come from for this 80 percent income tax increase? Are they going to go after the 47 percent who currently don't pay income tax? Are they going to get it from the wealthiest in our country? It's very doubtful. They will most likely be getting it from those of us who make up the highest percentage of the income tax paying segment.

Do you have a strategy to deal with this coming income tax increase? It is possible to access both your principal and your gains in a Bank On Yourself plan with no taxes due. It is a tax savings strategy, an income-producing strategy, and a purchasing strategy all rolled into a neatly designed system to promote your financial success.

Any time you make any financial decision you should have a checklist and evaluate your financial decision based on these factors: risk, taxes, penalties, inflation, fees and expenses. You will find the Bank On Yourself strategy to be the best solution to address all of these factors. I encourage you to be an independent thinker. Don't get swept up by the Wall Street mentality and the 401(k) crowd. Make wise decisions. With proper planning and by using the right investment vehicle, you will be able to prosper financially and leave a legacy for your family.

About Ron

Ron Campbell, CFP®, RFC®, is the founder and principal of Campbell Financial Services. He has more than 35 years of "in the trenches" experience in the financial services industry. He has served as an adjunct faculty member for adult education in financial planning at various high schools and community colleges, and also has taught those same courses at several companies. Ron has served as host of radio's "Successful Business Hour" and has been quoted and published in various publications.

In specializing with retirees or those about to be retired, Ron uses strategies that focus on guaranteed income and preservation of capital. What worked in the accumulation phase of one's life may not work as well during the distribution phase. Ron believes when it comes to investing, there is more to be gained by avoiding losses than picking the apparent winners. With the changing demographics and our country's fiscal woes, Ron believes risk, taxes, penalties and inflation need to be considered before implementing any investment strategy.

His memberships include The Better Business Bureau, Financial Planning Association, International Association of Registered Financial Consultants, and Wealth and Wisdom. He regularly conducts educational events throughout Anne Arundel and surrounding counties.

Ron resides in Lithicum, Maryland, with his wife, Cheryl. They have four daughters and seven beautiful grandchildren.

To schedule a time to discuss your financial future, contact Ron at Ron@RonCampbell. net or call (410) 766-0900 today.

7310 Ritchie Highway, Suite 700 Glen Burnie, MD 21061
Phone: (410)766-0900   Fax: (410)766-0908
www.RonCampbell.net

CHAPTER 33

FINDING THE RIGHT FINANCIAL ADVISOR

BY RUSS GRZYWINSKI

Since choosing a financial advisor is one of the most important decisions that you will make, I believe it is important to know a little more about that person than what's presented in their bio. So here's my story.

As far back as I can remember, I have had an interest in money, investments and wealth accumulation. As a teenager, I clearly remember reading stories in the newspaper about the wealthy, and I would pay particular attention to programs on TV that had anything to do with the wealthy, and what they were doing to earn high incomes and build wealth. When initially deciding on a career path, I had determined that being a computer operator/programmer would be my road to a high income future. As it turned out, although I was earning a very good income as I progressed in the data processing field, I determined pretty quickly that working in the corporate world was not for me.

So in 1974, I began selling real estate. My thinking was that by becoming a real estate broker, not only would I have the ability to control my income, but it would also give me the opportunity to identify good investment opportunities for personal investment. As I became more experienced and successful as an investment real estate broker, I opened my own real estate firm in 1978, which specialized in commercial and investment real estate. I primarily worked with high-income individuals who were interested in large tax write-offs and building a personal investment real estate portfolio. During that time, the strategy was to leverage real estate investments at the maximum level possible, and to take full advantage of accelerated depreciation that was available to shelter one's income from taxes.

In the early 1980s, inflation was out of control, and interest rates were at historic levels, reaching a high of 21.5 percent in June 1982. At those interest rates, few people were able to qualify for a mortgage or justify the purchase of an investment property, because the cash flow did not cover the debt service. To make things worse, tax laws were changed and the accelerated depreciation write-offs for investment real estate were also significantly reduced, making investment real estate even less appealing. As a result of these changes, I was effectively out of the real estate business, and my personal real estate portfolio had to be liquidated at a significant loss.

Around that same time, a fellow real estate broker called to ask how my business was doing, and to tell me what he was doing to help people with their finances. As it turned out, he was showing people how to buy term insurance and invest in tax-deferred annuities. So in 1981, I obtained my insurance license, and that would be the beginning of what would become a long and successful career as a financial advisor. In 1983, I joined a large financial planning firm's training and mentoring program to become a full-service financial planner. In January 1987, I started my own financial planning practice, then co-founded an independent fee-based investment advisory firm in 1995.

So what does all of this have to do with you, and why should you care? Well, I believe that it makes me highly qualified to help you reach your financial goals, and that you will benefit from the lessons and experiences I have had in regard to real estate risk, the impact of hyperinflation and double-digit interest rates, the importance of diversification, as well as truly understanding the meaning of investment risk and how to correctly manage it.

Chasing unrealistic rates of return and basing long-term financial decisions solely, or primarily, on return simply doesn't work. Most people don't really appreciate the significance of how the inevitable financial losses that will occur in their investments can impact their overall returns. They also let their emotions affect the decisions they make regarding their investments.

What I have also learned is that most of the time, taking extreme positions with one's investments, such as having excessive allocations in gold, silver, currencies, commodities, real estate, etc., is rarely successful over the long term, and that well-balanced diversification among noncorrelated financial vehicles has historically provided the best and most consistent long-term returns, without all of the sleepless nights that can be the result of chasing the highest return or the latest fad. Greed also causes most people to make really bad financial decisions, and often times chasing those unrealistic returns will end up costing them significant losses, or even the loss of their entire investment.

So my approach to wealth accumulation is a balanced approach. I believe that the best plan you can have for long-term wealth accumulation should include wealth-building vehicles and strategies that are safe, liquid, predictable and guaranteed to grow, such as Bank On Yourself, as well as investments that are appropriate for one's individual financial situation.

As an independent financial advisor, I am able to review and perform my own due diligence on financial vehicles and strategies, to determine if they may be appropriate for my clients. Typically, the majority of things I have reviewed over the years have failed my personal due diligence, and are not presented to my clients. However, there are times when a unique or little-known financial vehicle or strategy comes to my attention and meets my requirements. One such strategy that passed my test was Bank On Yourself. It is a proven strategy for wealth accumulation that is safe, liquid, predictable and guaranteed to grow.

Bank On Yourself also gives you the opportunity to create your own source of financing, and this is one of the most significant aspects of the plan for this reason: **It is far more important to eliminate what you're paying out in interest charges, rather than trying to chase the highest returns (and highest risk of loss) with your investments.** In the majority of cases, significantly reducing or eliminating high interest charges that you pay during your lifetime (financial loss), will have a much greater impact on the success of your overall wealth accumulation plan, compared to what you are consistently able to earn on your investments.

In my opinion, Bank On Yourself is the best way to *start* a wealth accumulation plan when you have limited funds available and can't afford to put those funds at risk of loss. On the other hand, if you already have a significant portion of your money invested and at risk of loss, *it provides the perfect diversification and complement to your risk-based investments*, by adding a degree of safety and predictability to your overall plan.

To demonstrate how you may benefit from this strategy, I'd like to share a few examples of how I'm helping clients reach their financial goals.

Jim is a lieutenant with the Chicago Fire Department. He was referred to me by Jim's father and his wife, with whom I have worked with for more than 20 years. Jim is married, has two young boys, and is a disciplined saver. Jim told me that he was concerned about his retirement and paying for his boys' college education. One of the reasons he contacted me was that he had been looking at his retirement plan account statement from the Chicago Fire Department, and based upon his estimation, **after 10 years, his account value was approximately the same as it was 10 years earlier.**

What appealed to him about Bank On Yourself was that it is something that is safe, predictable and guaranteed to grow. After reading Pamela Yellen's book and having a conference call with me, during which we discussed how Bank On Yourself could put him on the path to reaching his financial goals for his family, Jim asked me to design some plans based upon his situation. After reviewing the plans with him, he decided to implement a Bank On Yourself plan not only for himself, but for his wife and children, as well. Jim's plan is primarily being funded by the money he was previously directing to his CFD retirement plan.

Joe and Jamie, in Charlotte, North Carolina, are in their 30s, have one son, and enjoy two very successful careers. I started working with Joe when he was still single, and even at that time, Joe was doing well in his career, was financially disciplined, and was saving a portion of his income. Initially, I set Joe up with a basic investment plan, which was the start of his long-term financial plan at that time. I learned from working with Joe that he was somewhat conservative, and did not want to take a high degree of risk with the money he was able to set aside. Fortunately, as he continued to work hard and enjoy success in his career, he was not significantly increasing his lifestyle to match his increasing income. Quite the contrary; he wanted to set aside more money as a result of his higher income. So in 2004, I introduced Joe to Bank On Yourself. Based upon the safety, liquidity, guaranteed growth and opportunity to create his own source of financing with a Bank On Yourself plan, it was obviously a perfect fit for Joe's conservative approach to wealth accumulation.

Not too long after Joe and Jamie were married, they started a Bank On Yourself plan for Jamie, and over the years, they have used their plans to self-finance vehicles and pay off a mortgage, and they may possibly use their plans to purchase a lot for a future new home. When it comes to college education funding for their son, instead of using a 529 Plan, their Bank On Yourself plans will be a far better option. Although Joe and Jamie are using their plans as the foundation of their long-term financial plan, we continue to have an allocation to investments, which I believe is appropriate for a well-diversified long-term financial plan.

Jeff, in his early 60s, and his wife Dianne, in her early 50s, live in South Carolina. They initially looked into Bank On Yourself because they were interested in reducing the risk to the funds they had available and also having an opportunity to supplement their retirement income. In our initial conference call, we reviewed their current financial situation and financial goals. During that discussion, we actually determined that a typical Bank On Yourself plan was probably not the best solution in their particular situation. As an alternative, I presented a strategy to Jeff and Diane that we refer to as Bank On Yourself for Seniors. I explained that for individuals who are approaching or already in retirement, have a lump sum of money available that they do not want to put at risk of loss, and are interested in having safety, liquidity and guaranteed growth on those funds, this lump sum or single pay plan was much more appropriate in that situation. After explaining the differences as well as the benefits of this particular strategy compared to the typical Bank On Yourself plan, they determined that the Bank On Yourself Plan for Seniors was much more appropriate and suitable for their situation. As a result, they have implemented their plan and are quite happy with the peace of mind that it has added to their financial situation.

There is an extremely important point to keep in mind when it comes to the Bank On Yourself strategy. Bank On Yourself is not an investment, and should it not be compared to an investment. By using the correct financial vehicle for its implementation, it does not expose your capital to market volatility and risk of loss. It provides a high degree of certainty, and as such, serves a very important role in your overall wealth accumulation plan. Unfortunately, as I cautioned earlier, the desire for always seeking the highest return tempts some people to try and "improve" a Bank On Yourself plan by using variable or investment-oriented vehicles when establishing a plan. By doing this, you have now introduced *variability* into your plan, and possibly even risk of loss. In my opinion, that is the biggest mistake one can make when starting a Bank On Yourself plan, because you are now eliminating the certainty, for the *possibility* of higher returns.

So what are the steps that you should take to implement a financial strategy that will provide you with a solid game plan to achieve long-term success and the opportunity to have financial peace of mind?

1. **Understand that there is no "one size fits all" strategy** when it comes to building long-term financial security. You need a plan that is appropriate to your individual situation.

2. **Avoid chasing unrealistic returns.** This is extremely important. Historically, those who chase unrealistic returns typically experience a significant loss at some point, or perhaps have even found themselves putting their hard-earned funds into what ultimately turned out to be a Ponzi scheme.

3. **Don't underestimate the importance of having a well-diversified and appropriate strategy to accomplish long-term wealth accumulation.** The financial pyramid has been around for decades, and continues to be the best approach for most people when putting together a financial plan. If you are not familiar with the financial pyramid, it basically indicates that the greatest portion of the money that you have available to save/invest should be in relatively safe, liquid financial vehicles. As you approach the top of the pyramid, you allocate smaller percentages of your available capital toward higher risk financial vehicles, so that you are not putting a significant portion of your capital into financial vehicles and strategies that have a high risk of loss. A well- diversified financial strategy that is adjusted

over time to account for changes in the financial sector, as well as changes that have occurred during your lifetime, will give you the best chance of accomplishing your financial goals and long-term financial security.

4. **Try to really understand your risk tolerance.** The truth is that people feel they can tolerate a certain level of financial loss in their investments, only to discover that in reality, when they experience actual financial loss in their accounts, they find their risk tolerance is much lower than what they actually believed it was.

5. **If you don't have a plan, take the time to establish one now.** Start with a plan that is conservative, then consider increasing the risk, within your comfort zone, once you have established the foundation for your plan. Once your plan is established, the next most important thing is to have the discipline to stick with it. If you don't know where to begin, seek guidance from an experienced financial advisor. If you don't know who to contact, you might want to reach out to someone that you know is financially successful, and ask them who they work with, or who they might recommend. That may potentially increase the odds of finding an advisor that you can trust. Once you have identified an advisor, be sure that you are comfortable with his or her personality and with the recommendations and guidance that the advisor provides.

6. **If you already have a plan, consider getting a second opinion.** You might be surprised to find out that your plan is no longer appropriate for your current situation. Changes in the economy, the markets, your current age, lifestyle and new financial strategies all have an impact on the success of your plan.

I wish you much success in your financial journey and remember that having a financial plan that is appropriate for your situation will also help you to sleep at night.

About Russ

W. Russell Grzywinski is the president of Oak Brook Financial Group Ltd., and a co-principal of Oak Brook Advisors Ltd., a registered investment advisory firm. He has been a financial counselor since 1982 and has a wide range of experience in the areas of retirement and estate planning, corporate employee benefits, 401(k), profit sharing plans, insurance and investments. He is also a *Bank On Yourself®* authorized advisor.

For over thirty years, Russ has been helping hundreds of individuals, business owners and other professionals take control of their financial future. He has provided his clients with strategies to help them build their wealth and reach their retirement goals, relative to their individual financial capabilities.

Russ has published numerous articles on personal finance, retirement and estate planning, as well as tax reduction strategies. He has been quoted in ***Entrepreneur*** magazine and his columns have appeared in the ***Charlotte Business Journal*** and ***Business Today.*** In addition to his appearances on **Fox News Charlotte, News 14 Carolina,** and **News/Talk 1110 WBT Radio**, he has also been a featured speaker at national and regional conferences on a wide range of financial planning topics. Russ conducts seminars and workshops on a variety of rather unique financial concepts and strategies, which are often overlooked by other advisors.

As a *Bank On Yourself®* authorized advisor since 2004, Russ has become one of the country's leading experts by helping hundreds of clients grow their wealth with safety and predictability, reduce their taxes and put them on track to achieve their dreams of financial security.

Community service is also important to Russ. He has served as an officer of the Rotary club and is past president of a suburban Chicago Chamber of Commerce. As an instructor for Junior Achievement, Russ taught students the basic concepts of investing and related subjects.

Though based in Charlotte, North Carolina, Russ works with clients around the country, and especially in the Chicagoland area. He is also available to speak at your company, organization or association.

To learn more about Russ, visit www.oakbrookfinancial.com, email info@oakbrookfinancial.com, or call (800) 884-6577.

W. Russell Grzywinski
Oak Brook Financial Group, Ltd • Charlotte, NC

CHAPTER 34

MY CANADIAN *BANK ON YOURSELF* STORY

BY STEPHEN DEVLIN

To say that life has its ups and downs is often an understatement. I don't know many people who haven't been slammed to the floor a few times, sometimes wondering if they should—or even can—pick themselves back up again. Many are down for the count, but my wife and I rose above it, tripping along the way and downright stomped on, but eventually standing tall and strong. There's no doubt that through our struggles we learn. Each fall is an opportunity to get back up again, each failure an eye-opening experience to build character and harden our resolve. But it takes time, patience, a bit of persistence and some really good advice along the way to help us regain our footing and come out of our trials stronger and more prepared than we went into them.

Growing up in Vancouver, British Columbia, I was the second to the youngest of five kids. My parents married young and the pressures of children and a difficult marriage proved too much. Their marriage ended when I was five. Our family struggled in every way imaginable—financially, emotionally and spiritually. My mother worked hard at her job at a telephone company, while my older siblings helped at home. However, my greatest struggles took place because of my own embarrassment about our family situation. My self-esteem suffered and I became shy and unsure of myself.

As with any person adrift in a sea of despair, we long for stability, yearning for solid ground beneath our feet, something to count on. We all thrive on security, knowing what to expect, knowing what is expected of us and knowing we have a support system should we need one. My rock appeared when I was 11 years old and my mother met her soul mate. One day, early in their relationship, they rolled up in Buttercup, our Volkswagen bus, as we kids played street hockey. They yelled excitedly to us, something about going to pick berries, and we were puzzled when they said we couldn't go along. What was the big deal? Well, you don't gain a stepdad from berry picking but you do when your mom gets married. Picking berries, getting married—that's close, isn't it? Adopted by my stepdad and taking his last name, I felt a sense of family again. My chin held a bit higher, I ventured into areas of childhood I had not yet felt confident enough try, such as baseball, hockey, and soccer, and with that came a social life and a sense of normalcy I had so needed.

I found security and the courage to grow up as an independent thinker—someone who would make his own decisions and enthusiastically pursue his areas of interest. At age 17, I was already living alone while my parents taught our faith in the Bahamas. Being the sole resident of our family home in New Westminster was my first real experience with responsibility and having already graduated, I was ready to carve out my way in the world.

However, youth and folly go hand-in-hand. Inexperienced with matters of money, I knew only what I had heard over the years—you put your money in a bank and it accrues interest, and that's called handling your finances. This was tradition, this was fact and this was the way things worked, right? Over the years, I learned very little more about money, except that I wanted to earn it—and preferably lots of it. No one had to teach me how to waste it—that came quite naturally.

After a failed marriage and a handful of deadbeat relationships, I turned to self-improvement books and became introspective. Then in my mid-30s, I carefully considered exactly what I wanted from this world, from a partner, from myself. It was time to grow up and set goals, stop wasting time and money, and be serious about setting up my future for success.

Sometimes we get what we need in life, at just the right moment. The first was my stepdad, the second was when I met Michele. I wish I could say we didn't meet in a nightclub, but I can't. (At least it was an upscale club—a collared shirt required). Michele was with her group of friends, I with my buddies. I caught sight of a beautiful woman with reddish-blond hair and knew I had to make a move. We ended up dancing and I made sure she left with my phone number. Thankfully she held on to it and called me.

Michele and I jumped right into deep conversations about religion and other heavy topics, finding a connection with each other that felt easy and right. Two weeks later, we were engaged. Six months later, we were married. Decisiveness like that, for the larger things in life, proved to be a great asset of our marriage. Coincidentally, another man with the last name Devlin approached her for a date earlier the week we met. I'm just glad she ended up with the right one!

Michele has everything I need in a partner—she's smart, dynamic and interesting; she can get dressed up for a sophisticated night out yet could turn around and build a fence the very next day. An excellent problem solver, she's crucial in our decision-making as a couple. Our shared enthusiasm for entrepreneurship led us to several business ventures over the years, most of which were successful, but one of which would prove nearly devastating.

I was in the dot-com industry when I met Michele. Things were going well, but we all know how the dot-com meltdown story ends, don't we? We watched our savings whittle away with the roof caving in on this once-promising industry. Michele and I took steps toward building our own business, doing marketing for realtors, and mortgage and life insurance brokers. Then Revenue Canada slammed us with a $30,000 bill we could not pay. We were naïve in money matters and misinformed by an investment company on how to manage a large severance package. My rookie mistake made five years earlier had caught up with me—which is not uncommon for someone who let the system play him instead of making it work for him.

Michele and I got smart fast, using a RRSP loan to get a huge tax rebate, halving our debt. A bit wiser, we quickly shifted gears and adopted a beefed-up online version of our product, a neighborhood website program, which proved very lucrative and the answer to our prayers. Soon our net worth rose to the $2 million mark. We were soaring high but were about to get our wings clipped.

Money was rolling in and we didn't really even work full time. Life was great as we welcomed our son into the family. We enjoyed those times. Who wouldn't? Nearly every weekend was like a long weekend, but I was traveling as much as I was home. A couple of years later, the market had become saturated. Dwindling sales and nowhere to go but down, we finally saw the light at the end of the tunnel: a fleeting success.

We had wasted money and invested poorly, all while using that same old traditional method of financial management that we had always known. You've heard that saying, "The definition of insanity is to do the same thing over and over and expect different results."

So try, try again, right? Onward we plunged into our next endeavor. We did our research, hired professionals and interviewed franchisees. Everything looked great, at least on paper. Our children's-directory publishing business had the makings of a great opportunity. Everyone told us so and we believed it, too. Despite our best efforts, which included me working with a severed Achilles tendon for 10 days before seeking medical attention and self-funding the venture, there just wasn't enough profit to be made. A year and a half later, we were $500,000 in the red and counting.

It's no secret that financial strain is a huge stressor. We had been suffering through many of life's difficulties, as well—from a miscarriage, debilitating injuries and illness, our parents' passing and moving. The worries were piling up and our finances were depleted. Turned away from the banks that had offered so much credit in our good times, the word "bankruptcy" loomed in the unspoken vocabulary between us.

But sometimes you get what you need. A dear American friend and mentor counseled me on our financial situation and introduced me to a debt-elimination concept that I had not heard about before. He recommended Pamela Yellen's book *Bank On Yourself*, an innovative and nontraditional approach to money management. Michele and I were exhausted and reeling going from one problem to another and were aching to get our feet once more on solid ground. We also had our young son to consider.

I hadn't realized how interest worked before. I had no idea how much money needlessly left my hands every single day. I thought money in the bank earned me more money, but I learned that this was far from the case. Money sitting in the bank is bankruptcy on a payment plan! As inflation increased and my interest rates stagnated, I was losing money—our money. We were paying interest on everything. I realized that something as simple as buying a house or car was killing us financially—the first few years of a mortgage or loan are the heaviest in terms of interest paid. I thought paying cash for things was the best way to deal with our debt issue. Wrong! I learned about "opportunity cost" and embraced principles wealthy people use and understand, including leverage, compounding, volume and velocity, and tax favorableness. We were getting smarter about money—finally!

The Bank On Yourself concept turned our traditional thinking on its head and opened our eyes to what financial freedom really looked like. But would it work as well here in Canada? The main component of Bank On Yourself involves buying permanent, dividend-paying whole-life insurance. But not all life insurance companies are created equally. After assessing a dozen U.S. companies compared with Canadian, I found the right fit. Armed with this knowledge and my past experience, I was getting the message loud and clear. I was heading for another business shift so I needed a life insurance license fast. Sounds easy, but the material was not for the faint of heart. Juggling family life and our business, and studying was grueling but I was up for the challenge because I loved it so much. Michele and I knew a better way and wanted whoever we could tell to know about it. This was just too good, too simple, and too life-changing to keep to ourselves.

I purchased my own policy and was now paying interest to myself. I had a safe and stable dividend-driven financial vehicle that paid me, and from which I could borrow and use for whatever I needed, and then just pay myself back. This was working. I was my own financing source, and was not subject to rejection based on credit, income, or whether or not the bank felt I was too much of a risk to lend money to. We controlled our own finances and we were seeing immediate results while crawling out of debt. Bank On Yourself helped us escape our dire financial situation and build wealth again, but this time with an epiphany about just how oblivious we had been to the hands reaching into our pockets all along. No more would my worthiness be held in judgment by banks, nor would my hard-earned money finance their investments instead of my own.

We were amazed how simple this concept was, and we celebrated finally having financial peace in our world. It was incredible to experience this secure asset, allowing us to borrow our money on our terms while our money still grew as if we hadn't touched a dime of it. All with the comfort of life insurance, among other benefits, we were scratching our heads as to why some people still had a tough time understanding how it all worked. We knew very few Canadian life insurance agents accepted Bank On Yourself could work here. I would prove otherwise, despite the naysayers, making myself and our company a Canadian leader in the Bank On Yourself concept.

It is most beneficial to invest early in permanent life insurance while you're healthy and before health concerns emerge. Eligibility can become complicated but not necessarily impossible. Health, age and income become restrictive, so as parents, we did what comes naturally and protected our son.

We bought a policy as an investment in his future. He understood from a young age the value of a dollar and the handling of money. CJ will not face the same challenges we endured through our years of money mismanagement and misunderstanding. We will watch him grow along with his guaranteed financial future. Just as my stepfather gave me security in the form of a family name, we are giving CJ security in the form of wealth and life insurance. He will have his own ups and downs, no doubt, but we feel we've done our part in protecting him from one of life's most destructive stressors.

CJ's options will be limited only by his imagination. Can you imagine what this can do for you? Help your child learn about money, use it to travel, make home improvements, or pay off your credit card—the possibilities are endless and tax-exempt if used correctly.

I believe whole-heartedly in this concept because I spend my days helping people realize their goals, coaching them, supporting them. I even have teenage clients paying into their own policies. It is absolutely empowering.

Our clients are our family. We want them to sleep easy at night knowing their money is safe and secure, knowing they have access to it when they need it. Michele and I assist people in breaking down the barriers to building wealth—the very barriers that held us back for so long, including lack of knowledge and capital, fear, debt and cash flow issues, taxes. We have made a successful life for ourselves by helping others claim their money for themselves. We passionately educate people about banking on themselves. MacDev Financial Group Corp. is now a full-fledged life insurance agency. I can gratefully proclaim that I am recognized as the Canadian expert in this concept, even having the honor of teaching industry veterans how to use it effectively.

This is where you come in. You can fund your own life. Ask yourself: What is my money doing for me? I have shared our hardships for you to understand wealth could have come easier. I wish I had known earlier that there was a way out. I'm grateful for what we now know, or rather what was shared with us. So in turn I share it so you may enjoy life, find financial security, create wealth and avoid the financial pitfalls that unnecessarily plague so many, just as it did me and my family. Do yourself a favor, read *Bank On Yourself.*

About Stephen

Stephen Devlin is the cofounder and president of MacDev Financial Group Corp., located in Gibsons, British Columbia, and is the expert *Bank On Yourself* financial advisor. Stephen has adapted the concepts of Pamela Yellen's business model to develop a simple and extremely effective money management system that leads to safeguarding finances and building wealth. Stephen is an agent and consultant for several major life insurance companies and is well-versed in the ways of business success.

Stephen is passionate about helping Canadian individuals, families and corporations become financially self-empowered by teaching them the key principles to creating long-term security and controlling their financial futures. The *Bank On Yourself* proven concept allows clients to benefit from increased cash flow, resulting in the ability to self-finance endeavors such as purchasing vehicles and real estate, opening a business or taking on whatever life goal requires funding. Stephen greatly enjoys coaching others and witnessing the results as businesses and families flourish under his guidance. Because of his own hard-earned wisdom gained through personal difficulties and life experiences, it brings him great joy to share the security that financial stability brings.

Stephen is one of Canada's leading experts in this concept and therefore is regularly sought out by business professionals in the life insurance and financial fields to share his experience and approaches to creating financial security in uncertain times. The *Bank On Yourself* system provides the safe and calculated results that are in demand for creating wealth and being in control of your own money. Stephen and his business partners regularly speak all over Canada on the *Bank On Yourself* topic to groups ranging from just a few to several thousand people. Speaking engagements to private groups can be made with him upon request.

Stephen lives on British Columbia's beautiful Sunshine Coast with his wife and business partner, Michele, and their young son. He loves spending quality time with his family and also enjoys traveling, cooking, golfing, hiking, kayaking, swimming, hockey and coaching youth sports. He is a licensed life insurance broker in British Columbia (resident providence), Alberta, Saskatchewan, Manitoba, Ontario and Nova Scotia (pending).

Additional brokerage information regarding MacDev Financial Group Corp. can be found at the Insurance Council of British Columbia at www.insurancecouncilofbc.com.

To contact Stephen Devlin and begin on the path to financial security, please call (877) 534-7266 or email stephen@macdevfinancial.com. You can also find him on the web at www.macdevfinancial.com, where you can also learn more about the many services offered by MacDev Financial Group Corp.

CHAPTER 35

THE LONG ROAD TO INSURANCE BLISS

BY STEVEN L. HOLTZ, CLU, CFP

I've always been a searcher. I was born with a natural curiosity that radiated in every direction. I was one of those kids who couldn't resist taking things apart to see how they worked. Unfortunately for my parents, I didn't always have the same knack for putting them back together again. This fascination, curiosity and desire to understand how things work still endure in my life today.

THE BEGINNINGS

A new kind of search began while I was in college, and it has served me well as a professional. In addition to pursuing a traditional education, I also began a spiritual quest in the desire to be a better person and endeavor to find the proverbial "meaning of life." Since then, I have participated in numerous seminars and read countless books by authors with intriguing ideas. The great value I have derived in pursuing this type of information is immeasurable. I strongly believe that I am a better husband, father and friend, and I also deliver much more value to my clients as a direct result of this particular aspect of my journey.

Although I didn't set out with a goal to enter the insurance business, it has worked out well. It was a struggle at the beginning, as is true for most. I am not sure of the statistics today, but when I entered the business 35 years ago, more than 95 percent of those who tried to make it a career were gone within two years. Why? Did they not like the business or did they find they couldn't be successful in it? My mentor often said that the insurance business offers tremendous opportunities to enjoy great success and can be quite rewarding, but it will be neither satisfying nor rewarding if you are just mediocre. Given my innate interest in taking things apart to see how they work, I set out to dissect the insurance business with the goal of understanding each piece, and was determined this time to successfully put them all back together again.

FACING NEW CHALLENGES

I wasn't the best candidate in the world to go into the insurance business. I was very shy and not the outgoing, gregarious type, so I wasn't exactly your stereotypical insurance guy. I was single and hung out with mostly single people, so I didn't have the greatest list of prospects upon whom to call. My education hadn't prepared me, either; I was a biochemistry major and hadn't taken much in the way of business classes in college. I had three strikes on me before I even had a chance to swing the bat.

Given the attrition rate of new insurance salespeople, you could reasonably conclude I would have been a hopeless case. But I did have a few things going for me. I had a natural curiosity about the inner workings of the business and financial world, along with a strong desire to help people. I was low-key and sincere, two qualities most people appreciate. Being single was also surprisingly an advantage in one very significant way: I didn't have a family to take care of, so I didn't have the financial pressure that having a family creates. That doesn't mean I didn't have financial pressures; I did need to make enough money to at least take care of myself.

I also had one other significant factor in my favor. The personal growth seminars and the self-help books I had read would yield huge benefits. I didn't realize it at the time, but in a lot of ways I was being given a template that showed me how to be successful not only in life, but in business, as well. The tools and ideas ranged from the simple to the sublime. They were concepts as simple as "never be late," which translated to being on time for all my appointments. "Be true to yourself and others" or if you say you're going to do something, follow through and do it.

PURSUING SUCCESS

By far the most important concept I had learned, though certainly a bit abstract, is how we influence personal success through our attitude and our thoughts. Every human accomplishment begins as a thought. Success is a matter of channeling our thoughts, turning them into actions, and then taking responsibility for the results, whatever they may be. Given that we are often our own worst enemies, it is very easy to forget that and to get caught up in the everyday frustrations that we all encounter. Looking back, I had plenty of hurdles and obstacles. In spite of what I knew on a conscious level about how things work, I wasn't without my share of fear and anxiety about the present and the future, particularly from a financial point of view. I had self-doubt about whether I could put all the pieces back together again.

My career has had its share of twists and turns. When I first started out, I was an agent for several different insurance companies that provided the support and structure I thought I needed. However, I felt torn in my loyalties between making sufficient sales numbers for the company versus providing the best product to my individual customers. Unable to completely reconcile the two, about 20 years ago I took the chance of setting up my own office. Finally, I could operate completely independently and feel free to be completely objective in my recommendations.

When I entered the insurance business, there were basically two types of life insurance: term and whole-life. There were many variations of each, but purchasing life insurance at that time was basically a choice between one or the other, or a combination of the two. Whole-life, at that time, as was always the case, was a safe place to put your money. But your equity grew at a snail's pace, and you didn't have much equity in the early years. While many of my colleagues sold lots of whole-life, it didn't appeal to me as a wealth-building tool, so consequently I couldn't recommend it with a clear conscience. My goal was to find better ways to create financial security, not only for my clients, but for myself as well.

MY NEW STRATEGY

This was a very interesting and dynamic time to be in the financial services business. There was a confluence of events leading to some exciting changes. Personal computers were coming into vogue, and this new computer age not only enhanced productivity but led to the development of new products. The information superhighway was born with the development of the Internet. This was clearly an opportunity to elevate what I could do for my clients, and I gravitated towards the burgeoning area of financial planning. I became securities-licensed. I enrolled in certified financial planning courses and took all the necessary exams to become a CFP. I felt I was well on my way to finding the "Holy Grail" in my pursuit of providing financial security. Clearly, my puzzle pieces were beginning to form a recognizable shape.

I became very focused on recommending securities-type vehicles to my clients in meeting their long-term goals. I became a strong "buy and hold" advocate. Being that this was the early 1990s, this happened to be a very good time to do so as we were entering one of the best bull markets in our nation's history. I was using various types of mutual funds for both qualified retirement plans (IRAs, 401(k)'s, etc.) and nonqualified accounts. for life insurance needs, where it was appropriate, I was recommending the purchase of variable life, where the cash values could be invested in a host of mutual funds, with the idea being that cash value growth would be superior to other types of policies. I instituted for myself and my family all of these recommendations. I purchased a variable life policy when my daughter was born, and I was funding my retirement and my nonretirement accounts with the same mutual funds I recommended to my clients. In other words, I was employing the same conventional wisdom in my personal life to achieve my goal of financial security.

The market did have a couple of small hiccups during the 90s. But conventional wisdom taught that through a buy and hold strategy and methodical, regular investing (dollar cost averaging), the ups and downs didn't matter because you would do well in the long run. Of course, this assumed ever-upward trends in the market. This strategy worked well until the year 2000 came along and brought with it the burst of the dot-com bubble. Over the next three years, a lot of people lost a lot of money, including me and my clients. I began to worry that the puzzle was incomplete. Were there missing pieces? Leftover pieces? Something needed to change.

A WHOLE-LIFE REVELATION

Towards the end of this three year swoon, I was introduced to a financial concept using dividend-paying whole life insurance that would change the course of my practice. Whole-life? That antiquated, stodgy, painfully slow-growing financial vehicle I had turned away from two decades earlier? Although I was skeptical at first, this wasn't the same whole-life I had forsaken; this was clearly a new and improved version. There were new riders (which are options that could be attached to policies) that significantly accelerated the growth of the equity within a policy. Combine that with the timeless features of a whole-life policy—safety of principal, tax-deferred growth, and absolute access to one's cash value if or when needed—and you had a pretty compelling case for an incredible financial planning tool. Not only that, but with the right guidance and coaching, anyone could actually grow their wealth by using this policy as a source of capital to replace outside financing.

Best of all, no one, including me, had to worry about what was going on in the stock, bond or real estate markets. Every year, a policy's value would be greater than the year before, unless the policyholder had taken out some of his or her equity. That certainly reduced stress and anxiety for those who would like to see their money grow (and who doesn't), but who have a hard time handling the ups and downs in the market. You truly cannot measure the value of reducing one's stress, particularly in regards to money; it clearly has a positive impact on a person's health and general well-being.

The reliability of a properly arranged policy in furthering the pursuit of financial security became quite evident in late 2008/early 2009 when the markets—virtually all markets—took an absolute beating. If you had any money in stocks, bonds, mutual funds or real estate, you suffered a loss, and in some cases, a very large loss. Even the most conservative mutual funds may have lost 30 percent or more of their value. But here is where it gets exciting. With this wonderful financial tool—a uniquely designed whole-life policy that I was using for both my family and my clients—not only did we not lose any of the insurance policy's equity, but the policy's growth continued its expected upward trajectory. This reality had a huge impact on my financial planning perspective.

UNDERSTANDING LIQUIDITY

Another lesson that The Great Recession, which had just begun in late 2008, taught me was the value of having access to one's assets. Some of my clients did suffer financially during this period. Many had to reduce or eliminate contributions to their policy, use some of their equity to maintain their standard of living, or even borrow from themselves in order to avoid a financial calamity. Imagine how relieved clients were when I reminded them that we design these plans to provide flexibility when needed and there is always ready access to one's equity. The goal is to pay back what's been removed, with interest, and this can be done within the constraints of what a policyholder can afford. It was a new paradigm in the world of financial strategies, and I am pleased to say that when I put together all the pieces of what I'd learned over the years, the puzzle was not only complete but relayed a message of hope and reassurance to my clients.

Everyone knows that setting aside money, saving and investing are critically important for a positive financial future. I've learned and now taught that it's not the only facet in achieving financial security or independence. Over the years, I have reviewed and analyzed many people's financial situations. The most common problem I have encountered, when there is a problem, is a basic lack of liquidity. This seems so simple, but it's truly astounding how many people find themselves with a liquidity problem at one time or another in their lives.

The causes are many. Sometimes it's just a matter of overspending or living beyond one's means. It's so sad to see the number of people who use credit, particularly credit cards, without thinking about the financial ramifications, both short- and long-term. A person's financial energy can be changed so dramatically when valuable, oftentimes limited resources are not wasted in paying large amounts of interest to credit card companies and other financing companies. These entities really take advantage of consumers in the way they compute the interest due and the level of interest charged, in addition to other fees. If you are struggling to get ahead, tailor your cost of living to your income and try to create a surplus so you can start saving and create that all important liquidity. It's critical to get out from under the negative compounding factor of interest accrued on credit card debt, and use that same compounding factor in a positive way to maximize savings in the future.

THE COMMON MISTAKE INVESTORS MAKE

One of the most common reasons I've seen for a lack of liquidity is what I would describe as a misallocation of one's assets. I can't tell you how many people I've worked with whose money is basically locked up in two places—their home equity and their retirement plans. Most of us probably view our home equity as readily available, but that is not always the case. There are times when it is not easy to qualify for a home equity loan, particularly if you want to access your equity because you just lost your job. Or what if home prices plummet like they did in 2008? Home equity may disappear, and you risk being underwater on your home loan with no equity left at all. Lenders can also freeze your loan or even "call" it whenever they feel the need. Worrying about these risks is counter-productive to achieving a feeling of financial security and wellness.

Accessing one's retirement plans for liquidity needs can be quite costly. You can always take money out of your IRAs, but after paying the penalties and taxes, at most you'll end up with 60 cents for every dollar you take out. Many 401(k)'s have provisions for making a loan, and this should probably be your first choice for obtaining needed funds, but borrowing from your 401(k) can be problematic, as well.

Retirement planning is extremely important and a goal for most people with whom I meet. Thanks to government inducements (tax deferral, tax-deferred growth), many people contribute to their employer 401(k) plans and/or personal IRAs. I, too, used to contribute the maximum allowed into my retirement accounts. (There's that darned conventional, maybe outdated, wisdom again!) For years I never questioned the efficacy or the ramifications of putting as much money as possible into my retirement plans. But it does need to be questioned when you consider what is actually happening: Depending upon your tax bracket—let's say it's 30 percent—for every dollar contributed, you are saving 30 cents in taxes but you're giving up access to an additional 70 cents. You are losing 70 cents of precious liquidity. For what? So you can postpone the taxes to a later date, and who knows what those tax rates will be when you are someday forced to pay them on every single dollar that you take out in the future? This doesn't even take into consideration that once your money is in a qualified retirement plan like 401(k)'s and IRAs, the government is making the rules and it can change them anytime it wants. Do you trust the government to have your personal financial security at heart, or would you prefer to make those decisions yourself?

THE LESSON

If you have concerns about your financial future, give some thought to the foregoing. Take advantage of what I've learned and observed in my 35 years in the financial services industry. Don't necessarily follow the path of conventional wisdom, for it might be a road that's been laid out not for your benefit, but rather to take advantage of you. Try to avoid the past mistakes that both my clients and I have made and instead take advantage of the lessons that we have learned and proven true. Make sure you have liquidity so you can avoid the clutches of the banks and finance companies. Then you'll be in the best position to take advantage of opportunities as they present themselves. With your financial future secure, free from the stress of worrying about how world events may or may not affect your personal portfolio, you'll have greater peace of mind and a more enjoyable life.

About Steven

Steven Holtz is the founder and owner of Holtz Insurance Services, a full-service insurance agency located in Los Angeles, California. Steven is both a certified financial planner and chartered life underwriter, so he is eminently qualified to assist clients in their quest for financial security and wealth accumulation. He has expertise in a number of different areas, including estate planning, retirement planning, employee benefits, long term care planning, and college funding.

A native of Los Angeles, Steven graduated from UCLA with a bachelor of science degree and entered the life insurance business shortly thereafter. He enjoys working with and assisting a wide variety of clients, including professionals, executives, business owners and many others. From the beginning, his motto has always been to "put the client's interests first" and to deliver the highest level of service, both personally and through his agency.

Steven is very involved both in his profession and community. He is a member of several professional organizations, including the National Association of Insurance and Financial Advisors and the National Association of Health Underwriters. He regularly donates his time to a variety of charities in the Los Angeles area and is a member of his local chamber of commerce.

Steven is married to his lovely wife, Vicki, and together they have raised two beautiful children. Besides spending as much time as possible with his family, Steven is an avid reader and likes to keep up with current events and politics. He enjoys many outdoor activities, including walking and hiking with his Labrador retriever, sailing, gardening, and travel. He also enjoys a wide variety of sports.

To learn more about Steven and his insurance agency, please visit www.holtzinsurance.com, or call him at (310) 553-2220.